# Violet Trefusis

Other Works by Philippe Jullian

*Edward and the Edwardians*
*Robert de Montesquieu*
*Oscar Wilde*
*Flight into Egypt*
*Dreamers of Decadence*
*D'Annunzio*
*The Symbolists*
*The Triumph of Art Nouveau*

And, with Violet Trefusis,

*Memoirs of an Armchair*

# Violet Trefusis

## A Biography

INCLUDING CORRESPONDENCE WITH
VITA SACKVILLE-WEST

Philippe Jullian and John Phillips

A Harvest/HBJ Book
Harcourt Brace Jovanovich, Publishers
San Diego   New York   London

Originally published in the United States as *The Other Woman: A Life of Violet Trefusis*

**HBJ**

Copyright © 1976 Philippe Jullian and John Phillips

All rights reserved. No part of this publication may be
reproduced or transmitted in any form or by any means,
electronic or mechanical, including photocopy, recording,
or any information storage and retrieval system, without
permission in writing from the publisher.

Requests for permission to make copies of any part
of the work should be mailed to: Permissions,
Harcourt Brace Jovanovich, Publishers,
Orlando, FL 32887.

LIBRARY OF CONGRESS CATALOGING IN PUBLICATION DATA

Jullian, Philippe.
  Violet Trefusis.

Reprint. Previously published: The other woman.
Boston: Houghton Mifflin, 1976.
  Includes index.
    1. Trefusis, Violet Keppel, 1894–1972—Biography.
Sackville-West, V. (Victoria), 1892–1962.
    2. Trefusis, Violet Keppel, 1894–1972—Correspondence.
    3. Sackville-West, V. (Victoria), 1892–1962—Correspondence.
    4. Authors, English—20th century—Correspondence.
    5. Novelists, English—20th century—Biography.
    6. Novelists, French—20th century—Biography.

I. Phillips, John.  II. Title.
PR6039.R39Z72  1985    823'.912 [B]    84-22358
0-15-693555-4 (pbk.)

Printed in the United States of America
First Harvest/HBJ Edition
A B C D E F G H I J

# *Acknowledgments*

LORD KINROSS has been especially helpful in the preparation of this book. We also wish to thank Lady Diana Cooper, Dame Rebecca West, Mrs. Lesley Blanch, Robin McDouall, Raymond Mortimer, the late Cyril Connolly, and Derek Hill. And we would like to acknowledge the assistance provided by our translator, Charles Bricker.

Among Violet's friends in France we are most especially grateful for the help given by Monsieur le Président Gaston Palewski, the Duc d'Harcourt, the Baron Philippe de Rothschild, Monsieur Maurice Goudeket, Monsieur Hervé Mille, Monsieur Jacques Février, Monsieur Henri Sauguet, and Monsieur Jean-Pierre Grédy. Madame Nora Auric has given us permission to reproduce the fine portrait she painted of Violet. Many anecdotes were recounted by the following friends: the Marquise de Chabannes-la Palice, the Comtesse Amédée Costa de Beauregard, Madame la Générale Catroux, Madame la Générale Béthouart, Madame René Massigli, and Madame Gaston Bergery.

Violet's friends in Italy who were helpful include His Royal Highness Prince Paul of Yugoslavia and Sir Harold Acton, to whom we are especially indebted for many amusing stories and permission to quote from *More Memoirs of an Aesthete*. The Vicomtesse de Dampierre and Lady Enid Browne, as well as Violet's cousin the Viscountess Bury, have given us their support in this project as have Violet's numerous Italian friends.

Permission to quote material from Vita Sackville-West's novels *Challenge* and *The Edwardians* has been given by her literary executor and the publishers William Collins, Sons & Co. Ltd., and Curtis Brown Ltd.

# *Foreword*

VIOLET TREFUSIS was the lesser known of the protagonists in the extraordinary story of her love affair with Vita Sackville-West. One wonders whether she would have relished all the fuss over someone who had eventually become, as she herself put it, "a very conventional old lady." She detested scandal, and nothing about her later life suggests that she would ever have laid herself open to it.

Violet may well have turned over a time or two in her grave while the ashes of this famous affair were being raked. But in her lifetime, every inch a woman of letters, she used to like attracting the attention of literary critics. The publicity which has rescued her name from oblivion, the reviews which have praised her talent may in some other world be offering consolation to a self-esteem which to her regret used to receive bigger boosts from the *beau monde* than from the world of letters.

This cosmopolitan, who wrote charmingly in both English and French and left behind a book of sparkling memoirs, will finally find her place among the great writers of love letters. She may have had a premonition of it when she used to say to friends: "You'll see, people will talk about me a good deal after I'm gone." The friends agreed politely, thinking this was just another sign of the megalomania which so often put her in the wrong.

In fact, those who encountered Mrs. Trefusis only in her old age and who knew her superficially often formed an impression of a notable eccentric dissipating her waning energies in one last social round. The luxury of her houses, the excellence of her table, her taste for outmoded splendors placed her squarely in a bygone era. It was as though at her mother's death she assumed her weighty role of Edwardian *grande dame*. Yet with her oldest and closest friends, she could revert to the superbly vivacious style of conversation which more than anything won her the friendship of Paul Valéry, Jean Cocteau, Colette, and a host of others during the 1920s, and made her one of the most sought-after women in Paris.

The authors of this book have attempted to refurbish the image of the real Violet Trefusis. Vita Sackville-West was certainly a more widely known writer and she must be credited with the immense prestige of having inspired Virginia Woolf's *Orlando*. But this does not mean that the woman Vita loved was superficial. A perusal of Violet's letters is proof enough of that. We will see that in the years after the breakup of their affair Vita and Violet's relationship endured. But Vita had her husband, her sons, and her garden. And Violet, despite the love she bore her mother and a host of friends, was essentially very much alone. Her life lacked the coherence of Vita's. Their love was an upsetting, but perhaps not the most important episode in Vita's life, but for Violet it was really her only serious love affair. The fact is that she preferred the company of men to women. Thus, in Violet Trefusis's life as described here, the liaison provides the substance for only three chapters out of fourteen. The book as a whole recounts the life of a woman whose name deserves to be remembered as much for her role in what went on in Paris between the wars, and her special gifts as a writer in both French and English, as for her passionate involvement with Vita Sackville-West. Perhaps this work will be called trivial by those critics who judged these two ladies severely because they were rich and aristocratic. Both did attach a great deal of importance to their genealogies. Vita retreated from the world beneath the branches of an illustrious family tree which included some of England's greatest names, but the tree had undergone an exotic graft in the person of Pepita Duran, her Spanish-dancer grandmother, and it bore some singular fruit.

Violet's family tree also had had an exotic graft, a Greek great-grandmother. But Violet liked to climb higher in search of royal names that could satisfy her sense of grandeur and fantasy. Today the two friends' behavior appears incomprehensible unless you take into account the coats of arms, the heraldic bearings, the castles and legends which dominated their upbringing like so many tapestries hung as a backdrop to their children's pastimes. It may be futile to recall these splendors, and snobbish of the author to stress them, but they do explain the difficulties of adjusting to a world which was rapidly putting light years between itself and the world in which such values were respected. Vita became an eccentric in private; Violet, when she entered a drawing room. Both were specimens of a breed on its way to extinction.

There is no question that Violet liked, among other things, dining at the Ritz. But so did Proust and Firbank. Despite her attachment to *The Guermantes Way* and her excursions into the *Cities of the Plain,* Violet Trefusis was in many respects a Firbankian heroine: eccentric, discontented, witty, whimsical. Firbank certainly knew about Vita and Violet, and we get echoes of their adventures in *Valmouth.*

Like a Firbank heroine, Violet loved beauty above all things, and to have access to it she risked scandal in her youth, and in her old age sometimes courted ridicule. Vita had a more rational attitude toward Beauty. Violet was undoubtedly sensitive to the beauty of both sexes, but perhaps she appreciated beautiful objects most of all. She was a considerable connoisseur, and like all connoisseurs, not exceptionally creative: her novels are often echoes of her sparkling conversation, and her masterpieces were her houses. At the close of her life, she preferred people who were capable, like herself, of falling in love with a Venetian mirror or a Meissen vase, and who, out for a walk, would find their gaze caught by the same face or landscape which held her own attention.

Another writer prominent in the 1920s, Thornton Wilder, seemed to have prefigured Violet in *The Cabala,* a novel in which he reincarnated the gods of ancient Rome as wealthy and eccentric aristocrats in the Rome of 1925. They pursue fantastic intrigues in magnificent villas. Wilder's description of one of these characters perfectly fits Violet: "For the first ten minutes she said many foolish things because her mind was afar off; one felt vaguely that it would come around in its own time. This it presently did, and with considerable impact."

All this helps explain why the present book came to be written. As

to how it was written, John Nova Phillips, Violet's literary executor
and faithful friend during the last fifteen years of her life, discovered
among her papers a correspondence with Vita Sackville-West dating
from 1940; a second volume of memoirs, this one in French, called
*Triple Violette* and meant to complete *Don't Look Round* (1952);
and various other letters including some from Edward VII to Violet's
mother, Mrs. Keppel. These papers, with extracts from *Don't Look
Round,* have served as the basis for this life of Violet. A selection of
letters kindly lent by Vita's heir and edited by Mr. Phillips has been
included at the end of the book. Since they form a unit, it seemed a
better idea to group them in one place than to scatter them through the
text. There are also quotations from Vita Sackville-West's novel
*Challenge,* whose central characters, Julian and Eve, are none other
than Vita and Violet.

The author knew the postwar Violet, and met her friends, French
and English, during his visits to St. Loup and l'Ombrellino. Besides
relying on the papers put at his disposal by Mr. Phillips, he has inter-
viewed several of Violet's friends in order to reconstruct her life in
Paris between the wars.

The author extracted a good deal of information from Violet about
her mother and her circle in the course of writing *Edward and the
Edwardians* (1967), and during a visit to l'Ombrellino in 1952, Vita
Sackville-West discussed Mrs. Keppel at length with him. Notes taken
on those occasions, supplemented by Sonia Keppel's charming memoir,
*Edwardian Daughter,* have aided him in re-creating a childhood so
fabulous that the rest of Violet's life was completely disoriented by it.

# Contents

APPENDICES/INDEX

# Illustrations

# THE LIFE

By Philippe Jullian

# 1. *"Dear Mrs. George ..."*

VIOLET TREFUSIS' whole life was dominated by the extraordinary personality of her mother, the Honorable Mrs. George Keppel. Thanks to Mrs. Keppel, Violet's childhood was something of a fairy tale. Later, in her early twenties, she briefly tried to break the spell, but in no time her mother's magic reasserted itself. In many ways, Violet remained a little girl all her life and at Mrs. Keppel's death she must have felt lost in a world of adults. Toward the end of her own life, during a skirmish with Harold Acton, Violet suddenly stopped and seized his hand, crying, "Mama was very fond of you, so we must be friends."

In fact, Mrs. Keppel was much more a fairy godmother than a mother. Regally beautiful, she had the highest in the realm at her feet, and with a word or a smile she saw to it that her smallest whim was fulfilled, a wonder she eventually worked for her daughter too. In *Don't Look Round* Violet said of her:

My mother began as an atmosphere, a climate, luminous, resplendent, joyously embattled like golden armour; it was only later that I became conscious of her as an individual.

I basked in the climate of her love without asking myself any questions, until I was about five. Very soon she hit upon the right technique in dealing with me. Once, when I was very small, and of the opinion that I was not getting enough attention, I announced that I was going to run away. "Very well, run then," came the bland reply.

I started on a singularly flat fugue, pushing my little wheelbarrow in front of me. Nobody called. Nobody came. It was a complete fiasco.

(In later life, other fugues were to be nipped in the bud by the same method.)

My mother never lost her temper. When roused to anger, which was seldom, she would let fall a few icy sentences. She never bore malice; was always the first to say she was sorry. She not only had a gift of happiness, but she excelled in making others happy. She resembled a Christmas-tree laden with presents for everyone. There was no limit to her largesses. In her large, many-chambered heart, the humblest had his niche. Old bores, old governesses, poor relations, were welcomed as though they were the cat's whiskers.

Today Mrs. Keppel might appear to symbolize the Edwardian era in the same way that Madame de Pompadour incarnates the rococo. But where the arts were concerned, unlike the favorite of Louis XV, Edward VII's friend exercised little influence on the taste of her time. She was inclined to know many more bankers than writers or painters.

At the side of this fairy godmother there reigned an old enchanter, all-powerful and good-natured:

Once upon a time there was a little girl who was usually exhibited when coffee was served. Her interest was centered mainly in the *canards,* those lumps of sugar grown-ups would dip into their coffee for her, a favour she used to ask of a fat, bald gentleman who smelt of cigars and eau-de-Portugal, whose fingers were covered in rings, and to whom one curtsied endlessly. One day she took advantage of a lull in the conversation to inquire, "Mama, why do we call Grandpapa 'Majesty'?" A glacial silence ensued, in which you could have heard a pin drop: "No more *canards,* darling, you don't look terribly well. Alfred, take Mademoiselle upstairs." Aware that she had uttered an enormity, the little girl let the footman lead her off to the nursery. Not Grandpapa — but who? What? *

And then there was her father, so handsome, so beautifully dressed, so consummately tactful. The King valued nothing so much as the kind of tact which smoothed over all obstacles, cast a veil over difficult situations, and let everyone go on believing that all was for the best in the best of all possible societies. That Colonel Keppel had had nothing to do with the vast fortune amassed by his wife, that he had

* *Triple Violette.*

watched her become the first lady at court without indulging in the sort of outburst with which Monsieur de Montespan greeted Louis XIV's expropriation of his wife, and yet that he had not forfeited the esteem of a single friend all certainly added up to a masterpiece of tact. But it was also proof of the deep love he bore Mrs. Keppel. On her side, Mrs. Keppel's regard for her husband was so great that she would never have dreamed of compromising him in the least. In short, they got on to perfection in a world in which the one unforgivable sin was to provoke scandal. Only once was Colonel Keppel reminded publicly of his wife's role: at Baden, where a grand duke remarked to him with an unpleasant laugh, "So you're a Keppel. Are you related to the King's mistress?"

Love was at the root of this very estimable partnership. Alice Edmonstone and George Keppel had a good many points in common. Though they shared youth, looks, and aristocratic family backgrounds, neither had much money. Alice's father, Admiral Sir William Edmonstone, had six children and extensive but unprofitable estates in Scotland. The Keppels had to some extent been ruined by a grandmother who adored gambling, and Lady Albemarle was trying to rebuild the family fortunes. In this respect, except for her eldest son, the children's capital consisted exclusively of their name, their connections — and their looks. It seemed only natural that Alice Edmonstone was destined to marry a very rich man and that George Keppel would have to find himself an heiress. But this sort of scheming was foreign to their natures, and having fallen in love at first sight, they were married in 1891 to the immense satisfaction of both families, neither of which thought money the most important thing in life. This was a characteristic Violet inherited, for whatever snobberies she may otherwise have indulged in, she was never a money snob.

Unhappily, it was not long before the dearth of funds began to weigh heavily on the young household, launched as it was into the thick of the most brilliant society in London, a society which gravitated around Marlborough House and was regulated according to the whims of the Prince of Wales. One of the most attractive members of this circle was William Beckett (who in 1905 succeeded his Uncle Edmund as Lord Grimthorpe). He belonged to a banking family with estates in Yorkshire and an exceptionally magnificent villa at Ravello. Following the Prince of Wales's lead, he drifted from one woman to another, and when I saw Vita Sackville-West in Florence in 1950, she told me that Beckett was probably Violet's father. The liaison of William Beckett and Alice Keppel might have blown up into a scandal (there was talk of elopement and even divorce) if George Keppel had not forgiven his wife — on one condition: that he should have a child by Alice too.

The daughter Mrs. Keppel christened Violet was born on June 6, 1894 — and it was not until 1898 that her mother met the Prince of Wales for the first time, at the races. The Prince dined with the young couple on February 28, and from that evening on the Keppels moved with the Marlborough House and Sandringham set. According to Anita Leslie in *The Fabulous Leonard Jerome,* the meeting had taken place two months earlier, at Sandown. When the Prince came to the throne in 1902, Mrs. Keppel's position at court was supreme; at the coronation, where she sat in the box the King reserved for his intimates, she was the most talked-about woman in Westminster Abbey. She drew even more eyes than Sarah Bernhardt, who was there dressed all in white, or that pretty schemer Baroness de Meyer (no one ever found out whether she was the King's daughter or his mistress — no doubt her path crossed Violet's more than once).

Chronology makes it reasonable to discard as pure fantasy Violet's hints at royal ancestry and the notorious "secrets" with which she shrouded her childhood. And yet one is often tempted to go along with her endeavor to enshrine myth as history. Was it through a kind of osmosis, or the need to play out a role, that her profile took on a clearly Hanoverian cast as she approached fifty, and that she carried herself ever more regally? And did not Vita Sackville-West write a series of poems evoking Violet that she called "King's Daughter"? Anyone who enjoys an air of mystery is free to believe that the Prince of Wales had had a deeply clandestine liaison with Mrs. Keppel and that the encounter at the races was simply a scenario contrived as a way of introducing the young woman into the Prince's circle.

There too tact triumphed over jealousy and prudishness. Mrs. Keppel was sought after even by those who sometimes resented her, like Queen Alexandra and her daughter-in-law. The Queen contented herself with the occasionally childish dig, like the day at Sandringham when the King and Mrs. Keppel drove up and descended from their car, Edward enormous and his mistress by this time rather billowy. With a quick gesture, Alexandra mimicked Mrs. Keppel's ample figure and smoothed her own slim waist, which hadn't altered in forty years. When Mrs. Keppel was present, the King did not lapse into the black moods which so upset his entourage. She had the gift of making even the most ordinary gathering amusing. She knew what to do with an offending guest the moment the King began to toy with his watch fob, always the first sign of royal displeasure. She arranged bridge games and *dîners intimes* with pretty women. She herself remained above jealousy.

Mrs. Keppel's influence also made itself felt in official circles. Lord Hardinge of Penshurst, the head of the Foreign Office, wrote:

> I would like here to pay a tribute to her wonderful discretion, and to the excellent influence which she always exercised upon the King. She never utilized her knowledge to her own advantage, or to that of her friends; and I never heard her repeat an unkind word of anybody. There were one or two occasions when the King was in disagreement with the Foreign Office, and I was able, through her, to advise the King with a view to the policy of the Government being accepted. She was very loyal to the King, and patriotic at the same time.
>
> It would have been difficult to find any other lady who would have filled the part of friend to King Edward with the same loyalty and discretion.*

The Prime Minister, Mr. Asquith, paid homage to Mrs. Keppel too. In a letter he wrote in April 1908 after a stay at Biarritz, he thanked her for "your kind words and wise counsels, which I shall treasure and (I hope) profit by."

Mrs. Keppel, very much a supporter of the Entente Cordiale, was received in France as something of a queen incognita. It is not hard to understand how all these honors went to the head of the little girl who shared in them, and that she should have tried in her old age to

* Sir Philip Magnus, *King Edward the Seventh* (London: John Murray, 1964).

recapture their splendor by assuming a role: asides to ambassadors, allusions to information from very highly placed sources, conversations with more the ring of the Congress of Vienna than the Europe of Yalta. Violet played to an audience that was sometimes bored but sometimes amused, since her inventiveness was quite equal to the role she had created for herself from her mother's life.

The King often wrote to Mrs. Keppel, brief missives drenched in a very Victorian sensibility: he would send her edelweiss from Austria or from Scotland a feather taken from the first grouse of the season. His letters sounded as though they came from a sentimental godfather, and they always began, "Dear Mrs. George . . ." Only a few of the King's letters survive: the handful that Violet had kept at St. Loup, which are now part of the Royal Archives at Windsor, the gift of John Phillips to H.M. the Queen.

Other letters, written by the King to Lady Warwick under the spell of ardent emotion, had caused such a scandal during his career as Prince of Wales that he no longer took chances. Mrs. Keppel, however, was more adventurous. Vita Sackville-West alludes to this in *The Edwardians* (for "Romola Cheyne" read Alice Keppel):

"Speaking of Romola Cheyne, wasn't she staying here last week?" Lucy knew from her tone that some revelation was imminent, and when she saw Lady Roehampton take up the blotting-book she instantly understood. "How monstrous!" cried Lucy, moved to real indignation; "how often have I told the groom of the chambers to change the blotting-paper, in case something of the sort should happen? Well, what is it all about? It makes one's blood run cold, doesn't it, to think of the hands one's letters might fall into? I suppose it's a letter to . . ." and here she uttered a name so august that in deference to the respect and loyalty of the printer it must remain unrevealed. "No," said Lady Roehampton, "that's just the point: it isn't. Look!" Lucy joined her at the mirror, and together they read the indiscreet words of Romola Cheyne. "Well!" said Lucy, "I always suspected that, and it's nice to know for certain. But what I can't understand, is how a woman like Romola could leave a letter like that on the blotting-pad. Doesn't that seem to you incredible? She knows perfectly well that this house is always full of her friends," said Lucy with unconscious irony.

The Edwardians valued nothing more than their comfort; they may not have indulged in more affairs than preceding generations, but they took more bother over them. Thus country-house weekends were always straightforwardly arranged according to Mrs. Keppel's favorite maxim, *"A chacun sa chacune,"* and lovers were assigned rooms next door to their mistresses. This shocked foreign guests; the Duchesse de Noailles was astonished to hear her hostess ask whom she would like to have installed next to her, and Daisy of Pless was amazed — very much the Prussian princess — when at a luncheon party *entre femmes* the guests, who included Mrs. Keppel, talked openly of their lovers. They all agreed, however, that it was in bad taste to display a lover's photograph instead of a husband's on one's dressing table. Both Violet Trefusis and Vita Sackville-West were brought up by mothers with relaxed morals but uncompromising manners.

In *The Edwardians* Vita Sackville-West succeeded in doing Mrs. Keppel justice but not in conveying the charm which saw her through every difficulty. Violet, on the other hand, was particularly sensitive to this charm, which prevailed even under circumstances fraught with tension. In a letter written in August 1920, Violet lamented to Vita concerning their respective mothers: "Oh the charmers of this world, what an unfair advantage is given them."*

Now to trace with Violet the two branches of the family, beginning with the maternal side, the Scottish Edmonstones. Violet Trefusis always claimed Scotland, not England, as her homeland: the marriage of an Edmonstone and a Stuart in the fifteenth century was something she never forgot. She adored her Scottish grandmother, who had been brought up in Greece where her father was governor of the Ionian Islands. He had married a Greek girl of considerable beauty, and Violet liked to recall this romantic lineage:

My grandmother was wooed and won, and taken to live in Glasgow. From Ithaca to Kelvinside! What an odyssey! How she must have loathed and resented the indefatigable rain, the sulphurous fogs, the grim bewhiskered elders!

Apparently, she bore it all with stoicism and philosophy. Year after

* Letter No. 42.

year she gave birth to daughters; the long-awaited heir died in his infancy. At last, in 1868 she was rewarded. My uncle Archie was born, to join a plethora of sisters. Meanwhile, my grandfather had succeeded to the title and estate.*

Quantities of cousins lived in rambling Scottish castles, where despite the lugubrious architecture, fantasy reigned continually. The most remarkable was her Uncle Graham, Lord Advocate of Scotland and later Lord Dunedin. Extremely cultivated and a gifted linguist, he also possessed the romantic attraction of having been the Queen of Rumania's lover. There was nothing like this among the Keppels, who were perfectly correct but not very original.

Violet often liked to refer to her Dutch ancestry. Arnold Joost Keppel, of a noble Dutch family, then a handsome lad of sixteen, had accompanied William of Orange as Page of Honour in 1688. The family fortunes were due to the affection of King William, who showered titles on Arnold Joost. He became Earl of Albemarle, a Knight of the Garter, and eventually a major general who served under the Duke of Marlborough in a series of famous battles.

William-Anne, the second Earl, was named after Queen Anne, who was his godmother. He married the Duchess of Portsmouth, daughter of the Duke of Richmond, himself the illegitimate son of Charles II and Louise de Kerouaille, a personage who always appealed to Violet's imagination. They had fifteen children. Honors continued to be showered on the second Earl, among these in 1737 the rich governorship of Virginia. A lieutenant general, and colonel of the Coldstream Guards, he became in later years ambassador in Paris, and he was noted by Casanova and Horace Walpole, among others, for the splendid state he kept.

Other eighteenth-century Keppels became famous for their naval exploits, especially August Keppel, who had joined the navy at the age of ten, and at the age of fifteen accompanied Baron Anson on the voyage around the world. He became Rear Admiral of the Blue, leading the squadron in the attack on Havana under the command of his brother, the third Lord Albemarle. This great victory increased the

* *Don't Look Round.*

fame and popularity of the Keppels, and the naval tradition continued well into the twentieth century.

The family was always one of those closely associated with the court. Various Keppels held positions with successive sovereigns, including Queen Victoria, and so it was only in the natural course of things that Alice Keppel should become acquainted with the Prince of Wales.

In her old age, Violet often turned to her legitimate ancestors as though to seek respite from her mythical origins. She found them "much more chic than those fat Hanovers." Through them too she could claim descent from the Stuarts; through the Stuarts, from the Bourbons; and through the Bourbons, from the Medicis. In fact, like so many of the English aristocracy, the Keppels were related to the irregular descendants of Charles II by either Nell Gwyn or Louise de Kerouaille, the latter allowing Violet to claim the Rohans as her cousins. Though Violet gently poked fun at the Keppels in a letter to Vita Sackville-West, she realized all she owed them.*

Colonel Keppel played a decorative role in Violet's life, a walk-on, but he formed her masculine ideal, one she eventually proposed to admirers who were not always equipped to live up to it. He was a more detached figure, not directly concerned with his grand relations, but Violet loved him very dearly as a friend whom she greatly admired. He always believed the best of everyone and never criticized others. In every way he was an optimist. With him, however, certain matters were sacrosanct: his country, his friendships, and his family traditions.

Harold Acton, who met Colonel Keppel in Florence in the 1920s, has left us a fine portrait of the man in his book *More Memoirs of an Aesthete:*

Colonel Keppel was well matched as to height and size, tall, with broad shoulders and a narrow waist, and one could picture him waltzing superbly to the strains of "The Merry Widow." His nose was a touch too aquiline but he wore a bristling miniature moustache and looked every inch a colonel, with the hearty laugh that denotes a lack of humor. I remember how shocked he was to find my mother reading a

* Letter No. 24.

book about Oscar Wilde. "A frightful bounder, it made one puke to look at him," he muttered.

In 1900 Mrs. Keppel had a second daughter, Sonia, in whom all the Keppel family qualities were to be found. The late Victorian custom was to scatter straw to smother the noise of horses' hoofs in front of a house where anyone was confined to a sickroom. So many admirers visited the convalescent young Mrs. Keppel that Portman Square was littered with straw for several days. As for Violet, she ignored her little sister until Sonia was ten — and capable of carrying on a real conversation.

# 2. A Spoiled Child

WHEN JEAN COCTEAU used to say that Violet "rolled her hoop with a sceptre," he was both summing up a childhood spent in the shadow of the throne and poking gentle fun at the megalomania her memories of this childhood gave rise to. True enough: the years from four to twelve were literally the time of Violet's life, all the rest of which was spent trying to recapture their extraordinary atmosphere. Violet was a charming young woman, but she had been an unusually pretty little girl; at the age of nine, costumed as a bacchante for a fancy-dress party, she turned the heads of more than one of her parents' male friends. Extremely proud of her daughter, Mrs. Keppel kept her at her side almost uninterruptedly. The child was as amusing as she was pretty; quick to seize on the ridiculous, she perfected a prodigious gift for mimicry. Her chatter very quickly reached an adult level: she much preferred books to dolls. The King adored her and wrote her notes signed "Kingy," which became the Keppel girls' name for him in private. Sonia devised a curious game to play with Kingy. When His Majesty would come to tea and begin nodding in front of the fire, she used to slide pieces of buttered toast down the august trouser leg: the melting butter would speed the toast on its way. The King would wake up, launch another piece down his other leg, and they would place bets on the winner. But you had to be careful: the King's laughter could degenerate into one of those interminable coughing fits due to the chronic bronchitis which eventually carried him off.

Sometimes Mrs. Keppel would take Violet to Buckingham Palace: "Go and play in the garden, darling." Bored, the little girl caught sight one day of a tricycle. She climbed aboard and blithely pedaled off. But immediately a gardener, followed by footmen and an officer of the royal household, took up the chase, shouting, "The King's tricycle!" Terrified, and unable in any case to steer the thing, Violet sped into the palace lake. She was dragged out streaming with tears and mud while the royal vehicle sank into the muck.

Some years later, this enfant terrible led the elderly sovereign into an escapade which could have had disastrous results. From 1905 onward, the financier Sir Ernest Cassel rented an entire floor of the Hôtel du Palais at Biarritz, once the Empress Eugénie's private villa, so that Mrs. Keppel could be near the King, who usually spent March on the Basque coast. But let Violet tell what happened.

At Biarritz, I heard people talking about the imminent carnival at San Sebastián. Wouldn't it be wonderful to go there with Kingy, just ourselves, without anybody knowing, and wander as we liked among the Pierrots and Colombines? Two domino masks, one large, one small, were purchased in secret and we were off — with neither an equerry nor the silver trumpet the chauffeur normally kept at his side to announce the Royal passage and make other cars pull over.

In San Sebastián the motley, hilarious crowd swallowed us up. We descended from the car into the full flood of this tide of humanity, where confetti was stuffed into our eyes and mouth and ears. It didn't matter to me, but I saw that Kingy was in trouble: his face was scarlet, and he appeared on the point of suffocating. His bronchial tubes had always been susceptible to the slightest irritation. In a panic I tore off the mask which served as his disguise. *"Es el Rey!* Can't you see it's the King? You're suffocating him!" And all the dominoes emitted screams of laughter: "Isn't she marvellous! Let's see if that's a phony beard or not!" When they had proved that it was real, they let him go . . . We were able to clear ourselves a path to the car and the petrified chauffeur.

The adventure was not a success. My mother came back early from Bayonne and discovered at once that His Majesty and Miss Violet had vanished in the direction of the Spanish border . . . Mamma was waiting for us on the villa steps, and I was sent straight to my room. As for the poor King, it was decidedly the last time that he gave in to one of my childish whims.*

* *Triple Violette.*

At Biarritz the burden of keeping the King in a good humor fell exclusively on Mrs. Keppel; on rainy days — rather frequent on the Basque coast — this was a heavy responsibility.

Everyone returned to London for spring and the Season. The first item on the agenda was to pack the Keppel girls into the electric brougham and drive them off to Woollands, in Knightsbridge, to re-plenish their wardrobes. There they would run into the Ashley girls, Sir Ernest Cassel's granddaughters, the elder of whom grew up to become Lady Mountbatten. Once Violet's nannie remarked that the Ashley sisters had real lace on their knickers: "Mrs. Ashley can afford it; I can't," retorted Mrs. Keppel.

The house at 30 Portman Square was a comparatively modest one, several stories high, a good address, but for those days not very luxurious. Luxury came later, after the King's death: Mrs. Keppel's discretion had prevailed. But the royal friendship and the necessity for incognito imbued the fashionable household with an air of mystery which immediately struck Vita Sackville-West when she visited Port-man Square:

> . . . often when I went to their house I used to see a discreet little one-horse brougham waiting outside and the butler would slip me into a dark corner of the hall with a murmured, "One minute, miss, a gentle-man is coming downstairs," so that I might take my choice whether it was the King or the doctor. Often Violet would be sent for to come down to the drawing-room, when we said, "Oh bother!"*

Sonia has described those nursery days in her enchanting memoir, *Edwardian Daughter,* but Violet largely ignored her life in London in *Don't Look Round.* She seems not to have liked much of it except for the shopping expeditions, especially to bookshops, and Bumpus was almost on the edge of Portman Square. She recalled being taken to Duveen's in Bond Street.

> Sir Joseph [Duveen] was a friend of Mama's, and he had previously told her that he had just bought a charming old Victorian doll's house, with a lot of contemporary dolls, "for fun" . . .

* *Portrait of a Marriage* (New York: Atheneum, 1973).

"There!" beamed Sir Joseph, opening the doll's house. "She can have her pick. She's not going to leave these premises without a present!"

"May I choose what I like?"

"Of course, of course!"

The moment their backs were turned, I started prowling round the shop. What about the ring that looked like a large blob of sealing-wax with a tiny person in the middle? Surely this was just the thing for me? Twirling the ring round my thumb, I flew in search of my mother, and kind Sir Joseph.

"Hullo, hullo! What have we here!" exclaimed Sir Joseph with false joviality. "The Doge's ring! Now, what a clever little girl it is to have nosed that out!"

"Go and put it back at once, darling," my mother commanded.

"But it's my present!" I protested, clutching the ring with both hands. "Sir Joseph said I might choose what I liked!"

"He meant a doll, dear, not a ring. Go and put it back this minute!"

The tears welled up in my eyes. My faith in human nature was shaken.

Sir Joseph's eyes wandered distressfully from my mother to me. Would it not be a gesture on his part, so unsemitic, and, yes, lordly, to give a fifteenth century ring to a little girl of six?

"No, Mrs Keppel," there were almost tears in *his* eyes now, "she shall keep it, as she chose it. It will be something for her to remember me by, when she's grown up . . ."*

Years later Violet gave the ring to Vita Sackville-West, and after Vita's death, Harold Nicolson gave it back to Violet.

It was hard for Mrs. Keppel after Violet's triumph in Duveen's to employ her only effective mode of punishment (the only one she ever tried, perhaps). This was to breathe coldly: "You have no charm."

The reminiscences of both Violet and her sister imply that the girls spent vast amounts of time in trains. At Christmas, they went to stay with their parents' close friends Lord and Lady Alington at Crichel, their Dorset country house, where children existed chiefly to be brought in, smothered in lace, at teatime. Napier, the future Lord Alington, became a close friend of Violet's; exceedingly handsome

* *Don't Look Round.*

and exceedingly eccentric, he charmed both sexes. On Christmas Day, the party of nearly thirty guests exchanged gold boxes and Fabergé trinkets, whose magnificence diminished, of course, in ratio to personal fortunes.

Later the family went to the Earl and Countess of Ilchester at Melbury. Lord Ilchester was one of Mrs. Keppel's staunchest admirers. She called him "Stavey," recalling the days when he was Lord Stavordale. At Melbury life was more domestic, and children and dogs took charge. Easter was spent at the Keppel family seat, Lord Albemarle's Quidenham House, where life pursued its course plainly enough among crowds of cousins and horses.

But nothing equaled the summer holidays in Scotland at Duntreath Castle,* which began in August and ended in November. In her old age, Violet often recalled them with emotion.

I would wait eagerly for the moment when the clipped little hedges of England were replaced by rambling walls of crumbling stone; the moment when the sheep assumed the long, dark, melancholy faces of Spanish grandees; when railway-station names became more and more guttural . . . At Glasgow a car would wait to drive us to my uncle's castle a dozen miles or so into the countryside. The hideous Glasgow suburbs, teeming and raffish, at least contained a kind of Jacques Callot energy which seemed to be cocking a snook at Edinburgh's venerable rectitude.

Once the last slum was behind us and the car had grazed the last drunk, the moors would come rushing up to meet us. Then we would reach the tiny loch, lofty and lonely, set in the moors like a monocle. A pair of hills stood guard above the castle, and a leaping brook wandered about the foot of a hill in the park.

The first thing that struck us as we entered the castle was its smell of cedar, tuberoses — and gunpowder. The presence of these varied ingredients was explained by the greenhouses, which furnished tuberoses (my grandmother's favorite flower) all year round, and the lavatories' cedar panelling. The musty smell of gunpowder, particularly noticeable on the ground floor, emanated from the gun-room, where highly polished

---

* A fifteenth-century castle, one of the largest of this type in Scotland, it was acquired about 1434 by Sir William Edmonstone of Culloden. It was an uninhabited ruin until restored in 1854 by Sir Archibald Edmonstone.

guns were ranged in cases lined in green baize. Masculine odours mingled with women's perfumes . . .*

There were picnics on the banks of Loch Lomond, and the great Duntreath shoots were occasionally honored by the royal presence. It was at Duntreath that Violet began her friendship with Hugh Walpole, then an undergraduate at Cambridge, spending his summer holidays as her cousins' tutor, a young man who did not approve of the Edmonstones' smart carryings-on. He was yet to write his first novel, and he was always to remain one of Violet's faithful friends. Walpole's clergyman father was incensed that his son had accepted a post with the family of the King's mistress, but the youthful Walpole reassured him that everything was perfectly respectable — the notorious Mrs. Keppel spent her evenings at the bridge table.

Violet came back from Scotland with wonderful stories about family ghosts. Later in her life she told one to Jean Cocteau, who thought it was excellent material for a film:

Great-aunt Campbell used to have the same dream over and over again. She saw a feudal castle rise up before her with drawbridge, ramparts, keep — nothing was missing. She knew it by heart. Imagine how she felt one day during a walk in the country when she turned a bend in the road and found herself face to face with her dream castle! Her heart pounding, she crossed the drawbridge and rang the bell at the side of the great nail-studded portals. In a few minutes a forbidding old servant came to open them: "Who lives here?" asked my aunt in a quavering voice. "Nobody, madam. The castle is haunted." The servant looked her up and down carefully. "But you," he said, "ought to know that better than anyone. You are the ghost!"†

Violet kept house-party photographs where Mrs. Keppel had hung them, in the bathroom at l'Ombrellino. In one the King is seated in a row of princesses in tailored tweeds enlivened with furs. Mrs. Keppel emerges from a sable stole, and at her feet sits a glowing Violet, dressed to the nines. In the second row, reserved for guests of lesser

* *Triple Violette.*
† *Triple Violette.*

rank, there is a panoply of every possible variety of beard and mustache.

From time to time Mrs. Keppel would declare: "I detest child prodigies, but all the same we've got to think about educating Violet." So she hired a French governess who had brought up the daughter of Lord Derby. She was called Hélène Claissac and was a Protestant Republican from the Midi, totally unimpressed by royalty. Despite her democratic convictions, "Moiselle" (as she was rechristened) taught Violet French by giving her the novels of the Comtesse de Ségur, the "Balzac of childhood," to read. These charming stories of the Second Empire take place in the chateaux of congenial, aristocratic families who extend their charity to whoever of the deserving poor are possessed of sentiments noble enough to enable them to transcend their origins. The plots abound in amiable generals, benign prelates, faithful servitors, and sharp-tongued dowagers. Outside this world there is no salvation; there are only pretentious nouveaux riches, swindlers, and the poor who end up in the workhouse because they have failed to heed the curé.

Violet adhered all her life to the Comtesse de Ségur's code, confirmed as it was by Mrs. Keppel's frequently reiterated admonition, "Only the right people are right." Nancy Mitford's criteria for French society were the same. Violet remained very attached to Moiselle, who died a few years after the war. She never stopped thinking of her charge as a spoiled child. Once at St. Loup, Violet introduced her to her guests sentimentally as "the lady who brought me up: Mademoiselle Claissac."

The old woman looked at the others: "Do excuse me!"

I prefer her comment on Violet to the Abbé Mugnier's. The abbé was a fashionable priest who flattered himself with having reconciled Proust to his Maker. Introduced to Mrs. Keppel, he took her hands in his own and sighed feelingly, "The source! The source!" as though Violet were a fount of profundity.

Moiselle took Violet to spend six months in Paris. It was love at first sight, and, completely under the city's spell, the little girl began to keep a diary which somewhat resembled another young Edwardian's literary effort, Daisy Ashford's *The Young Visiters*. Her heart was torn between museums and pastry shops. On one memorable occasion, looking down from a balcony that gave onto the Rue de Rivoli, she glimpsed the young Spanish King go by on his way to call on President Émile Loubet. The moment she was back in London she began to sulk and refused to work. The only way to keep peace in the family was to send her back to France.

The following Spring, I returned to Paris with Moiselle. This time I was promoted to an apartment in the Quai Debilly . . . which my mother had rented from a friend. It was full of Empire furniture, engravings of *le Roi de Rome;* it pandered to my Napoleonic cult . . .

Then there was the Sunday treat of Versailles where the fountains looked as though they were spurted by subterranean whales; the Thursday treat of Rumpelmayer with its absurd mural paintings of the Riviera (still existent) and succulent chocolate éclairs.

My mother paid me the supreme compliment of coming to stay at "my" flat. In her opinion, a woman could not learn soon enough to serve food in its proper sequence. Accordingly, one day, she told me I was to order dinner for eight and gave me *carte blanche* as to the menu, with injunctions to the cook that it must be served exactly as I ordered it, on the principle that I could only learn by experience. To the embarrassment of her guests, mayonnaise sauce appeared not once, but three times; with the fish, the *rôti*, the sweet. It happened to be my favourite sauce at the moment!

I have vivid memories of the first time I accompanied my mother to the dressmaker, where she was received like a goddess, Monsieur Jean [Worth] supervising her fitting in person, the *vendeuses* quite shamelessly forsaking their other clients to vie with each other in flattering epithets. *Il y avait de quoi!* My mother was everything that could most appeal to them, lovely, vivacious, fêted, fashionable, with a kind word for each of the anonymous old crones who had been for years in the establishment.

Even I, *en plein age ingrat,* came in for a little vicarious petting. *"De Madame Keppel je suis la fille, je suis la fille!"* I chanted to the tune of "Madame Angot" as we were ushered out.*

* *Don't Look Round.*

Jacques Émile Blanche, who often went to London, where so many of the sitters for his portraits lived, in later life reminded Violet of their first meeting.

Do you remember how Mrs George Keppel invited me to tea one day in order to show me some Chinese lacquered furniture and how you, Violet, received me, for your mother had been commanded to appear at Court? How you in short skirts expressed yourself in Paris slang like the urchins of Montmartre and how you played the hostess like an expert society woman, and when you, like a true collector, led me to inspect the rare Chinese lacquer screens, you said: "How I should like to live in Paris!"*

* *Portraits of a Lifetime.*

# 3. A Friend

One day I allowed myself to be dragged to a tea-party at Lady Kilmorey's. There I met a girl older than myself, but, apparently, every bit as unsociable. She was tall for her age, gawky, most unsuitably dressed in what appeared to be her mother's old clothes. I do not remember who made the first step. Anyhow, much to my family's gratification I asked if I might have her to tea. She came. We were both consummate snobs, and talked, chiefly, as far as I can remember, about our ancestors. I essayed a few superior allusions to Paris. She was not impressed; her tastes seemed to lie in another direction. She digressed on her magnificent home in the country, her dogs, her rabbits.

I thought her nice, but rather childish (I was then ten). We separated, however, with mutual esteem. The repressions of my short life immediately found an outlet in a voluminous correspondence. I bombarded the poor girl with letters which became more exacting as hers tended to become more and more of the "yesterday-my-pet-rabbit-had-six-babies" type. Clearly, no letter writer. Our meetings, however, atoned for this epistolary pusillanimity. These were devoted mainly to the discussion of our favorite heroes — d'Artagnan, Bayard, Raleigh. We used to sit dangling our legs over the leather fender of my father's sitting-room (he was never in at this hour) until fetched by our respective governesses. Our friendship progressed all that winter.*

That is how Violet remembered Vita Sackville-West half a century after their meeting. Compare what Vita herself recalled a decade later, when their romantic friendship had turned to passion:

* *Don't Look Round.*

I acquired a friend — I, who was the worst person in the world at making friends, closed instantaneously in friendship, or almost instantaneously (to be exact, the second time we saw each other), with Violet. I was thirteen, she was two years younger, but in every instinct she might have been six years my senior. It seems to me so significant now that I should remember with such distinctness my first sight of her; we met at a tea-party by the bedside of a mutual friend with a broken leg, and she made to me some little remark about the flowers in the room. I wasn't listening; and so didn't answer. This piqued her — she was already spoilt. She got her mother to ask mine to send me to tea. I went. We sat in a darkened room, and talked — about our ancestors, of all strange topics — and in the hall as I left she kissed me. I made up a little song that evening, "I've got a friend!" I remember so well. I sang it in my bath.*

The already strongly marked destinies of the two girls — extremely precocious for their ages — shared a few points in common. For one thing, each had a domineering mother. Lord Sackville, courteous and self-effacing, was assigned an even more difficult role in life than Colonel Keppel's — as Lady Sackville was singularly lacking in tact. The illegitimate daughter of an English peer and a Spanish dancer, the gifts of her mixed heritage were too much at odds for them ever to exert a positive influence. Despite her beauty, admired by Rodin, and her lively personality, life with her was a series of dramas. We know what Vita thought of Mrs. Keppel; here is what Violet remembered about Lady Sackville:

There was much about her mother I was at a loss to account for. Her vivacity, effervescence, like new wine in an old bottle? She was a woman of about fifty. In her too fleshy face, classical features sought to escape from the encroaching fat. An admirable mouth, of a pure and cruel design, held good. It was obvious that she had been beautiful. Her voluminous, ambiguous body was upholstered, rather than dressed, in what appeared to be an assortment of patterns, lace, brocades, velvets, taffetas. Shopping lists were pinned to her bosom. She kept up a flow of flattering, sprightly conversation, not unlike the patter of a conjurer, intent on keeping your mind off the trick he is about to perform. Like

* Portrait of a Marriage.

the conjurer, she fascinated you, more especially as these monologues were uttered in a youthful, high-stepping voice, with a strong French accent.*

And, like Mrs. Keppel's, Lady Sackville's life centered round an elderly gentleman — more notable for his great wealth than for his influence: Sir John Murray Scott, the heir to Sir Richard Wallace. Most of the time he lived in Paris in a house filled with part of Sir Richard's famous collection. He used to give Lady Sackville large sums intended to help her maintain Knole, the Sackville estate; Vita called him "Seery" and adored him. A good many years later, Vita, who spoke excellent French, came to Paris to give a lecture on Pepita and the Sackvilles. Violet had invited the entire Faubourg Saint-Germain and several members of the Académie Française. In the course of her lecture Vita remarked that "I never knew whether my mother was Sir John's mistress or not." Afterward, the audience of indignant princesses protested to Violet: "How can this Mme Nicolson, who second to yourself is the epitome of all that is best in the English, bring herself to speak in public of her mother's lovers!" Violet often used to refer to their outrage to show how staid the French were compared to the English. But she planted herself squarely on the side of the French.

For the Sackvilles, however, scandal represented just another battle to be won, another trophy to snare for the great hall at Knole. Twice in five years the most intimate affairs of the Sackville family were blazoned across the front pages. First, when Vita's grandfather Lionel died, his illegitimate offspring began a court case over the fortune and the title of Lord Sackville. The title had gone automatically to Vita's father, Lionel Sackville-West, her grandfather's nephew. Then Sir John Murray Scott's family accused the new Lady Sackville of alienating their inheritance. Seery had left her an enormous fortune and a houseful of furniture fit for a king — which she immediately sold to Seligmann's, the antique dealer (some of it can now be seen in New York in the Frick Collection). With incomparable brio and a touch of duplicity, Lady Sackville vanquished the jury. There is a photo-

* *Don't Look Round.*

graph of the family on its ways to court. Lord Sackville is impeccably turned out; Vita, with the air of an infanta incognita dodging the press, is supported by her *meniña,* Rosamund Grosvenor, a slightly faded English rose. With his charming schoolboy's face, her fiancé, Harold Nicolson, seems to be meditating on the wisdom of an alliance with this florid and scandalous family.

Obviously, we are some distance from the Keppel concern with what's "done." Nevertheless, Mrs. George and Lady Sackville were close enough to find it entirely natural that their daughters should be thrown together much of the time.

Before long Violet was invited to Knole. The huge house, with its tapestry-lined galleries, its silver, its romantically named bedrooms with beds draped like catafalques, its family portraits, and its secret staircases, was a source of pride to Lord Sackville's daughter. Violet too fell in love with the splendors of Knole and became party to its secrets.

Vita's stature was magnified for Violet by all the glamour of Knole. Already houses and their atmospheres counted for her, more perhaps, than the people who inhabited them. Years later, her own houses were much more a matter of atmosphere than décor, and she could forgive anyone anything if she liked the house he lived in.

At Knole or in the Scottish castles of Violet's family, where they met as fellow guests, the girls became madly romantic. Their favorite author was Edmond Rostand. They knew *Cyrano de Bergerac* by heart, as well as the symbolist play in verse he had written for Sarah Bernhardt, *La Princesse Lointaine.* In 1910 Violet wrote to her friend from Ceylon, enclosing three lines from the play; for her, the Princesse Lointaine was Vita.

> *Le seul rêve intéresse*
> *Vivre sans rêve ou-est-ce?*
> *Et j'aime la Princesse Lointaine*

They read Baudelaire and Verlaine, too, but it was Rostand who held them in thrall. With Alexandre Dumas and Sir Walter Scott, his influence pervaded the historical novels the fourteen-year-old Vita began to turn out one after another: *The Earl of Dorset, The King's Secret, The City of the Lily.*

The last of these was written in homage to Florence, which she visited in 1908 with Violet and her nannie. Rosamund Grosvenor also went along. Before they left, Violet told Vita that she loved her. It was a tribute Vita accepted, flattered by the conquest of so elegant a friend, but that was as far as things went. Vita had been prepared for Tuscany by her favorite poets, and she was totally enchanted by it. Violet missed Paris a little, but both were alert to the attentiveness of Italian men, both those respectably introduced and the others in the street, who might vigorously launch an amiable remark or two in their direction. In 1951, Vita came back to Florence to stay briefly at Violet's. I remember a drive we all took through the city's crowded streets. The two women indulged in a leisurely survey of the pass-ers-by, their verdicts those of a pair of latter-day disciples of Oscar Wilde: "Ah, my dear, that profile: *pure* Donatello!" "Look, Vita! The flower-seller!" "Divine! A Botticelli!" "And do look at that one, a little on the heavy side, but *very* attractive!" "A Michelangelo, darling. Heavens, but these people *are* beautiful!"

When Vita came back on her own a year after her first visit, a young Italian aristocrat, the Marchese Orazio Pucci, began to pay her court. He even followed her to England. She treated him with more irony than compassion. But for Vita as for so many Englishwomen, Florence remained the "City of the Soul."

In September of the same year, Lady Sackville took her daughter to Scotland to stay with Sir John Murray Scott. Violet was at Duntreath, where she invited her friend to come:

> I remember various details about that visit: how Violet had filled my room with tuberoses, how we dressed up, how she chased me with a dagger down the long passage of that very ancient Scotch castle, and concluded the day by spending the night in my room. It was the first time I ever spent the night with anyone, though goodness knows it was decorous enough: we never went to sleep, but talked throughout the night, while little owls hooted outside. I can't hear owls now without recalling her soft troubling presence in my room in the dark.*

* *Portrait of a Marriage;* also see Letter No. 62.

At the time Vita wrote these lines Violet was also thinking about Scotland — and sent her a letter in the same spirit.*

During the next couple of years, 1909 and 1910, the friends rarely saw each other. Vita went to Russia with her mother and Sir John. In her diary, Daisy, Princess of Pless, noted that the Sackville-Wests stayed at Furstenstein Castle in Silesia, where the party was made up entirely of names from the *Almanach de Gotha:* Arenberg, Windisch-Graetz, Thurn und Hohenstein. In Russia, Vita was dazzled by the magnificent life her hosts led and by the splendors of St. Petersburg. Meanwhile, Violet went back to Paris for six months before the usual removals to Biarritz and Scotland.

Then, in November 1910, a pall descended over the Keppel household: the King was gravely ill. Mrs. Keppel remained in seclusion while she waited for the latest news to be telephoned from the palace. On November 5, she went to see her old friend for the last time. In his sickroom were gathered Sir Ernest Cassel, Mrs. Willy James, and other friends of his youth. The next day the King died. Queen Alexandra immediately notified Mrs. Keppel and herself escorted her into the room where the King's body lay. Sonia was astonished at the way his death had turned their family life upside-down. But Colonel Keppel explained: "He was a great king and a wonderful man." The Keppels closed Portman Square and went with their daughters to stay with Mrs. Arthur James.

Mrs. Keppel decided to stay out of sight as long as the official mourning lasted, and then to wait even longer before coming back to London. This was one of this remarkable woman's most intelligent decisions; she avoided the embarrassments of curiosity and compassion, the depressing influence of all the changes at court and society wrought by sovereigns very different from Edward and Alexandra. When she did return, two years later, her hair had turned white — and she was still only forty-three.

Thus, very soon after the King's death, Mrs. Keppel and her daughters, with Moiselle, Nannie, and a party of friends and relations, sailed for Ceylon, where Sir Thomas Lipton had lent them his luxurious bungalow, surrounded by his tea plantations. On the eve of the sailing, Violet

* Letter No. 42.

and Vita went to the theater together. After the play, Violet tried to persuade Vita to come with her in a discussion that grew so animated their car was forced to take several turns around Hyde Park.

From Ceylon, Violet wrote, usually in French. Her letters were flirtatious, romantic, and often extremely amusing despite her adolescent affectations and self-satisfaction in her own cleverness.* Ceylon bored Violet, however, and the East was never to hold any charms for her. Yet she later recalled, in a few glittering images, the island's hills and green forests.

Three months passed, and the family went their various ways. The grown-ups left for the East, where Mrs. Keppel and her husband had planned to spend a year in China. She adored Peking, she adored the Chinese, and it was China that perfected her taste for lovely things. She eventually came back to Europe with trunks full of marvelous objects, and a mind enriched with new understanding.

Violet returned from Ceylon early in 1911 with rubies for Vita, which she gave to her in Monte Carlo, where Lady Sackville had rented an enormous villa, surrounded by olive trees, for Vita to convalesce in; she suspected her daughter to be consumptive after a bout of pneumonia. Violet rejoined Sonia in Munich, where the girls had been to a kind of finishing school, and before long she was begging Vita to come and join her and her large circle of new friends. She went to the opera constantly, where she familiarized herself with the Wagnerian mythology. She even fell in love with a Wittelsbach prince: "I saw myself as a mixture of Lola Montez and the 'Winter Queen.' We met at the Nymphenburg house of a lady called Pepita de Carmendillas who specialized in pretenders and lost causes. It was bliss." And besides the opera and Bavarian princes, there were her painting lessons and her visits to romantic castles. It was in Munich that Violet acquired her pronounced taste for the *Mittel Europa* of the Orient Express. She dreamed of Warsaw and Vienna and Budapest, and as soon as she was allowed to travel on her own, she hurried off to see them.

* Letters Nos. 1 and 2.

# 4. The Reluctant Debutante

IN 1912 Mrs. Keppel came back to London and began to live in the splendor that good taste forbade while the King was still alive. Her new house at 16 Grosvenor Street was furnished luxuriously in accordance with the newly refined sensibility for which she had China to thank. She began to entertain constantly. In *Great Morning* Sir Osbert Sitwell left a charming portrait of the house and Mrs. Keppel. It must have been one of the most remarkable houses in London. Behind the dignified Georgian façade was an immensely light and spacious house which everywhere reflected Mrs. Keppel's love of splendor. The rooms were magnificent to the last detail. It was Mrs. Keppel who first introduced Chinese carpets to London, and with typical finesse she kept Angora cats to match, but as impressive as the décor, complete with the red lacquer cabinets and huge porcelain pagodas, was the way in which she as a hostess conducted the running of the house.

All who visited her spoke in later life of her ability to entertain and her gift of conversation. She was humorous, kind and, surprisingly for one who did not suffer fools gladly, displayed the utmost good nature to all with whom she spoke. A memorable figure in a fashionable world, she was exact and devoid of pettiness. Always she had a boldness and a power of enchantment. There too, as if to complement their mother, lived Violet and Sonia.

Once settled, Mrs. Keppel left for Munich to check on her daughters. She was dismayed to find that Violet had become a "budding Gretchen." More than ever, she wanted her back in England to prepare for her coming-out and to begin grooming herself for the marriage market. Still, the road from Munich to London took a detour through the fitting rooms of the Paris couturiers. While they were in Paris, Mrs. Keppel decided to let her daughter try her social wings, and took her to dine at Boni de Castellane's. It turned into one of the most delightful passages in Violet's memoirs:

Boni de Castellane was, I suppose, at the zenith of his prestige. Regarded with the irreverence of seventeen he had fuzzy pink hair set rather far back on his forehead, a fair drooping moustache, heavy-lidded sleepy eyes, and the staccato walk of an automaton. But he was very kind.

His house, lit exclusively by candles, was lovely, full of exquisite bibelots and family pictures, including a portrait of his great ancestor, Talleyrand. Hypnotized by all this, I sat silently at dinner, conscientiously drinking the wine that was poured into glass after glass. Accustomed to the most Spartan of evening meals based on biscuits and a glass of milk, I was determined to drink as to the manner born.

Presently, one of my neighbours remarked slyly: "You seem very young, Mademoiselle. Would this by any chance be your first grown-up dinner party?" This would never do.

"My first dinner party," I snorted. "I would have you know, Monsieur, that I have just celebrated my twenty-fifth birthday!" As ill luck would have it there was a dead silence as I uttered these words. My mother heard, and threw me a look of unadulterated fury. I collapsed into a crestfallen silence, and took a great gulp from one of my glasses.

Was it my imagination, or were there two Boni de Castellanes, or had he a brother who was very like him, a twin, perhaps? I blinked again. Curious that I shouldn't have noticed there were two of them . . .

I seemed to have some difficulty in articulating, could it be the wine? Horror! I put down the glass I was in the act of conveying to my mouth.

"If I were you, *chère Mademoiselle,* I think I would stick to one kind of wine," his voice was now definitely motherly, "mixtures are bad for the stomach. Personally, I drink nothing but Bordeaux."*

Violet was enchanted with Grosvenor Street. She was given a kind of minuscule studio at the top of the house, which she began to stuff full of antique brocades and vaguely Renaissance furniture. But

* *Don't Look Round.*

it wasn't long before the decorations were revised, and Bakst-inspired incense burners and piles of colorful cushions were installed under the influence of the Ballet Russe, now the toast of London. With her friends the Alingtons, Lady Juliet Duff, and others chosen from the more emancipated of her contemporaries, Violet gave intimate soirées in her studio. Did she see herself as Scheherazade? One evening, the younger brother of one of her guests was whisked into the studio, disrobed, painted black, decked out in a turban, and pressed into service as a slave to hand round the refreshments.

Diaghilev, Nijinsky, and Karsavina often came to dine in Grosvenor Street or at Lady Alington's, and Violet definitively forsook Germany for Russia. When she wrote to Vita now she signed herself "Lushka" and called Vita "Mitya." The Grand Duke Michael and his morganatic wife, the Countess Torby, were old friends of Mrs. Keppel's, and they helped add more luster to the land of Prince Igor. Once, Diaghilev even asked Mrs. Keppel to lend him her vast drawing room as a temporary rehearsal hall.

Soon Mrs. Keppel's own visitors began to wend their way up to the studio guided by the smell of incense. George Moore, temporarily abandoning Lady Cunard, came to read poetry to Violet — not necessarily his own. On the stairs he might pass Hugh Walpole, fresh from his first literary success, or a humorous politician like Lord Haldane. Violet set about writing poetry too — in English: she had already written a play in German. Some of her poems were gathered into a limited edition destined for her friends; some appeared in literary reviews. Mrs. Keppel detested earnest women intellectuals, and a reputation as a bluestocking was, of course, no help in matchmaking. Her tact deserted her for once, and she teased Violet. How much, she wanted to know, did an editor pay to publish one of her poems. "Almost nothing," was the reply. Mrs. Keppel suggested that in that case she might as well drop her ill-paid exertions.

Ever since her return from Germany Violet had wanted to see Vita, and eventually an invitation to Knole arrived.

If she expected a horizontal pseudo-Gretchen, I expected a "representative Englishwoman," perpendicular, gauche, all knobs and knuckles. No one told me that Vita had turned into a beauty. The knobs and knuckles had disappeared. She was tall and graceful. The profound, hereditary Sackville eyes were as pools from which the morning mist had lifted. A peach might have envied her complexion. Round her revolved several enamoured young men, one of whom had presented her with a bear, inevitably christened Ivan. Bears had taken the place of rabbits.

She had all the prestige that two years' precedence *dans le monde* can confer. I felt resentful, at a disadvantage. Surely she might have kept me informed of her evolution? "Do you like my dress? *Tu me trouves jolie?*" I questioned eagerly, reverting to the French of our childhood, pining for praise. *"Tu as beaucoup de chic,"* was the cautious reply.*

Violet persuaded Vita to share her enthusiasm for the exhilarating German music. Prince Paul of Yugoslavia recalled one evening with amusement. It was his first big dinner party in London at Mrs. Keppel's. All the most celebrated Edwardians were there, including Lady Sackville, who to him looked rather witchlike. After dinner somebody sat down at the piano, and Violet and Vita, who were not among the guests, made an entrance in eighteenth-century costumes and improvised a kind of dance or pantomime based on *Der Rosenkavalier.* Naturally, Vita took the role of Octavian. The guests quickly began to fidget: the exhibition was, after all, somewhat shocking. An embarrassed Mrs. Keppel put an unceremonious end to it.

Nevertheless, Vita didn't try to see Violet too often; her life was becoming rather complicated. For one thing, the tepid and clinging Rosamund Grosvenor would weep all night when she knew a visit to Violet was in the offing. For another, Vita had begun to feel a strong attraction to one of the most intelligent young men she had yet encountered in her round of London balls: Harold Nicolson, son of the English ambassador to St. Petersburg and nephew of a viceroy of India, the Marquess of Dufferin and Ava. But this family of impecunious high civil servants did not impress the Sackvilles. They wanted a much grander match for Vita. Viscount Lascelles, heir to Harewood House (who later married Mary, the only daughter of George V), and the Marquess of Granby, heir to Belvoir, were both in love with

* *Don't Look Round.*

the slender, slightly melancholic young woman whose personality is reflected in de László's 1910 portrait.

In his review of *Portrait of a Marriage,* Christopher Sykes very justly stressed the basic egocentricity of this young woman, who later obliged her husband to give up a brilliant career. Her self-centeredness explains the trouble she had in mustering much interest in her children. Romantic warmth, deep sensuality, and quantities of charm masked a toughness which turned all the crueler if her victim protested. That Violet was madly in love with Vita seems to have been an open secret at Knole. One day Lord Sackville remarked to Vita that Violet would turn pale when her friend came into the room. Violet might be deep in one of her brilliant conversations, or launched on one of her parodies, but she would immediately fall silent. If Vita was egocentric, Violet was — luckily for her — intensely frivolous. She would never lock herself into her room to shed tears, like silly Rosamund. No, she would flirt outrageously with the best-looking boy among the houseguests and put her love out of mind for a while.

It became clear, even before Violet was launched on her first season, that she was not going to be easy to marry off. Mothers found her too "fast," and she did not get on with girls her own age apart from Vita, whom she saw less and less. Yet she did have some suitors. If the confidences of an old lady can be believed, it was exclusively her own doing that she did not become the Duchess of Wellington or Lady Sitwell. Certainly both men remained loyal friends and used to share a host of old jokes with her. Proper young men kept their distance — Violet was a bluestocking, after all! But this failed to scare away Julian Grenfell, Lord Desborough's son, who had grown up among "souls."

I met Julian in the spring before war was declared, at Taplow. He resembled a young gladiator with his curly, bullet-shaped head, projecting lip, cleft chin, magnificent physique. The loveliest girls in London were there for him to choose. His deepest, implacable eye raked the room. I suddenly felt a hand on my shoulder. "Let's get out of here, come for a walk." Dumb with surprise and gratitude, I found myself being propelled at great speed through a still wintry wood.

"You see, I'm anti-social," he was saying. "I don't even possess a dinner jacket. I loathe parties. What the hell are you doing here?"

"But let me . . ."

"Yes, I know, you're a débutante and all that, but that's no answer to my question."

"As a matter of fact," I stammered, anxious to rehabilitate myself in his eyes, "I didn't want to come out, it was forced upon me."

"Oh well, there's some hope then."

Before I knew where I was, I began to tell him the story of my life up to date. Of course, I fell in love with Julian. Who didn't? His manner of wooing, if anything so tempestuous could be called by so mild a name, was unconventional to say the least of it.

He would arrive at Grosvenor Street dressed in an old sweater and crumpled grey flannel trousers, with frequently a black eye, and, more than once, a split lip (having been boxing the night before); would sweep aside the terrorized footman, mount the stairs four at a time, and burst into my so-called "studio" . . . (Let no one be under any misapprehension concerning Julian's intentions. He suggested everything, bless his heart, short of matrimony!) . . . Julian alternately fascinated and terrified me. On one occasion, I dragged him to a ball given by one of my relatives. Bursting out of hired "tails," he lured me to the ladies' cloakroom, where he locked us in. An awkward moment arose when a member of the Royal family asked for her cloak. Had he been less precipitate he would doubtless have won my consent to — anything.

Alas! His courtship was too spectacular, the ladies' cloakroom incident did not pass unnoticed. My father was infuriated by his dress, his recurrent black eye, his *sans gêne*. Julian was banned.*

Violet loved to dance, but not at the great balls, now that the gramophone let you dance whenever you liked. Two years before the First World War, this reluctant debutante gave her friends a foretaste of the twenties. The craze for the Ballet Russe had given way to a new craze for jazz. Violet found a kindred spirit in Nancy Cunard, who was also to become the despair of her mother. They joined forces with composer-painter Gerald Berners and took up everything his set found amusing.

* *Don't Look Round.*

Under the influence of this gifted circle, Violet before long decided she would write, and despite her frivolous side, she never deserted this vocation. She always had something in the works, and from the outset firmly enlisted herself on the side of Bohemia — in reaction to her mother's establishment background, where the principal diversions were bridge and horse racing. Naturally, the example of Vita, who had been writing from childhood, helped sway the highly talented Violet.

By 1912 Vita had more confidence in her own talents — and she made two decisions: to become a great poet and to marry Harold Nicolson. She spent very little time in England that year and the next. She went back to Florence with the faithful Rosamund and journeyed to her grandmother's homeland, Spain. I do not know how she and her mother took it into their heads that Pepita was the daughter of a Spanish grandee, but once Violet told this author that this grandfather — the Spanish ambassador to St. Petersburg — led so luxurious an existence that he maintained furnished houses in all the major cities between Madrid and St. Petersburg, each complete with servants and horses, so that he would never have to sleep under a strange roof: a story so extravagant it deserves to be true!

Her life abroad and her flirtations counted for little against Vita's decision to become engaged — which earned her a sarcastic letter from Violet. On October 1, 1913, she married Harold at Knole, with Rosamund as maid of honor. Violet did not attend. Next came a honeymoon in Italy, Egypt, and finally Turkey, where the couple spent the winter in Constantinople: Harold was an attaché at the British Embassy there. He introduced to Vita a Frenchman, a contemporary and an ex-lover. He was called Pierre de Lacretelle, slender, dark, vivacious, and highly intelligent. His brother Jacques, a novelist and member of the Académie Française, later became a great friend of Violet's. Pierre got over his affair, but at the age of eighty, he still used to recall Harold and their strolls along the edge of the Bosphorus with some emotion. Harold himself evoked the atmosphere of those twilight days of the Turkish Empire in his story "Professor Malone," from *Some People*.

The Keppels continued to give balls for Violet at which they managed to have a much better time than their daughter. The colonel methodically sorted guests into a variety of categories, keeping a precise record of these as well as acceptances and regrets. He drew up the seating plans for dinner too. Mrs. Keppel looked on serenely. If someone congratulated her after a party, she would say, "Oh, George did all that. I just picked up the cigarette ends." Paul Morand, in those days an attaché at the French Embassy, has left a dazzling souvenir of these evenings, *"Parmi les Laques Vertes."* The Keppels had no country house for matchmaking weekends, but they did have a friend, Baroness Daisy de Brienen, who lent them her eighteenth-century house built over a canal near The Hague. It was called Clingendaal:

> . . . shoals of guests, including a suitor or two, came to spend August and September with us. We used to bathe in the morning at Scheveningen, sightsee in the afternoon, sometimes dress up for dinner. In the summer of 1914, all the brilliant, doomed young men the war was to annihilate, George Vernon, Volley Heath, Patrick Shaw Stewart, Raymond Asquith, Bim Tennant, flocked to Holland. Diana Manners, dazzling, disconcerting, came with her mother, the Duchess of Rutland, Diana appeared, as it were, to people, lighting up the room with her flawless, awe-inspiring beauty . . .
>
> Lady Oxford and the epigrammatical Elizabeth also visited us: in fact, they were there when the war broke out. We all crowded on the night boat to Newhaven. The following morning, we breakfasted at 10 Downing Street, which gave us the momentary thrill of being behind the scenes, though, of course, we saw nothing, not even the dumpy, grumpy figure of the Prime Minister.*

Two of Violet's closest friends, Julian Grenfell and Willie Edmonstone, were among the first to die in the war, and it was during this period that Violet drew closer to her sister, Sonia, who, she had finally realized, possessed sufficient wit to carry on a conversation. Totally unalike but equally gifted, the two sisters admired but rarely understood each other. Still, they managed to share a great many good times. In 1917, Mrs. Keppel was put in charge of a hospital at Boulogne with Lady Sarah Wilson, and Colonel Keppel was sent to train recruits in Ireland. Violet felt lost in London and went for long visits

* *Don't Look Round.*

to Berkeley Castle as the guest of Margaret Dansey, called Pat, the niece of Lord Fitzhardinge. Here she lived in a medieval setting worlds away from the drama that was ravaging Europe. It was a setting that allowed her to indulge her half-historical, half-sentimental fantasies with no fear of interruption. And Violet could confide in Miss Dansey about Vita, whom she saw rarely, even though Vita had been back in England since June 1914.

Apparently the young Nicolsons were in transports of mutual adoration. Then, in August, they had a son, Benedict. Violet insisted on becoming his godmother, but aside from a lavish present on the occasion of his wedding, she took no more interest in this godson than in her other godchildren.

In March 1915, the Nicolsons bought Long Barn, a sixteenth-century farmhouse only two miles from Knole. Violet, who disliked the role of spectator to their domestic bliss, once complained after a brief stay: "The annoying thing about a Tudor house is that you feel as though you're living *under* the furniture, not over it." She did not pay them another visit until April 1918 — a visit which decided her entire life and led to one of those crises which the Sackville grandeur managed to take in its stride without much difficulty but which to the Keppels was anathema.

# 5. *Courting Scandal*

THE THREE YEARS of drama, elopement, and folly that marked the passionate relationship between Violet Trefusis and Vita Sackville-West have been so meticulously traced by Nigel Nicolson that it would be presumptuous to go over them again in detail. But a résumé of their affair will serve as useful background to Violet's letters, many more of which are reproduced here, and at greater length than in *Portrait of a Marriage*. These letters show Violet in a worse predicament than Vita because of her more pronounced femininity — and her terrible isolation. Vita was a Gibraltar of a woman who could, moreover, count in times of stress on a husband who was always there to tell her how wonderful she was and that he would love her forever. Denys Trefusis was less amiable than Harold Nicolson and bore the scars of a war Harold had not fought; he was both less flexible and more vulnerable. He is more to be pitied in his unhappiness. He felt himself cruelly betrayed, while Harold, once the crisis was over, resumed his role of indulgent comrade.

That Mrs. Keppel should have taken a strict line is understandable. In her youth she had steered a perilous and successful course between the shoals and reefs of scandal, and now all at once a passion she found unbearable to contemplate threatened to blacken the family name. The Edwardians took adultery in their stride, and a woman of fashion who was what we would bluntly label a nymphomaniac was simply a "poor dear." But they did not extend the same tolerance to homosexuals — of either sex. The Oscar Wilde affair had left a whiff of sulfur in the air, and for homosexuals with means, it was more prudent to go away to live in, say, Italy, if they wanted to avoid the nuisances of scandal and blackmail. It was to Italy that lesbian couples like Radclyffe Hall, author of *The Well of Loneliness,* and her friend, Una Troubridge, fled. Lady Troubridge had just stepped down from a central role in a divorce trial which must certainly have provided food for thought to the Keppels and Sackvilles. Her husband, Admiral Sir John Troubridge, had cited Radclyffe Hall as co-respondent — and not, as had heretofore been done, another man. The scandal was immense, for all that the families involved were far less prominent than the Keppels or the Sackvilles. Elsewhere, Vernon Lee (Violet Paget) held court on Bellosguardo Hill, overlooking Florence (where Mrs. Keppel herself bought a villa in 1927), and other women in this predicament withdrew deep into the country. Of course, male or female, many homosexuals were prepared to let discretion take precedence of passion and maintained their place in society at the cost of no more than a little mild gossip.

Lady Sackville, ordinarily so extravagant herself, was more vexed than outraged, and on the whole fairly reasonable. She held endless conferences with Mrs. Keppel on how best to lure Vita and Violet back to the fold. It was said that as a last resort the two mothers went to see the bankers who managed their daughters' various trust funds and persuaded them to disregard the couple's requests for money. Mrs. Keppel and Lady Sackville were certainly formidable enough to cow bank managers, but it seems that Violet had in any case always depended on her mother, and Vita partly on her husband, partly on Lady Sackville. Yet in February 1920 they had managed to scrape together enough to think of buying a house in Italy or Greece.

Vita had no illusions about her mother; she granted her a measure of charm, that was all. Violet, who adored her mother, felt nothing but guilt at wounding her this way, a guilt transformed into feelings of hostility. She called Mrs. Keppel *men Chinday* in the private language she used with Vita, whose strange vocabulary, mostly borrowed from Spanish Gypsy words, included expressions like *chapiscar,* "let's escape." Once when Violet was alone for a few days in her parents' house, she used words to describe the house that she might just as well have applied to her mother: "this inhuman detached disdainful house." In Vita's version of the affair, she calls her friend's mother a "demon of a woman." However, Mrs. Keppel was too intelligent to provoke a break; there were very few scenes, no estrangements.

Violet's mother's principal objection to her going off for good with Vita was certainly the opprobrium attached to such adventures. She explained coldly to Violet that she would forever be considered *à côté:* definitely on the sidelines. All her relations, the Edmonstones as well as the Keppels, would regard her as the black sheep of the family. "Very well," Violet replied, "then I'll become a bohemian," and she drew even closer to her Gypsy Vita.

For anyone who knew Violet in her later years, when she seemed to set so much store by society's opinion and remained concerned with propriety despite all her eccentricities, it is an extraordinary sensation to read letters as courageous and rebellious as those written during this period. She wanted to shout her love from the housetops, and her revolt was a harbinger of Women's Liberation. More precisely, she was both a lyrical suffragette and an aristocrat disdainful of convention.

In her letters, Violet often returns to her desire to lead an artist's life, perhaps in a shared Paris studio on £200 a year. When Vita went back to Harold — in Paris — Violet waxed satiric over the upper-bohemian life in store for her there as the wife of a future ambassador. She would end up exchanging witticisms with Jean Cocteau. In fact, this was the life Violet was herself to lead a few years hence. Renunciation of the advantages that were so much a part of her parents' world was an integral part of the need she felt that she required to serve Beauty. Violet and Vita had been shaped by the aesthetic movement; spiritually, they were the daughters of Christina Rossetti and Oscar Wilde (with, as we have seen, a romantic legacy from Edmond Rostand). They dreamed of dedicating their whole existence to Beauty. Vita would become a great poet, a lesbian Byron, with Violet as her muse. Irresistibly, the wonderful lesbian ladies Ronald Firbank put into *Caprice* and *Inclinations* come to mind, so affected but sincere in their quest after the Beautiful. In one of her letters Violet wrote: "I feel a Beauty I cannot express, my life is an altar, my being is a sacrifice. If ever I could make others feel the universe of blinding beauty that I almost see at times I should not have lived in vain."

One speculates that had they succeeded in spending their lives together they would probably have settled down in Andalusia, out of Violet's love for Vita, her taste for the romantic, and attachment to the feudal order. She had decided very early in life that Spain was her spiritual home. She had had a Spanish admirer, one of Mrs. Keppel's friends, a man she loved when she was sixteen and made fun of when she was eighteen. But he floated back into her memories when she was seventy:

I fell irretrievably in love with an "old man" of thirty-five, a friend of my parents and a scion of Seville to his fingertips. At that age one tends to look on the fleeting as eternal, and I held my peace . . . I pined. Life was drained of meaning. I would not have admitted to my infatuation for an empire. On the eve of our departure for England, he came to pay a farewell call. Mama wasn't yet ready, so I received him in the drawing-room. My heartbeats were deafening, but I said not a word. "What's wrong, *Mademoiselle?* You seem so sad." And I replied, throwing caution to the winds, "It's because you don't like me, *Monsieur.*" He drew himself up to his full height: "And . . . if . . . I love you," he stammered, "is it any concern of yours?"*

Violet's tensions and raptures smoldered away with occasional bursts of affection until she came to spend a few days alone with Vita at Long Barn at the end of April 1918. Two years afterward, Vita set down all the details of that day, the climax of a hitherto not overly successful visit. She had been afraid that Violet was bored — Violet, who was in fact enthralled by her friend's boyish clothes and high spirits. Then came the evening, and they fell into each other's arms. From the beginning Violet assumed the "feminine" role: "She was far more skilful than I. I might have been a boy of thirteen and she a woman of thirty-five," Vita recalled.

The early days of their liaison were ecstatically happy; the friends went off to Cornwall for a fortnight. Sometimes they would travel to Plymouth to visit a music hall, where they tasted the pleasures of incognito before those of the transvestism to come.† Then Vita had

* *Triple Violette.*
† Letter No. 9.

to go back to Long Barn; she did not like to leave Harold alone for very long. But for most of July, Vita and Violet stayed in Cornwall, this time in a house Hugh Walpole lent them. Before long, Violet could only think about running away with Vita and starting a new life. This impulse to flee appears in most of the letters Violet wrote to her friend when they were separated — one a day, or two or three in times of crisis, and all of which Vita carefully put back into their envelopes and saved. Denys Trefusis destroyed Vita's letters to Violet.

At the beginning, neither family thought much about it when the two eccentric friends left for the seaside; Harold was the first to start worrying, followed by Mrs. Keppel, who decided to marry Violet off as soon as she could. She was convinced that marriage would cure her of her childish whims. Violet, despite the tensions involved, remained under her mother's spell. On August 27, 1918, she wrote to Vita, somewhat cynically:

> Chinday has been so marvellously "witful" here that I could forgive her anything. She is a clever woman: I do admire her. I adore the unparalleled romance of her life. My dear: our respective mothers take "some" beating! I wonder if I shall ever squeeze as much romance into my life as she has had in hers; anyhow I mean to have a jolly good try! *À tout prendre, j n'ai pas trop mal débuté* [everything considered, I haven't made a bad start!].

Was it to justify this cynicism that Violet eventually agreed to marry Denys Trefusis? Things became difficult every time one of her fiancés began to turn serious. Here is how she saw it all thirty years later:

> I got engaged more than once, with varying motives; compassion, curiosity, boredom, physical attraction. I got engaged, but somehow shied at matrimony . . .
>
> Then, the last year of the war, I met Denys Trefusis, who, like Julian Grenfell, was an Elizabethan. He had a pale arrogant face, whose logical conclusion would seem to be a pointed beard; I mentally added a ruff and one pearl earring. It was impossible to look better bred, more audacious. Slim and elegant, he could not help dramatizing his appearance; like Lord Ribblesdale, he made the most ordinary clothes

appear picturesque. Intrepid, rebellious, he had led an adventurous, exciting life, having run away to Russia when he was little more than a schoolboy, refusing to accept money from home, living on the proceeds of half a dozen improvisations. More Russian than English, he returned to England at the outbreak of war, where he joined the "Blues."

Who was I to withstand such nomadic prestige, such intransigence, so many challenges to my imagination? In fact, the only time I ever succumbed to *le charme slave* was with Denys. I was by no means the only girl to set her cap at him. Never did I work so hard. At long last, he began to respond, taking care to explain that, like Julian, he was anti-matrimony . . . Why did I always want to marry people who had a prejudice against what is called "settling down"?

On his return to the front, I wrote innumerable, and judging by the result, successful letters. On his next leave he reluctantly proposed.*

Everyone was under the young officer's spell. Vita, who quickly came to hate him, nevertheless had to admit that Denys was exceptionally intelligent and sensitive. Violet began to call him Loge, after Wagner's elusive god of fire in *Das Rheingold*. The Keppels might have preferred someone with more money, or the heir to a great name, but his family was otherwise impeccable, one of the oldest in Cornwall. Denys' grandfather was the twentieth Baron Clinton; the family had important connections and would establish others. Yet there *was* a touch of eccentricity. Denys' elder brother had married the daughter of Lord Hardinge of Penshurst, a woman so much older than himself that he had served as a page at her first wedding.

In October the friends saw each other daily in London. At the beginning of their liaison they had started on a novel, *Challenge,* whose protagonists were portraits of themselves. Vita is "Julian," a young Englishman whose family is the richest family in a vaguely Hellenistic republic, and who aids a vassal island offshore to gain its independence. Violet is "Eve," his cousin, who joins him in the adventure but ends by betraying Julian. She wants him to herself, without having to reckon with his newly won power over the islanders. Julian proceeds to humiliate his cousin — and to retain her — by proposing marriage, but in her pride in her own independence she drowns herself (like

* *Don't Look Round.*

Sappho). While this might make a good film script, it is not a very good plot for a novel. Some of the amusing secondary characters are reminiscent of Norman Douglas' *South Wind:* Balkan ladies and diplomats whose originals Vita must have encountered in Constantinople.

Eve represents the eternal feminine, heightened by Violet's fantasies:

> . . . Eve's world, ephemerally and clandestinely populated. He contemplated it in fascination, acknowledging that here was an additional, a separate art, insistent for recognition, dominating, imperative, forcing itself impudently upon mankind, exasperating to the straight-minded because it imposed itself, would not be denied, was subtle, pretended so unswervingly to dignity that dignity was accorded it by a credulous humanity — the art which Eve practised, so vain, so cruel, so unproductive, the most fantastically prosperous of imposters!

With all the fervor of youth, the friends did not hesitate to include a good deal of purple prose, which is nonetheless meant perfectly seriously. Some of these passages were underlined in pencil by Violet herself when she reread *Challenge* in 1922, just after the final break. J. W. Lambert very fairly noted in his *Sunday Times* review of the book:

> Eve (a portrait, much enjoyed by its original, of Violet Trefusis) is an appalling young creature. More described than created, until she goes into action as a sexual suppliant, she draws from her author repeated chains of doting adjectives ("meddlesome, elusive, tantalising, detached . . . selfish, jealous, unkind, pernicious, indolent, vain"). [He concludes by summing the novel up as] a daydream which sweeps along with all the exhilarating courage of its own absurdity . . .

Violet soon found herself unable to endure long separations from Vita, who had truly become Julian,* and immediately after the Armistice, the two friends decided to leave for Paris. A friend, Edward Knoblock (the author of *Kismet*), lent them his pied-à-terre in the Palais Royal. Like Hugh Walpole, he was a fashionable homosexual. The idea of becoming accomplices in an adventure as romantic as it

* Letter No. 9.

was aristocratic, but which also defied society with more courage than either of these gentlemen had ever been able to muster, must have enchanted them. For the two young women Paris still kept its shady turn-of-the-century reputation. The city where Oscar Wilde spent his last days, where every artistic audacity could be indulged, was also the Gay Paree of more or less ill-frequented nightclubs and the apache haunts near the Place de la Bastille.

They spent ten insanely happy and recklessly foolish days. Vita, dressed as a boy, would go out dancing arm in arm with Violet. Violet never forgot a moment of this long week. Their families, who had no idea what a scandalous existence their daughters were leading in Paris, were seriously worried nevertheless. Too bad for them: unable to endure the thought of being parted, instead of returning to England the friends slipped away to Monte Carlo, to the villa Lady Sackville had rented there, Château Malet. Once more they haunted the popular dance halls, Vita always dressed as "Julian."

Harold Nicolson spent a wretched Christmas at Knole with his in-laws — who were having their own problems. Lord Sackville wanted to install his good friend Olive Rubens in Knole — and her husband! It was decided that the best plan of attack would be to persuade Vita to stay in Paris with Harold, there as an attaché at the Peace Conference. She agreed. Later Vita regretted that she and Violet had not by-passed Monte Carlo and gone to Greece, which they considered their spiritual home. Perhaps she had feared that so far-flung an adventure would have decided things forever: she never really burned all her bridges.

Violet returned to London to find Denys Trefusis out of the army and still decided on marriage. Mrs. Keppel's feeling was the sooner the better. Violet wrote a letter on March 30,* which, despairing as it was, nonetheless suggested that a compromise had been reached which would permit Vita to tolerate the idea of the marriage. Denys was to promise Violet that it would remain unconsummated. And here we come to the most difficult knot to unravel in the whole business. It is hard to see how, despite his gallantry, an officer only just back

* Letter No. 10.

from a war could agree not to lay a hand on his young wife. This suggests a singular degree of masochism, or the resignation of impotence. On the other hand, the horror with which Violet contemplated marriage, and her string of broken engagements, might have had an explanation more physiological than psychological. Much later in life, she suggested to an old friend that a physical anomaly had made marriage if not impossible at least unpleasant to contemplate. But after a few months of married life, a minor operation put things to rights. Here is perhaps the origin of Violet's obsession with Elizabeth I, a Virgin Queen in spite of herself. Denys' renowned discretion may explain why he seemed preferable to any of her other suitors.

On March 26, their engagement was announced. Rarely has an engaged couple ever appeared less expectant. To his future sister-in-law, Sonia, Denys seemed excessively reserved and Violet as distraught during her dress fittings and the dinner parties in the engaged couple's honor as she had been six years earlier at those debutante balls she found so tiresome. When she had a free moment, she would run to her room and dash off a heart-rending note to Vita.*

Vita had other things to think about, however: her mother had left Knole for good. Harold showed himself extremely useful to her in this crisis, and Violet turned deeply jealous of him. She wrote bitterly to Vita† when Vita went off to Paris with her husband. Violet looked on this as a double betrayal since Paris was "their" city; her letters fluctuate between sarcasm and despair. Violet guessed that Harold was bestowing on Vita what she was incapable of giving: tranquillity, an even temper, a talent for turning everything into a joke to be laughed over once passions had cooled. Harold suffered, of course, but philosophically. In fact, he was having an affair with a young friend of Proust's, Comte Jean de Gaigneron, whose portrait he painted unsparingly as "the Marquis de Chaumont" in Some People. And like the hero of the story, Jean de Gaigneron was eventually to rater son Jockey: a blackball dashed his consuming ambition to be elected to the exclusive Jockey Club.

Violet was left completely alone to withstand family pressures and

* Letters Nos. 10 and 11.
† Letters Nos. 11 and 13.

scenes with Denys. As the wedding day approached she threatened to do her worst. But sometimes her imagination gained the upper hand and she could invent, in a very Firbankian vein, fanciful newspaper accounts of the engagement in a letter to Vita.* After a good many hemmings and hawings, the date was set for June 16, 1919, and by some miracle the wedding took place on that day. Colonel Keppel surpassed himself in his arrangements for the ceremony and reception. There was an air of magnificence: the music included Purcell's "Trumpet Voluntary," Gounod's "Ave Maria" — sung by Dame Nellie Melba — and the "Wedding March" from *Lohengrin*. Violet appeared radiant — and still distraught.

Until the last minute she had hoped that Vita would rescue her, but, no, Vita had too much common sense. Before she left for the church, Violet wrote to her: "You have broken my heart, goodbye." At the same moment Vita sat in Versailles, watch in hand, ready to follow the proceedings in her mind's eye — heartbroken, of course, and wild with rage that her inamorata could give herself to a man.

Breathing a long sigh of relief, Mrs. Keppel put the newly-weds aboard the train that was to take them to France. Scenes — cruel, ugly ones — marked their arrival in Paris. The contempt for the feelings of others which manifests itself throughout Vita's writings — a point we will return to later — and the brutality of her passion are frightening. Whether she took herself for an Elizabethan, a Gypsy, or the Julian of her novel, the aspect of fiction impinging on real life is what strikes us more than the passion itself. Though the terrible scenes between Vita and the Trefusises occurred at the Ritz, their tone was much less Firbankian and much more that of the savage lesbian episodes in Proust:

On Tuesday night Violet and Denys came to Paris. On Wednesday I went to see her, at the Ritz. She was wearing clothes I had never seen before, but no wedding ring. I can't describe how terrible it all was — that meeting, and everything. It makes me physically ill to write about it and think about it, and my cheeks are burning. It was dreadful, dreadful. By then I had left Versailles, and was living alone in a small

* Letter No. 15.

hotel. I took her there, I treated her savagely, I made love to her, I had her, I didn't care, I only wanted to hurt Denys, even though he didn't know of it. I make no excuse, except that I had suffered too much during the past week and was really scarcely responsible. The next day I saw Denys at an awful interview. Violet told him she had meant to run away with me instead of marrying him; she told him she didn't care for him. He got very white, and I thought he was going to faint.*

Nor did the honeymooning couple find any more peace of mind at Saint-Jean-de-Luz. Despite the charms of Saint-Jean-de-Luz and the Basque countryside, despite their pleasant hotel and the proximity of Spain, their wedding trip was a disaster, judging by the almost daily letters Violet sent to Vita.† When the Trefusises came back to England, things calmed down a little because Violet and Vita were able to meet several times a week. They took a house in Sussex. Then all at once there were new scenes, and Mrs. Keppel threatened to stop Violet's allowance. Violet faced the prospect of poverty with relative equanimity:

> Chinday was so unkind to me last night that I went to bed in tears. All these rows will probably end in my being quite penniless. She already seems to think that I should "support myself" but I won't, no I won't let things like being jewel-less and impecunious distress me: Loge doesn't mind, so why should I? I shall have to become a governess or something . . . When I think that Chinday has at least £20,000 a year! However, *parlons d'autre chose.*

On her return to England, Violet had been put through a kind of family council during which she again told Mrs. Keppel and Denys that she was resolved to live with Vita. She had been so resolute that they proposed a compromise: "Very well, but wait until Sonia is married: a scandal like this, and her wedding will never take place." The younger of the Keppel girls had just become engaged to a young officer, Roland Cubitt, the son of Baron Ashcombe and heir apparent to the enormous building concern founded by his grandfather Tom

---

* *Portrait of a Marriage.*
† Letters Nos. 17, 18, et seq.

Cubitt. She might have made a more striking match: the Grand Duke Dmitri was one of her suitors, but Mrs. Keppel did not put much stock in Russian refugees. Once the engagement was announced, Sonia's godmother, Mrs. Ronald Greville, drove in her enormous Rolls-Royce to Denbies, the Ashcombes' ungainly Sussex house, where she summoned Lord Ashcombe outside to the car to announce brusquely: "I find that Miss Keppel is marrying beneath her station." She drove off leaving a stunned Lord Ashcombe behind her. He had another shock in store when he discussed the marriage settlement with Mrs. Keppel, who, he found, required from someone as rich as he was a generosity equal to her own.

# 6. *Separations*

NEITHER VIOLET'S LETTERS to Vita nor Vita's manuscripts provide any easy clues to the chronology of two hectic years, nor is it easy to divine even an approximation of the truth among so many contradictions and distortions. Lies told to assuage wounded sensibilities, to put people off guard, grew more tangled, sometimes turning the courageous lovers into characters from farce — a little as though they had abandoned the dignified robes of Shakespeare for the dishabille of Feydeau. In the final weeks and months, a note of moral deterioration sounds, brought on by exhaustion. The struggle had gone on too long. Character flaws were intensified: Vita turned hard, Violet unstable, Harold rather weepy, and Denys stood revealed in all his weaknesses.

As for Mrs. Keppel, she seems to have been annoyed to discover that money does not always buy the last word. Violet was probably deeper in the morass of deception than Vita, who had no accounts to square with her mother. Vita appeared to have been detached, lying simply to be left in peace. Nor did she attach much importance to it: Lady Sackville wanted to know everything, manage everything, and would stop at nothing to do so. Vita even entered into a kind of collusion with Denys Trefusis at one point, and throughout she had a confidant: Harold. Violet's lies were told to a mother she admired, which made lying harder, and to a husband she valued and to whom she was in some degree attracted. She also, fortunately, had a confidante in Pat Dansey. In her feminine way, Violet would have been more at ease in her lies than Vita if confusion and fantasy had not driven her to mixing them up, or to pushing credibility too far. Thus, after the drama of Violet's marriage — and a few happy weeks on their own — the two friends failed in their try at establishing a permanent liaison. Family and society were able to separate them because too many misunderstandings divided them in the face of the enemy. Their lies demanded continual coordination, and separation only made things worse. Violet eventually lost confidence in Vita to such an extent that she stood on the brink of suicide. Her endless letters were repetitions of a single plea: "Come! I can't live without you; don't believe anything they've told you!"

She was referring to the most serious of their misunderstandings, centered on something to which far less importance is attached today: virginity. Like many lesbians, Vita looked on herself as a kind of vestal virgin, and she felt that the loss of virginity was the ultimate degradation. In any case, she thought of sexual relations with a man as ridiculous, if not repellent. Violet did not feel the same way, and eventually she agreed to sleep with her husband (but how far did she really go?). This "betrayal," she later told Vita, took place on the eve of the friend's departure for Lincoln on February 3, 1920. Vita chose Lincoln because she wanted to make some notes for a new novel, and it was at Lincoln that they once again resolved to live together and made new plans to elope.

On February 9, Violet left England by herself, leaving Vita behind at Dover. Vita crossed the Channel — with Denys! — and from February 10 to 13, the women stayed at Amiens, as Violet was ill. And on February 14, Denys arrived at Amiens with Harold in a hired plane. Even Colonel Keppel appeared. There were scenes in hotels, railway waiting rooms, and buffets; there were missed boats; there were the husbands in joint pursuit of their wives; there was Colonel Keppel, totally adrift in the maelstrom. Everyone proceeded at the speeded-up gait of characters in a badly projected silent film. The self-parody of which the English are capable once self-control deserts them overshadowed the drama. In the confusion, everything was begun over again at least once a day. Nobody seemed capable of sticking to a decision. Why, for instance, did Vita confide the little hoard they had saved for their house to Denys? Why did he later return it to Violet? Then later she made Violet swear that she would

not kill herself. In all of this Vita seemed culpably indecisive; after
all, she was the "man" of the pair — it was her job to arrange their
flight, to summon up the courage to burn bridges, or else to say: No, I
prefer my life with Harold. But jealousy thwarted all sensible behavior. Denys' silence spurred Vita to believe that he was "really
married" to Violet; Violet, caught in the crossfire, defended herself
badly. Pain and rage drove Vita back to Harold and consolation. Violet
tried to sort things out in a letter written on the evening of that crucial
day in Amiens.* Her confusion and cunning might have unsettled
any man who agreed to marry her, but if Denys had been sure of her
love he might have come through it all, taken her firmly in hand,
and avoided all this time lost in railway-station waiting rooms. Vita,
too, failed in her masculine vocation; after all, at twenty-six, Violet
was still a girl. The Feydeau farce of Amiens behind them, Violet
and Denys started south.

The trip was a nightmare. We can reconstruct it from the letters
Violet sent two or three times a day to Vita, who had taken refuge
at Long Barn. From the first, she assured Vita that "our separation
is due to a misunderstanding. There has never, never, never in my life
been any attempt at what you thought from that person . . ." From
then on, Violet shared Vita's hatred of Denys, whose indiscretion (or
lie?) had destroyed her love. Denys, exhausted by Amiens, fell ill to
the point of delirium, and they were forced to break their journey in
a deplorable hotel at Gien. "I will kill him if I stay with him," Violet
wrote, and Denys was well aware of it. When she came to see how
he was, he shouted, "Go away! You hate me; it is in your face. Go
away!" They drove in their big car to Nîmes via Bourges and Vichy,
each staring out his own window, Violet crying to the chauffeur to
go faster over the bad roads. It was quite a journey, and Violet began
to look on the husband beside her as her jailer, even if he was rather
ridiculous: "How I hate Denys with his tears and humility and utter
dependence on me." It must be remembered that Denys didn't have a
shilling, something that made the situation even more humiliating;
Mrs. Keppel was paying for everything. At Nîmes Violet had news:

* Letter No. 30.

there was to be a two-month separation from Vita, time enough for passions to cool. Now she became very jealous of Harold and begged Vita not to wear her wedding ring.

On February 24 at Toulon, the Trefusises met the Keppels, who had just come from Saint Moritz. "I am trapped on every side," wrote Violet. Negotiations began. At first, Mrs. Keppel insisted that the young couple go on a year's trip around the world. Then she modified her proposition to a long stay in Tangier with the painter Sir John Lavery — unless Denys would prefer the romantic surroundings of Ragusa, perhaps? In any case, Mrs. Keppel was resolutely set against divorce, and when Violet suggested an annulment based on non-consummation of the marriage, she threatened her with the humiliation of a medical examination. If there *were* a divorce, Mrs. Keppel promised to cut her daughter off without a penny — and never to see her again. After a good deal of to-ing and fro-ing, Violet promised her mother to stay with Denys until May. Vita seems to have provided her friend with very little support during this difficult time, and one wonders what went through the telegraph operators' minds as they transcribed in their countrified hand the desperate appeals of Violet, partly coded in the friends' private language: "AH JULIAN, JULIAN. SIR TRAN RASTAGEL TIRA MITYA. I'VE WRITTEN YOU AT LEAST TWICE A DAY AND SENT INNUMERABLE WIRES. IF YOU GO TO CHINA PROMISE NO LONGER HOLDS. MENTILICHE DON'T TORMENT ME. VIENI." It was probably around this time that Violet — held prisoner by her family, threatened with the loss of everything if she went back to Vita — wrote a poem strikingly akin to one Vita published in 1921 called "Bitterness." Vita's poem must have been written during this episode too.

Despite her promise to spend another two months with her husband, Violet went to stay with Pat Dansey at Bordighera. Violet has left us a charming portrait of her friend Miss Dansey:

> She was small and quick and done in various shades of brown, her hair was the colour of potato chips, her eyes were like bees, her face had the texture and hue of a pheasant's egg. I have made her sound edible, but she was too brittle and furry to make really good eating.

She had a stutter that sounded most incongruous in her small neat person, for it gave one the impression she was slightly intoxicated.*

Pat Dansey had left the shadowy splendors of Berkeley Castle to share a house with her girlfriend "Joan," and immediately, in a letter with a slightly amused ring to it, she invited Vita to join them: "Dear Vita, It is a queer world! You and I mutually agreed we loathe each other and here I am having to take as much trouble and worry over your and Violet's affairs as I might be expected to take if I entertained feelings of great affection for you. It is a mercy I can see how comic my position is . . ." But Vita stayed with Harold, where she contented herself with composing infrequent and evasive letters and telegrams. Denys settled into the Hôtel de Paris and scrupulously paid a call on his wife every evening at Bordighera, obedient to the wishes of Mrs. Keppel. The two things that really kept him at Monte Carlo were the Casino and Nancy Cunard. As for Violet, the coming of spring and the comfort of Pat Dansey's villa restored a measure of calm to her life, and in her letters supplications and explanations gave way to anecdote.

But before very long, tormented by Vita's silence, Violet started going to the Casino too. At the tables she could forget her unhappiness, though gambling brought her other problems. One evening she lost 10,000 francs. That week or two at Monte Carlo was the most wretched of her life: she felt herself turning into one of those *déclassée* women whose only resource is coquetry. She looked up a little dressmaker who had admired Vita the first time they went to Monte Carlo: "You're such a lonely little thing, drifting like a soul in torment," the girl consoled her. "Let's have lunch together." And the orchestra, playing the serenade from *Les Millions d'Arlequin,* brought back those evenings in the arms of "Julian."

A family council sharpened her feeling that she was a fallen woman. Mrs. Keppel had a very precise idea of Violet's predicament, and she perhaps repeated to herself the French phrase Violet later used to apply to some of her own friends: *"Quelle dégringolade!"* — "What a come-down!" Coldly, she suggested that she and her daughter might

* *Don't Look Round.*

not meet again. She put it simply: "Do as you like, the important thing is that Denys go back to England to tend to my affairs." Sonia was hardly in a position to offer any more comfort to Violet; the scandal compromised her marriage, and her engagement was dragging on. Mrs. Keppel did not want to sacrifice Sonia's happiness to Violet's passion, and in this light her attitude appears as something more than a concern for what society might say. She was, however, desperately afraid of being cut out from Violet forever. On the evening of their meeting, Violet received a letter from a family friend: "Your mother is a brave woman and I admire the courage she displays amongst this fire of hateful gossip."

Acquaintances snubbed Violet in the Monte Carlo shops, and she wrote to Vita: "I come to you all bleeding and hurt, knowing that you have been spared the ghastly day I have just been through, knowing that you are surrounded by sympathy and affection . . . How can you expect me not to find it unjust? It is as though two people had been caught stealing but one is put in prison and the other is not"

Pat Dansey and her friend, Joan, finally persuaded Vita to go with them to Venice. On the way, she joined Violet in Avignon on March 20. But Violet, who knew the reconciliation was only fleeting, was upset, and their reunion contained no more than a few brief moments of happiness. Later the two friends regretted that they had not left then for Greece or Egypt. Violet never looked back on Venice with much pleasure, nor did she ever return there willingly. She had also conceived a loathing for the Côte d'Azur, and much later in life she would do all she could to avoid passing that way when she went to Italy.

On April 10 Violet and Vita returned to London. But it was only natural that first Grosvenor Street and then the house that Denys had rented on the outskirts of Reading should quickly become prisons for Violet. Yet Denys showed himself a very tactful warder; he would go away from time to time so that Vita could come to spend the night with Violet. He began to appear in a more sympathetic light, though Violet complained. "Denys has got one of his Julian Grenfellesque fits of morbidness and is talking of killing himself," she wrote in one of her daily letters to Vita, letters already calmer in tone and hinting at the approach of a more resigned attitude. She had obviously been affected by her Scottish holidays and relations; she really was not of this world but an elusive Melusina. The truth for her was as changeable as the weather. She dreamed of living with Vita forever, but she must have sensed that that was not to be. A most curious letter from Pat Dansey to Vita is revealing. She was "a trick monkey . . . a child," wrote Miss Dansey, whose dislike of Vita had certainly altered during the trip to Venice. "Think of yourself and less of her . . . I'm bringing you a few Macedonian cigars." Certainly Violet had a rather vague conception of the truth and was terribly confused. This explains the letter she wrote to Vita after they had gone to a performance of Barrie's *Mary Rose* on May 7.*

Violet and Denys occasionally saw Sonia and her fiancée, to whom they appeared "formally happy." The younger couple had a splendid wedding in the autumn of 1920, and things seemed to be settling down at last. Certainly during the previous spring the Trefusises' social life had been very quiet. Nevertheless, at a party Violet met Raquel Meller, a great screen beauty who later played the Empress Eugénie in *Violettes Impériales*. In a Spanish whose gestures spoke more than words, Violet invited her to come to the country with her, perhaps as a way of provoking Vita's jealousy, for Vita was just then on a cruise with Harold on Lord Sackville's yacht. To amuse herself, Violet would roam antique shops; one morning she bought "the largest piece of blue John I have ever seen, a colossal goblet like the Holy Grail, and a lovely Tanagra." Then she set about an autobiographical novel.

At the same time, Vita began putting the story of their affair on paper, the manuscript which her son Nigel discovered fifty years later in a Gladstone bag at Sissinghurst. When anyone begins to write a story of an affair, its end is in sight. Still, perhaps because the emotions were somewhat calmed, Violet's letters to Vita became more literary, the letters of an aesthete. Certainly Beauty and Vita were synonymous for Violet, but passion can be sublimated. From a weekend house party

* Letter No. 33.

where she found herself sequestered with a crowd of bridge players, Violet sent a description of her mortal boredom to Vita.* Yet she could not refrain from reproaching her for not having sent a birthday present (which, in fact, arrived a few days later). Her friend Winifred Ashton, the novelist Clemence Dane, had at least written to her. Around mid-June the friends went together on a visit to Berkeley Castle.† It was also about this time that Violet's letters began mentioning attractive strangers she had run across: Denys' own sister, a mysterious Spaniard called Alfonso. After a two-month truce, things once more began to deteriorate between the Trefusises; Violet discovered that Denys had burned all her letters from Vita — "I always tear up the more indiscreet ones, thank goodness!" — and here the affair took a turn straight from Alexandre Dumas.

The angry Violet returned to her idea of an annulment for non-consummation and received a sarcastic reply from her mother. Mrs. Keppel did on occasion take a hard line with her spoiled child — somewhat belatedly — and she tried to prevent her from getting into debt. Violet's very generous allowance didn't keep her from running up enormous bills with antique dealers and dressmakers. Mrs. Keppel's daughter was in many ways irresponsible; moreover, she had to be watched so that she couldn't borrow enough money somewhere to buy a house for herself and Vita. Her mother relied on her son-in-law to apply the brakes on Violet's reckless spending, and she also needed him to head off a divorce, one which couldn't fail to make the front pages and disgrace the family publicly. As it was, in society the scandal was already almost irreparable. Perhaps she also feared that Denys would cite Vita as co-respondent, a move that would be utterly catastrophic for both families. They undoubtedly had vivid recollections of Lady Troubridge's divorce.

Mrs. Keppel was afraid that left on their own Violet and Denys would only make things worse, so she had the happy idea of taking Violet with her to Scotland. Back among the souvenirs of Vita's childhood visit to Duntreath, she calmed down a little. Her cousins

* Letter No. 35.
† Letter No. 36.

were delightful company, and the pain of her love affair seems to have eased.* She announced that she was about to fall into the arms of a very young, very handsome cousin, a youth who was not yet twenty: "Really young, darling, not faked young like you and me!" Decidedly, Violet's great love was Beauty: too bad if it had first shown itself in feminine guise.

Mrs. Keppel decided to return to Holland, getting up a house party as she used to do before the war. She took along her daughters, her sons-in-law, and a few guests, including a socially prominent American couple, the Harry Lehrs, and an old friend, Lady de Trafford. They played bridge most of the time, which left Violet nothing to do but wait for Vita's infrequent letters. The tensions between Violet and Denys and Violet and her mother led to embarrassing scenes. Violet's only confidante was a Russian émigrée who had been invited along out of charity. A plan was even worked out for meeting Vita in Prague.

As always with Violet, it was difficult to define the border between reality and fantasy. It sounded like fantasy when Violet wrote to Vita that Sir Basil Zaharoff, the famous munitions maker and one of the world's richest men, wanted her to become his mistress. But it was the absolute truth.† Resuming the role she used to play on their first trip to Paris, Violet's letter was written in the style of a demimondaine writing to her *amant de coeur,* and enclosed was a remarkable pen and ink fantasy drawing of Sir Basil and Violet bedecked with pearls at Deauville. A few hours later Violet, afraid that Vita might take her seriously, sent a telegram to reassure her. One thing, however, *was* true. Violet was becoming one of those women to whom such propositions can be made; quite a few years later, she was linked with someone in this way, someone infinitely more attractive, Comte Jean Ostrorog — Sir Basil's son-in-law.

Between letters she read the latest novels, books like *Tamarisk Town* and *Green Apple Harvest.* Vita, perhaps annoyed by too many complaining letters, wrote to Violet, just when she was at her unhappiest, that she never thought of her these days (July 25, 1920). But then out of pity — no, rather in one final resurgence of passion,

* Letters Nos. 42, 43, 44.
† Letter 34.

or in preparation for the final break — Vita agreed once more to leave her family to spend six weeks with Violet in the south of France, at Hyères and Carcassonne, in late winter.

When they returned to England at the beginning of March, things went from bad to worse. Violet wanted to speak to her husband, then in Cornwall, but her mother-in-law forbade her to enter the house. Mrs. Keppel's patience was exhausted, and to head off a new scandal, she sent her daughter to Italy under the eye of Moiselle. This ir-reproachable Protestant was a strict guardian who saw to it that Violet observed the prohibition on communication with Vita. So Violet made Pat Dansey her go-between, sending her long letters to pass on to Vita. Curiously, these arrived accompanied by rather ambiguous letters from Pat. The confidante referred to Violet as an unhappy but wayward child, taking care to underline the dangers the relationship posed for Vita. In short, she concluded, it would be better to break it off as quickly as possible. And then Pat Dansey, obviously infatuated, flattered Vita and her poetry, which was beginning to meet with a good deal of success (one more reason not to reopen the scandal).

There is something unsettling about Pat Dansey, this superficially discreet woman. She had lived among the ghosts of Berkeley Castle; her dreams were full of omens; she had dabbled in black magic. Pat wrote to Vita on November 12, 1921, exerting all her will to divide the two friends — or rather, to get Violet to stop importuning Vita: "Look here — I will make my bet extend over 6 months! And if I am really mischievous I can will it to happen before the end of 6 months. I haven't your *beauty,* your *charm* — nor your brilliant, brilliant brains — but — when I choose to use it, I have the most *wicked* hypnotic will, and with no boasting spirit — the few times I have used it, it has been successful!"

At about this time Violet's letters disappear from the correspondence Vita later saved so carefully, but Pat, who appears to have embarked on an affair with Vita, is much in evidence. From time to time she takes a dig at Violet: "I simply fail to see why people don't see through her," or "the cute little creature."

Violet's life while Pat Dansey was trying to pry her away from Vita was miserable, but it had its moments. She spent the spring in

Italy, as planned, and Mrs. Keppel joined her there. Apart from a tantrum or two, Violet gave the impression of never having been so happy to be with her mother. So one of Violet's old friends recalls; she also remembers running across Violet with a daughter of William Beckett, Lord Grimthorpe: "Don't you think we look alike? It's not so surprising — we have the same father!" They went to Florence, they went to Rome. They stayed in a palace and went out constantly: "It amuses me to think that I have been brought here to be 'reformed.' The Italian society is the most corrupt I have ever come across . . . I don't suppose that anyone here has ever really *loved* anyone in their lives." In this worldly inferno she at least had an ally in a friend she had come across in Florence, Rebecca West, "brilliantly clever with the only true and just conception of cleverness — namely that it is of such secondary importance, and that one's emotions matter so infinitely more. She was very kind to me, because she knew I was desperately unhappy." There were no letters from Vita, no money to run away with.

July was spent at Clingendaal under the watchful eye of the Baroness de Brienen; Mrs. Keppel was in England with Sonia, who was expecting a child. Violet, very much alone now, tried to return to the novel she had been working on now and again for the past two years, a project that undoubtedly had rescued her from despair. On July 23 she sent a letter to Pat — for Vita's eyes — declaring that she felt old and ugly.* Reading D. H. Lawrence's *Women in Love* only made her neurasthenic condition worse. The end was at hand: there were no more letters. All is silence between that summer of 1921 and the following winter, when Violet, apparently reconciled with her husband, went to live with him in Paris.

For more than a year, Vita had forced herself to go into society with her husband, where, as their son Nigel has amusingly remarked, "They were almost the only people not to speak about the scandal." She made her peace with her mother, and, as a token of her change of heart, promised to stop the publication of *Challenge*. Lady Sackville had shown the manuscript to Mrs. Belloc Lowndes, the novelist,

---

* Letter No. 52.

a goodhearted, sensible woman who felt that it wasn't worth risking more trouble for. She simply asked Vita: "Would you publish this book if Violet were dead?" Vita had to acknowledge that she wouldn't and took the manuscript back from her English publisher (though the book appeared in an American edition in 1924). Violet, who had helped Vita with *Challenge* and hoped to enter posterity under the guise of Eve, was terribly hurt by her friend's circumspection. What would remain of their love, of all they had gone through, if not this book? Only Violet understood Vita's dedication when the book did come out. Written in their secret language, it was undeciphered until 1973, when a *Sunday Times* reader, Mrs. Ridler, discovered that its vocabulary came from George Borrow's *The Zincali, or the Gypsies in Spain* (Vita, proud of her Gypsy grandmother, knew everything the author of *The Bible in Spain* had written):

> This book is thine, honoured witch;
> If thou readest, thou wilt find thy tormented soul
> Changed and free.

The passages Violet marked in her copy of *Challenge* reassured her that she had been the object of an incomparable love.

> Whatever she might do, whatever crime she might commit, whatever baseness she might perpetrate, her ultimate worth, the core, the kernel, would remain to him unsullied and inviolate. This he knew blindly, seeing it as the mystic sees God; and knew it the more profoundly that he could have defended it with no argument of reason.

What balm the novel would have provided for so many wounds if only it had turned out to be a masterpiece; if only Vita had become, as she wanted to, the last of the great romantics. *Challenge* would have brought immortality with it. But by a twist of fate, it was Vita who was immortalized, in Virginia Woolf's masterpiece, *Orlando*.

We can get an insight into Vita's passion for Violet by reading *Orlando*. Virginia Woolf transforms Violet into a Russian princess, capricious, voracious, chaotic, and irresistible, undoubtedly relying on what Vita had told her. A few phrases show how potent Violet's charm still was for Vita: "the extraordinary seductiveness which issued from the whole person" . . . "she talked so enchantingly, so wittily, so wisely (but unfortunately always in French . . .)." As with Violet, there is a mystery about Sasha's origins: "the Muscovite Ambassador, who was her uncle perhaps, or perhaps her father." But at heart the Princess is a "fox," like Violet, who sometimes admitted this cunning side to her personality. She even used to wear a brooch in the shape of a fox's head, given to her during the last war by a friend who called her "Foxy": "For in all she said, however open she seemed and voluptuous, there was something hidden; in all she did, however daring, there was something concealed." She was a half-human creature, who succumbed to every whim, yet succeeded in gaining pardon. "Sasha hung over him, passing his dizzied eyes softly, sinuously, like the fox that had bit him." And like the liaison between Violet and Vita, the love of Orlando for the Princess "became the scandal of the Court." And so did their frustrated elopement. Sasha sailed off in "the ship of the Muscovite Embassy," leaving the raging Orlando with nothing but the password of their flight, *"Jour de ma vie!"*

Virginia Woolf met Violet on no more than two or three occasions, though years later Vita told her that Virginia had thought of her "as being all chestnut and green in colour." The novelist met Mrs. Keppel only once:

> It would have been difficult to find two people more dissimilar than Virginia Woolf and my mother. Yet, strange as it may seem, they were deeply interested in one another, and longed to meet.
>
> Raymond Mortimer got wind of this, and with typical mercurial mischief offered to sponsor an encounter. He was to bring Mama to tea with Virginia in Tavistock Square. Meanwhile, Virginia had steeped herself in Edwardian memoirs, while my mother struggled manfully with *Mrs Dalloway* and *To the Lighthouse.* Off we set. Raymond and I had agreed that it would be more tactful, after the first *échange de politesse,* to eclipse ourselves; there was a drawing-room, at the extremity of which we sat, well out of earshot.
>
> After about half an hour's spasmodic conversation, we were longing to see if the experiment had been a success — we unobtrusively moved nearer — they certainly seemed very animated; "Personally, I've always

been in favour of six cylinders though I know some people think four are less trouble."

"My dear Mrs Keppel, you wouldn't hesitate if you saw the *new Lanchester with the fluid fly-wheel!*"

Neither knew a thing about motors; both thought they were on safe ground, discussing a topic on which they could both bluff to their heart's content.*

I once asked Violet if Vita had really been in love with Virginia. "Not for a minute," she replied with a trace of ill-concealed spite. "Virginia ran after her, and she couldn't get rid of her. She found her so sentimental."

Violet continued to see the Nicolsons after the chaos of the preceding three years died down, but she saw them a good deal less, for now she lived in Paris. Years later, in 1938, Vita came there to give a lecture. Violet introduced Vita to her friends, and brought a number of them to hear her talk — in the spacious reception rooms lent by Comtesse Georges de Castellane in her house in the Rue de Varennes. In the garden outside played the elegant Hubert Robert fountain that Proust borrowed for the garden of the Prince de Guermantes in *Cities of the Plain.* Everyone from the English Embassy was there, for fame had long since effaced any taint of scandal.

* *Don't Look Round.*

# 7. The Princesse

THE YOUNG TREFUSISES were together again for better or worse. But it was out of the question for them to live in England: what their families wanted more than anything else now was to avoid all reminders of scandal. There could be no chance of a meeting with the Nicolsons, who for their part had been managing to look society straight in the eye. Italy and Spain had overtones of exile: obviously, the answer was Paris. Mrs. Keppel found her son-in-law a job, allotted a generous allowance to her daughter, and before long the dust began to settle. Once Denys' authority over his wife was confirmed, he seems to have fallen rather quickly into a way of life which excluded her. He had a weakness for the pretty Russian émigrées who in those days filled the Paris couture houses and the Gypsy cabarets. But Violet was jealous, and family quarrels straight out of Noël Coward, spiced with divorce threats, became the order of the day. Still, none of this held a candle to what they had already gone through. Since Violet had never enjoyed staying up late, and dropped with fatigue and boredom in nightclubs, her husband ended by going out on his own nearly every night.

One of Denys' close friends was Felix Yousoupoff,* and Violet used to say that it was a dinner she agreed to arrange for the Yousoupoffs that gave rise to one of the most celebrated gaffes of the twenties. The dinner was to be held at the house of Madeleine le Chevrel, a friend of Violet's whose salon was just beginning to be talked about. The Russians accepted, but only on condition that the evening's conversation would be kept scrupulously free of references to Rasputin, the

* The assassin of Rasputin.

subject of a current and scandalously overblown film. Of course, Mademoiselle le Chevrel promised, nobody would breathe a word about Rasputin. On the night of the dinner party, she dutifully warned everyone: "Not a word about Rasputin!" The guests of honor arrived last, and the proud hostess began to introduce her guests, one by one, to "the Prince and Princess Rasputin."

Once Violet had found herself and Denys a house at Auteuil, the first of many houses on which she lavished quantities of time and money, things began to improve between them:

In 1923 we found the home we had always longed for; a diminutive house in Auteuil, facing full South, looking on to a garden full of gnarled old trees, uneasy to find themselves in Paris. A magnificent chestnut towered over them as a conductor lords it over his musicians. In winter, with its denuded branches (I had nearly written "antlers"), it put one in mind of a vigilant stag; in March, the young sticky leaves drooped like the ears of a bloodhound; later, it turned into a periwig. We hastened to furnish the house, regardless of nationality or period. There were Chinese rugs with geometrical patterns. Venetian mirrors full of reminiscences and plots, glass pictures, one of which was given me by my mother. It represented a Chinese lady smiling at a small grey parrot perched on her arm. She attempts nothing to detain it. Its cage is in her eyes.

After a year or two of relative content I realized I was married to Lohengrin, or Odysseus? His latent nostalgia for Russia asserted itself more strongly. Roused and anxious, I would accompany him on his nightclub expeditions. I awoke to the fact that the wasp-waisted Caucasian dancers had probably more in common with him than I had. Not for nothing did they sing: "Ulié tai na Krilieh viétra" — approximately, "let us flee on the wings of the wind."

Go he must. It so happened that a friend of his, Fred Cripps, was being sent to Russia on a mission. Denys, with his knowledge of the language, would be invaluable. He did not hesitate. For several months I was practically without news of him, owing to no fault of his: the posts were irregular and his letters censored.*

Before he left, Denys introduced his wife to an old friend who shared his love of music, the Princesse Edmond de Polignac. Born Win-

* *Don't Look Round.*

naretta Singer in 1865, she was the daughter of the inventor of the sewing machine and joint heiress to his immense fortune. She was born and brought up in Europe, like her sister Isabelle (who married Duc Decazes and died unseasonably young). Winnaretta's first marriage, to Prince Scey-Montbéliard, made little impact on her life; her second, in 1893, was to a delightful man a good deal older than herself: Prince Edmond de Polignac, a talented amateur composer and a close friend to the Comte Robert de Montesquiou and Charles Haas, the original of Proust's Charles Swann. To the Polignacs and their innumerable relations Winnaretta was to become "Aunt Winnie." De Montesquiou arranged the Prince's marriage to the American heiress, and at the reception announced (in an allusion to the fashionable custom of dining at a flock of little tables instead of a single large one): "Supper will be served off little sewing machines." The union was on balance a happy one: the Princesse saw to it that her husband's compositions were at last performed, and the Prince filled her salon to overflowing with the wittiest and most illustrious personalities Paris had to offer. The Singers added a pinch of eccentricity. Handsome Paris Singer, the Princesse's brother, took Isadora Duncan as his mistress. The Princesse's niece Daisy Decazes, who first married a de Broglie prince, then the Honourable Reginald Fellowes, acquired a reputation for maliciousness and elegance at twenty that she kept the rest of her life.

With her huge fortune and famous family behind her, the Princesse kept more than one iron in the fire — and wielded them with a dexterity which warded off jealousy and malicious gossip. She was an artist, an aristocrat, and an adept at the art of love. Her taste and generosity won her an important position in French music circles. A fervent Wagnerian, she helped finance the Paris Opéra production of the *Ring,* and from 1895 onward, nearly all important musical premières took place under her roof. She was an intimate friend of Gabriel Fauré's, and was instrumental in the triumph of the Ballet Russe. The Princesse supported Stravinsky in the face of the hostile reception accorded *Le Sacre du Printemps* and commissioned *L'Histoire du Soldat* as well as Manuel de Falla's *El Retablo de Maese Pedro* and an orchestral suite from Erik Satie. Ravel dedicated his *Pavane pour une Infante défunte* to her; Fauré, his *Mélodies Vénitiennes;*

Darius Milhaud, his *Orphée*. She encouraged Nadia Boulanger in her early days, as well as a whole new generation of composers who became friends of Violet's: Francis Poulenc, Georges Auric, Henri Sauguet, Germaine Tailleferre. And the Princesse herself was an accomplished organist and a remarkable pianist who played duets with Artur Rubinstein, including a Bach concerto and Chabrier waltzes. She was a skilled painter, too, and built up an impressive collection of Impressionists as well.

Intelligent and generous, the Princesse nonetheless could be intimidating. Jean Cocteau, who thought she had the profile of Dante, used to call her, in an impolite French pun, *"Mère Dante"* (*"emmerdante,"* an adjective derived from *merde* that is applied to anyone or anything exceedingly annoying). In the Avenue Henri-Martin she built a vast mansion in the style of Louis XVI. Its grand staircase led up to a music room with a ceiling full of somewhat too intimately entwined nymphs painted by José Maria Sert. In this room, for over forty years, she sponsored concerts at which her musical friends mingled with her society friends. Besides her Paris house, the Princesse kept another in Venice, one of the most imposing palaces along the Grand Canal, and she filled it with guests at Easter and in September.

She was a close friend to Anna de Noailles and her sister Hélène, the Princesse de Caraman-Chimay. They brought Marcel Proust to the Avenue Henri-Martin, and the story goes that Proust heard a sonata there by a Belgian composer called Guillaume Lekeu which he took as a model for the *Vinteuil Sonata*. But the Princesse developed an antipathy for him which deepened to hostility when she discovered that he planned to dedicate *Cities of the Plain* to her in memory of the Prince (who had died in 1901). Indeed, in this the novelist showed a want of tact, for beneath the surface of her fashionable existence, the Princesse led a stormy private life. Yet despite her decidedly masculine appearance and her tailored clothes, her exalted position in society was never threatened by scandal. Her most celebrated affair occurred just before the First World War with the same Baronne de Meyer who may have been the daughter of Edward VII, and who was a friend of Diaghilev's. The Princesse had also been the inamorata of Romaine Brooks, a remarkable American portrait painter taken up by

Paris society during the war decade. Mrs. Brooks later recalled the Princesse as she sat to her for a portrait. Meryle Secrest quotes her in *Between Me and Life:* " 'The head is bent forward with profile emerging from a profusion of dark hair. The lowered eyes escape detection. The nose is arched, strong, atavistic ruthlessness ever active in self-defense.' "

By the 1920s, the Princesse had become a legendary figure. Her acid remarks are still famous, and Violet used to repeat some of them in excellent mimicry of her half-American, half-aristocratic accent, delivered through permanently clenched teeth. Once a sexually ambiguous and invincibly snobbish gentleman presumed to address her as "Aunt Winnie." "Auntie yourself!" was her annihilating reply. And to a woman who simpered to her, "So, Princesse, you are in Paris for some time?" she snapped back: "For thirty years, if I'm not mistaken!" One of her many Polignac nephews, vexed at his failure to touch her for a loan, complained bitterly: "After all, my name is at *least* as good as yours." She glared at him: "Not at the bottom of a cheque, it isn't!"

If her affairs of the heart sometimes drew this imposing personage into relatively delicate situations, we can be sure that she was seldom nonplused, even when she met her match. The Princesse once lured a young wife away from her husband and received a visit from his seconds, who bore a message: "If you're the man you think you are, accept my challenge to a duel."

The Princesse died in London during the last war, leaving her house and part of her fortune to a research foundation. Once a year, a concert in her memory reunites some of the composers she helped and some of the survivors of her salon: *Time Regained* indeed.

An honored guest at the Polignacs', Violet found herself swept into a circle which suited her exactly and helped refine her social criteria. She brought to it youth and imagination. There is little doubt that the Princesse was very much in love with Violet for nearly ten years. And it is possible that for Violet, whose love for her mother had made her a perennial adolescent, there was a transfer of affections to this remarkable and much older woman. She could again stand in awe of an exceptional intelligence, and indulge herself in childish behavior.

And again it was Mrs. Keppel's tact which warded off if not gossip at least outright scandal. She resumed her role as chaperone. If Violet were invited to Venice, Mrs. Keppel, sometimes accompanied by the colonel, would promptly show up too. It is not surprising that so august a lady should cast a protective veil over her daughter's amours: her presence fended off all indiscreet talk, and as a good Edwardian, Mrs. Keppel had a proper respect for the Princesse's money. As a good American, the Princesse respected the Keppels as the height of chic. And with her mother and the Princesse thus allied, Violet played the enfant terrible. In perfect accord, the two women moved to head off any caprice which looked like it was going too far.

One winter the Princesse hired a *dahabeah* and set off on a Nile cruise. As well as the Keppels, she had invited a good-looking young pianist, not much more than a boy, called Jacques Février. Violet was bored by the boat's slow progress upstream and the succession of ruins, all more or less alike. She amused herself by flirting with Février, or locked herself into her cabin for endless siestas. On deck, the Princesse and her parents played bridge. Sometimes Mrs. Keppel would interrupt the game and spread out a map: "Look, Georgie, that's ours," she would say, pointing to the location of some lucrative investment Sir Ernest Cassel had advised her to make. On a trip to Morocco, the grandson of one of the Princesse's friends, a handsome spahi officer called Olivier de La Moussaye, served as their guide — and Violet was soon up to her old antics.

What she really liked were their Mediterranean cruises. It was aboard the Princesse's yacht that she finally discovered Greece, and with Greek blood in her veins, she was in raptures. She agreed with Cocteau's comment on Greece, and repeated it often: *"Rome s'enfonce, Athènes s'envole"* — "Rome digs in, Athens takes wing."

In an old copy of French *Vogue* photographs of a Polignac cruise show the women, hatted and gloved, riding donkeys on the island of Thera, or in rapt contemplation of the Parthenon. It is a far cry from Lady Mendl's summing up of the temple: "Beige! Just my colour!" Violet had very little to do with Lady Mendl and café society; Elsa Maxwell was not at all her cup of tea. The quality she valued more than any other, besides Beauty, was probably intelligence. At the

Princesse's, she became the friend of several Polignac relations, Edwige de Chabannes, who was both beautiful and intelligent, and of Marie Blanche Lanvin, the wife of Comte Jean de Polignac. But Marie Blanche's beauty and her wit had an affected quality which Violet found off-putting. Daisy Fellowes bothered her too because next to Daisy even the most smartly dressed woman took on a frumpy air. Daisy was malicious as well, and like all childlike people, despite her sophistication, Violet was undone by malice.

She visited Greece again — on Daisy's yacht. Mrs. Fellowes chose her guests not so much to give them pleasure as to get her chosen victims fixed firmly at the center of her web. It was in this spirit that she prepared a surprise for Violet, who hadn't yet found her sea legs. She went down to her cabin just after a lavish lunch to discover an anatomy textbook on her bed, opened to the most repellent plates it contained. She was sick at once.

In 1927 the Trefusises went to the United States. Despite the warmth of American hospitality, the English couple were bored. In New York their cousin by marriage, the department store magnate Marshall Field, gave parties for them where the free flow of drink snuffed out all worthwhile conversation. Violet went to Washington too, where Rebecca West ran into her with the Princesse as they were on their way to the White House. Why? A mystery unless they were invited simply as distinguished tourists. Then they went to Palm Beach, Florida, as the guests of the Princesse's brother, Paris Singer, then president of the luxurious and exclusive Everglades Club. The opulence of Palm Beach with its concentration of millionaires and lack of any signs of intellectual life was not at all to Violet's taste. She was delighted to leave for Cuba, then a tropical paradise with a Spanish flavor. They liked the florid architecture and the colorful cuisine, and while there they were given an audience with the President, Machado y Morales.

At the Princesse's Violet was taken up by two women who admired her intelligence, said so, and took steps to assure her success, issuing her an official passport into the Paris literati. They were Anna de Noailles and Colette. Her portrait of the Comtesse de Noailles is one of the best things in her memoirs:

Tiny, brilliant, restless, she lived in a tropical turmoil of flowers and furbelows. Never relaxed, never silent, she twittered, twitted, perorated. She was always to be found at any hour of the day in precisely the same room, in precisely the same chaise-longue, in precisely the same state of combative inanition, vowing she would be dead before the year was out — to a philosophical audience who knew perfectly well that on the stroke of eight she would leap to her feet, galvanize her servants, don veils and feathers, and be fetched by two doting slaves who would conduct her to some restaurant which she would dazzle and bewitch until two in the morning, when she would suddenly recollect she was a dying woman and would practically be carried to her grave by the conquered diners. The French are creatures of habit; the unexpected makes no lasting appeal. They like to feel that Anna was always to be found in her bedroom from 12 A.M. to 8 P.M. It was comforting to know that she died all day and dined all night.

Madame de Polignac would take a mischievous delight in confronting what she called the "thoroughbred" with the "Percheron"; in other words, Anna de Noailles with Colette. Colette on these occasions would behave like a somewhat grumpy gardener who has been dragged away from his work.*

But death didn't interest Colette, "not even her own"; her likes and dislikes were ranged on the side of life:

To use a word that must astonish those who do not know Colette, she was "cosy." She loved mixing the sauce vinaigrette that accompanied her home-grown salad; her kitchen was more familiar to her than her drawing-room. She adored comfort and disdained luxury. She had many phobias; any kind of snob, social, literary, political. Especially she disliked women whose conversation was as skimpy as their diet.†

The first time Colette glimpsed Violet she cried, "Violet? *Mais non!* Geranium!" What she saw was a young woman in the pink of condition, her transparent complexion as rosy-cheeked as an eighteenth-century portrait. Violet loved good food at a time when dieting was coming into fashion. Paul Valéry punned *"Madame Très Physique"* ("Madame Very Physical") because, without making much of a fuss about it, she had become the very picture of health. Jacques Émile

* *Don't Look Round.*
† *Don't Look Round.*

Blanche painted her during this period of her life, and she would go to sit for him in the famous studio not far from her own little house. As an Anglophile, Blanche showed the greatest consideration for Mrs. Keppel's daughter. And as a disciple of Proust's, he was fascinated by a scandal whose repercussions had reached Paris considerably muffled. He asked Violet why she preferred Paris to London. "Because here one is freer to say and do what one pleases, without conventional constrictions" But Blanche suggested another reason: her ambition to become a writer. "You want to compete for the Prix Femina." He went on: "Why do your smart friends all want to be taken for professional artists? Isn't that a new type of snobbery?"

# 8. The Novelist

JACQUES ÉMILE BLANCHE guessed rightly that Violet's ambitions lay much more in the direction of literature than frivolity. She liked to write, and she had an excellent gift for observation sharpened by her talent for mimicry and flair for décor. She could create an atmosphere in a novel as easily as in a drawing room. In the best of Paris traditions Violet presided over a salon.

Paul Morand, Jean Giraudoux, and a sprinkling of diplomats were among the regulars. Lady Crewe, the wife of the English ambassador, would bring along English friends beset by qualms about being introduced to the scandalous Violet, but they always went away vanquished by her charm. Nothing about this elegant young hostess bespoke Lesbos; she seemed even more at home in smart society than in literature.

Things were settling down. Her position in society safely reconquered, Violet was now after fame rather than notoriety. She started to write, more carefully than before, but less weightily too. During this period women writers, always more respected in France than in England, basked between the wars in the light reflected by two stars in particular, Anna de Noailles and Colette, not to mention all those other Egerias, speakers, and literary-jury chairmen, who were the focus of a certain interest. Each pursued her speciality: Myriam Harry, the Middle East; the Princesse Bibesco, international society; Lucie Delarue-Mardrus, the French provinces. Violet's speciality was England, and she always wove into her plots the sort of complications that ensue from involvement, whether through family connections or sentiment, with two countries, France and England.

In 1929 *Sortie de Secours* (*Emergency Exit*) was published. The plot is simple: an independent young woman of means has a very handsome but somewhat lukewarm lover. To arouse his jealousy, she sets out to seduce a famous painter old enough to be her father. She succeeds, and even falls in love with the personable old man, when she realizes that jealousy and love are less important in life than independence. The theme of the novel was pinpointed for her by Misia Sert (Nathalie Styx):

> 'In each human being there is an emergency exit: that is, the cult of self under a multitude of manifestations, which means that when an obsession becomes too violent you can escape, vanish with a snicker . . .' It was that diabolic Nathalie who unconsciously opened that door for me!

The novel is written in the first person by a woman who has decided she's finished with suffering. What Violet writes about this sort of affliction is both amusing and revealing:

> Happiness for me lies in things, not people. Should I ever be unfaithful to Drino, it would be with a country or a city. You could say that my irresponsible and evasive nature can't support the heavy trappings of love. And, when someone does impose them, it becomes as grotesque as a little girl dressed in grown-up finery. It knows what's expected and wanted; flattered, for a little while it will turn grown-up: voice, gestures, gait, everything will be faithfully reproduced. But the result is caricature. The voice will be sterner, the gait more pompous, the adult evoked through a pitiless stress on the comic. I am ridiculous when I'm in love — more ridiculous than other people. Like the little girl, I take my part terribly seriously; every ounce of moderation and taste desert me: I trip over my train.

At thirty-five, Violet looked back on the dramas and follies of her twenties with ironic contempt; she would never be caught off guard again, that was certain. Her despair, at least so it appeared, had dwindled into a few melancholy reflections she scattered here and there, more heavily laden with irony than drama: "The sea you drown in can be a lovely shade of blue." "Death — what I am waiting for? I've loved enormously, suffered enormously, travelled enormously. I should die, rich in all that love, all that pain, all those countries." "I shall say: God, let me give back to you what's left of my life; I don't like carrying small change."

The book leaves the impression that passion and its attendant dramas are to be considered in the worst possible taste. There is in it the sometimes slightly pedantic offhandedness of Giraudoux, the sensuality of Colette. What Violet writes about Cuba is entirely characteristic of her aesthetic greediness:

> Blue, pink, green, adorned with a little of everything, niches, pillars, busts, pineapples, these overfed houses contemplated life with a replete smile. Crowded, pulpy, plump, they looked like fat ladies nodding into their siestas after too much lunch. Everything was voluptuous, beginning with the food. The red- and black-lacquered Moro crabs with hooked claws like parrots' beaks; saffron rice mixed with red peppers, green fruit with black seeds, small scented pink bananas like a pianists's stubby fingers.

The mood is far removed from *Challenge.*

*Écho,* published two years later, takes place in Scotland. Better received than *Sortie de Secours,* it was even something of a best-seller. Its style is more finished, less fidgety, and the plot more original. A delightful Parisian visits her Scottish aunt in her gloomy castle. There she charms her inseparable twin cousins, a brother and sister. The sister is sure that her French cousin has become her brother's mistress and she drowns herself. The brother banishes the Parisian. A host of reminders of Violet's Scottish holidays are cleverly counterpointed with the wit of a Paris salon. Yet this book, which Somerset Maugham might have turned into an excellent short story, interests us less than *Sortie de Secours:* Violet had become an accomplished novelist, but we lose sight of her.

A third novel, *Broderie Anglaise,* is full of oddities but had a certain success. In it, Violet succeeds in showing us England through the eyes of a Frenchwoman as she spends her holidays moving from one country house to another. Her last novel in French was finished in January 1940 and published by Gallimard a year later in occupied Paris, which meant that it went virtually unreviewed. Its title, *Les Causes Perdues*

(*Lost Causes*), suggests the pessimism of its story, which unfolds among a greedy and grasping aristocracy, with its ridiculous cortege of female companions, grumbling servants, and slightly too handsome chauffeurs. In her English-language novels we find the same qualities that distinguish her French style — high spirits, the *mot juste*, graphic description — and some of the faults as well: occasional tedium and a snobbery rather reminiscent of the turn-of-the-century attitudes E. F. Benson echoed in his novel *Dodo*. The characters and the atmosphere are the same ingredients Nancy Mitford employed, and Violet's novels are now considered delightful period pieces.

*Tandem* was published in 1933. It is the story of two Greek sisters, one married to a French duke (an amusing sketch of Anna de Noailles), the other the wife of an Englishman whose family seat bears a strong resemblance to Knole. The latter dies in a riding accident, and her elder sister pursues a brilliant but lonely career. Violet caught to perfection the disenchantment which began to create a void around the Comtesse de Noailles once the "sublime" had gone out of fashion. The supporting characters are inspired: a music-loving Rumanian aunt, a duchess addicted to play-acting (Anna de Noailles again), an Irish governess, a fat lady from Bordeaux, a laughable but successful Don Juan (based on the playwright Henry Bernstein). They display Violet's prodigious gift for mimicry, but very little of Violet, except perhaps in this exchange:

"You are a queer little thing, aren't you? Have you never been physically attracted by anyone?"

"Superficially, yes," she sighed. "And I am content with the most superficial caresses. Le dénouement!"

The novel is full of epigrams that she sometimes borrowed to sprinkle through her conversation: "She was the last representative of a milieu to which she never belonged." Or a variant often applied to her scheming friend Lady D—: "She is the sort of woman she would not ask to her own parties." Her comments on France have a charming ring of entente cordiale: "France is no young hussy, impudent and *court-vêtue,* she is elderly, possibly a little stout, philosophical, very greedy. She understands everything and is — kind." "In England they like a foreigner to be typically a foreigner; it satisfies their craving for the picturesque; in France the foreigner is popular who is as much like a Frenchman as possible." Violet very accurately noted that it was much pleasanter to be a writer in France than in England. In Paris people would ask you, "What are you working on? When is your next book coming out?" while the English would inquire casually, "I hear you've published another book?"

Her next novel, *Hunt the Slipper* (1937), was aptly reviewed in the *Times Literary Supplement:*

This is an amusing, detached, penetrating study of mental and physical love as the pastime of persons of assured income, literary education and cultivated, acquisitive good taste. Its theme recalls those emotional Baedekers of the seventeenth century in which Mlle de Scudery and her followers planned out, with a detailed and exquisite accuracy, a wealth of helpful comment, the grand tour through the Pays du Tendre . . . Miss Trefusis writes with a charm that has been disciplined into a technique; with butterfly brevity, and with a connoisseur's appreciation of unique specimens of personality.

It is a delightful book, which ends on a sad misunderstanding. There are a number of brilliantly witty epigrams, one of which applies exactly to Violet: "He was helpless to the point of genius about the things which did not interest him."

After the war, Violet Trefusis published *Pirates at Play,* the story of a band of handsome Florentines on the lookout for rich mistresses. It is amusing, but less charming than its predecessors. Several members of Florentine society are recognizable, including the old Marchesa Serristori, who was one of Florence's leading hostesses. The heroes have something of Louise de Vilmorin's brothers about them.

Violet's novels come straight from her address book; they concern exclusively the rich and fashionable, with their hangers-on-servants, governesses, dressmakers, secretaries, florists. She worked out her plots with the same care she would devote to seating a large dinner party: she strove for a harmonious blend of the correct and the congenial. And the reader comes away as though from an extremely successful dinner given in a very pretty house. During the evening, the smartly dressed and witty guests have from time to time let drop a remark that suggests that they too know what it is to love and suffer. But however intense their emotions, it is hard not to think that a longish cruise, or plans for a party, or a flirtation or two wouldn't lighten their mood, transmuting despair into an intriguing melancholy. Proust once noted that for the Duchesse de Guermantes arranging a luncheon party could put everything right, an observation that recurs to the reader of these novels written by a woman who did indeed enjoy lunching out. Her plots often have the charm of those confidences, which stop just short of indiscretion and whose only harm is in their teasing allusions. Philippe de Rothschild, who knew Violet when he was a small boy (their mothers were good friends), recalls that as a woman Violet took more pleasure in intimate gossip than in her own love affairs. And she used her voice, the most fascinating thing about her, in her probings of the affairs of others, or in her hints about her own lovers, to create a pervadingly sensual atmosphere. Perhaps, suggests her old friend, some tempestuous love had come too close for comfort. But she would have been put out had no one made her feel desirable, a trait found in a number of her characters: they set out to conquer, then retreat on tiptoe.

Had Violet needed to earn her living, she probably would have become a more prolific and better-known writer. She wouldn't have been distracted by constant temptations. But travel and the social round dissipated her attention, and her novels remained simply the products of a highly talented woman of the world. Curiously, her French novels met with much more success than the English ones. She missed the Prix Femina by only a vote or two, having begun the traditional round of visits to jury members with "one of the most influential," the widow of Alphonse Daudet:

> . . . a visit to her house was indispensable. "Whatever you do," my friends recommended, "do not let her think you're well off." I accordingly borrowed an old suit from my maid, taking the métro, not a taxi, to her distant *quartier*. A few days later I sent the old lady a few mangy marigolds. *"Quand je pense,"* she bewailed, *"que cette petite veuve* si méritante *a dû se priver de manger pour m'envoyer ces fleurs!"*

["When I think that this *so deserving* little woman had to go without a meal to send me these flowers!"] *

Yes: Violet's friends had been mistaken; she would have done better to pull out all her aristocratic stops. Madame Daudet was a snob if she was anything. Violet's success did not sit well with Daisy Fellowes, who had literary ambitions herself. But before getting down to work, Daisy wanted a publisher, and she set about exerting all her charms on Gaston Gallimard, the head of the house of Gallimard (Violet dealt with the charming and vaguely melancholy literary editor at Plon, Georges Poupet). Eventually Daisy pounced on her victim, fragile and transparent as crystal: "You know, Violet darling, I call M Gallimard 'Gaston' these days." "Is *that* all?" Violet flared, making a rapid-fire pun on the French word for "doll": "I call my editor at Plon 'Poupée'!"

Violet Trefusis is one of that handful of English authors who have written so delightfully in French: Anthony Hamilton, with his *Mémoires de la Vie du Comte de Gramont;* William Beckford, with *Vathek;* Oscar Wilde with *Salomé;* Ronald Firbank with his early symbolist tale, "La Princesse aux Soleils (Romance Parlée)." Moreover, she shared with these writers an instinct for elegance, a leaning toward fantasy. Paul Morand once told Jacques Émile Blanche that Violet was a better writer than himself, and until the war she in fact won considerable acclaim. Critics compared her with the Princesse Bibesco — who built a more durable reputation on her abilities to work hard and survive the tedium of the more academic of the salons. But the two women were the best of friends nevertheless.

Violet came to know Jean Cocteau through Anna de Noailles and the Princesse de Polignac. And through Cocteau, impelled by her curiosity and her fascination with *la vie bohème,* she met Maurice Sachs and Sachs's current lover, Max Jacob. But Max's sexual proclivities didn't prevent him from proposing to the newly widowed Violet in 1929:

> *Écho* brought a lot of new friends in its wake. I realized I was a self-made woman, and also, in spite of appearances, a lonely one. I received

* *Don't Look Round.*

a proposal. Max Jacob . . . called on me one afternoon, dressed, he imagined, for the part of a suitor. A small dapper Punchinello, he wore a top hat, white spats, gloves the colour of fresh butter. He hung his hat on his stick which he held like a banner between his legs. He was irresistible. I longed to take advantage of his proposal which was couched in terms that sounded as though he had learned them out of a book on etiquette. We examined the pros and cons. St Loup, far from being an asset, proved a stumbling block.

"*Je déteste la campagne,*" said Max, "*tout y est trop vrai!* The nearest I ever get is the Bois, and that is bad enough, because it *reminds* me of the country."

"What about travel?"

"That is different, the place doesn't belong to me, there are no responsibilities. *C'est comme si je mangeais au restaurant.*"

A great advantage, he pointed out, was his being about twenty years older than me. "I have waited forty years before proposing to anyone. I am not likely to propose to anyone else."*

The Princesse de Polignac also introduced her composer protégés to Violet, among them Francis Poulenc, who shared with Violet a liking for pretty houses and good food. Sometimes she would visit him at his house on the banks of the Loire, and he frequently came to see her at the Tour de St. Loup. He used to drive out in a taxi because he had a crush on the driver, so Violet called him Prince Thurn and Taxis. Other composers were regular guests: Georges Auric (with his beautiful wife Nora) and Violet's close friend Henri Sauguet, whose lively presence could be depended upon to thaw the most icebound of luncheon parties. Part of this musical circle were the painter José Maria Sert and his wife, one of the first couples in Paris to take the young Englishwoman under their wing.

Physically, Sert resembled a portly Franz Hals, with his splashed-on moustache, his jovial baldness; a fat cat purring by a well-fed fire, fed by his wife, Misia, whose terribly intelligent eyes sparkled with wit and ferocity. A mixture of Puck and Sans Gêne, she would overturn with a shrug doctrines hatched in the morning of Time, canonize with a word artists no one had ever taken seriously. Queen of burlesque, she

* *Don't Look Round.*

whisked the spectacles from the nose of the sage. Under her tuition, people behaved as in a ballet; the universally respected statesman would suddenly discover himself to be animated by a Petrouchka-like passion, the dowager forsaking her train for pink tights.*

At Misia Sert's Violet would see Paul Claudel and André Maurois. Paul Morand and his wife and the Princesse Soutzo would be there, and Jean Giraudoux, and of course Jean Cocteau — forever captivated by Violet and her "hoop and sceptre."

* *Don't Look Round.*

# 9. St. Loup

VIOLET NOT ONLY maintained her salon in Neuilly, she established herself in a country house worthy of a character from one of her novels. Its setting was wonderfully romantic, and she found it under illustrious auspices:

> The year before Marcel Proust died I had the privilege of meeting him at a luncheon party given by Walter Berry. He was a disappointment, only emerging from his shawls to complain about his health, which was manifestly deplorable. A pair of Indo-Persian eyes, so heavily-lashed, so gaudy, as to make their owner appear overdressed, were imprisoned in a face the colour of tallow. At the end of the meal he became more objective. Turning to me, he inquired if I knew *les environs de Paris?* Without giving me time to reply he amplified: "I'll wager you have never heard of St Loup de Naud, though perhaps you are familiar with the person of that name in my book. Yes? Well, you should visit the place which inspired it. It is about eighty kilometres from Paris, on the road to Provins. A lovely surprise. It is an aquiline little hamlet perched on a hillock *en pleine plaine.* The steep village street leads to one of the finest Romanesque churches in France. Poor church, it is sadly neglected; some allege it is disfigured. I would say it is embellished by great smears of green mould which make it look as if it had been reclaimed from the sea, *la cathédrale engloutie.* Go to see it — *vous m'en direz des nouvelles!"**

"It is not an exaggeration," Violet wrote, "to say that places have played at least as important a part in my life as people."

Colette had another name for St. Loup, La Mélisandière, chosen to

* *Don't Look Round.*

suit its Gothic atmosphere; it is easy to imagine Mélisande letting down her long hair from one of the tower windows. The fifteenth-century tower, all that remains of a much larger chateau, is a sharply angled mass surmounted by a steeply pitched roof. The tower dominates a park which slopes down to a little wooded plain. Violet quickly added a more comfortable wing to this austere keep and brought statues from Italy for the garden, through which a long flight of stairs descended toward a parterre laid out in hedges of clipped box. The apse of the neighboring church juts up between the tall elms at the bottom of the garden. In the park are the remains of the tenth- and eleventh-century Abbey of St. Loup, including a marvelously preserved tithe barn or refectory, a vast ogival structure supported by a row of columns, the perfect setting for a Gothic novel. Frankly, in spite of its charm, St. Loup is not a reassuring place: beneath the dining room are deep oubliettes, and many of Violet's English guests used to claim that the tower bedrooms were haunted. They insisted on sleeping in the new wing, where Violet had prudently installed her own bedroom. But French guests imperturbably relished the big tower rooms with their canopied beds and tapestries — just the sort of thing, they felt, one was likely to find in an English castle. Violet wasted no time in adorning St. Loup with furniture and pictures which immediately looked as though they had belonged there forever.

She liked magnificently framed looking glasses, whose mottled depths turned anyone who gazed into them into an old portrait. There were looking glasses surrounded with colored Venetian glass, with silver Stuart frames, with mahogany Chippendale pagodas. Violet also loved hangings embroidered with coats of arms, flowers, fantastic birds. Her taste sometimes partook of whatever it was in Edith Sitwell that made her "Elegy for Dead Fashions" such a wonderful, nostalgic catalogue of a poem. Her interiors had little to do with what was fashionable, but they were all the more successful for that. Her occasionally audacious color sense never failed her: the mauve velvet of her dining chairs against the white and yellow tiles of the dining room is a case in point. Tall Venetian blackamoors held candelabra, and a pair of faience lions stood guard over the Gothic fireplace. In her tiny library Violet housed a collection of rare bindings, mostly of the seventeenth and eighteenth centuries, and ornamented with illustrious coats of arms. Not surprisingly, she collected books of royal provenance. A descendant of the Stuarts through the Edmonstones, she especially cherished the Book of Common Prayer, which had belonged to James I, bindings with the arms of Charles II and the Old Pretender, and a manuscript that had belonged to the last of the Stuarts, Cardinal York. A history of the Stuarts once owned by Madame du Barry had the advantage of satisfying Violet's ancestor worship along with her fascination for royal mistresses. In the latter vein, she collected books that had belonged to Madame de Maintenon and Madame de Pompadour. And the better to identify with the sovereigns for whom she occasionally took herself, she acquired volumes that bore the arms of Elizabeth I, Catherine the Great, and Marie Antoinette. She was especially proud of a binding from the library of the Duchesse de Montpensier, the Grande Mademoiselle — perhaps because this cousin of Louis XIV had inspired a book of Vita's, perhaps because like Violet she had dismissed so many distinguished suitors.

More than a decorator, Violet was a stage director who used her rooms as sets against which she could act out the luxurious scenarios of an imagination overtaken, as the years went by, by a veritable mythomania. This urge to assume another identity lay behind her special fondness for costume balls. In 1939 she made a wonderful entrance into a Louis XIV ball given by the Comte Étienne de Beaumont: she was dressed as the Duchesse de Bourgogne in a red hunting habit trimmed in gold braid, a wig, and a tricorn, all copied from a portrait in her own collection.

The count, who dominated smart Paris society between the wars, quickly saw that Violet's touch of fantasy could do much to enliven the fancy-dress balls which every season brought the fashionable rich who knew how to spend money in touch with artists who knew how to turn this luxury to creative ends. They soon became friends, and among the people she ran across at his house were the Baronne de Meyer and her fleshy husband, now a well-known photographer. "Dirty *Boches!*" murmured the Princesse de Polignac when she too came across her former friends. Violet got to know Tony Gandarillas, who later on took charge of the Baronne's ashes when her husband had her cremated —

and once, in an after-dinner haze, Tony and Princesse Violette Murat mistook them for cocaine. But this was another milieu entirely: except for the sleeping pills she took in her latter years, drugs were never a part of Violet's life.

Etienne de Beaumont was like a prancing circus horse as he shook his imaginary plumes — but he was the ringmaster too, and he knew just how to make his friends trot in the direction he wanted them to. Edouard Bourdet's play *La Fleur des Pois* (1932) has left us a caricature of the de Beaumont set. Bourdet himself was a good-looking man who managed to be both morally austere and fashionable, and in other plays he portrayed social circles which, to a lesser degree than that in *La Fleur des Pois,* were those which molded Violet. *La Sexe Faible* (1929) takes place at the Ritz, and it was filled with characters she could recognize; she was a close friend of the original of the old Polish countess whose dismal evening sans gigolo remains one of the play's set pieces. And in *La Prisonnière* (1926), with its then scandalous story of a triangle in which the wife's lover is disclosed at the final curtain to be another woman, Bourdet rattled one or two of the skeletons in the Princesse de Polignac's closet. Violet was a friend of Bourdet's lovely and intelligent wife, Denise. A deep-rooted coldness and a tendency to nag would have made her rather disagreeable if she had not also possessed the ability to laugh. Her outbursts, orchestrated with the peals of Jacques Février or Christian Bérard, still echo through St. Loup. But outside her circle of intimates she chose to remain as forbidding as Minerva.

Since Violet's own house was much too small, Étienne de Beaumont urged her to hire the first level of the Eiffel Tower for a costume ball. This she did, in June 1937, asking her guests to come dressed in what Parisians might have worn for the tower's inauguration in 1889. People warned Violet that the times were not as propitious as they might be for such a gathering: the Popular Front held sway, and many of her friends were convinced that public opinion would be aroused to the point at which working-class hecklers would pelt the guests with rotten apples. Instead, the guests arrived courageously decked out in ostrich feathers or false beards to the applause of curious bystanders. Violet had also asked her mother's old friends, one of whom

came in a dress cut very low. "What a marvellous false front!" commented Serge Lifar. "It's my own, monsieur!" came the haughty
Edwardian rejoinder. "I had no idea that tonight was going to be
fancy-dress."

When Violet became a widow she was besieged with imagined
"fiancés" — but some were more likely candidates than Max Jacob.
For a moment, on the advice of her friend Marie Murat, she thought
of accepting Comte Stanislas de La Rochefoucauld. The count was a
rather imposing man, undeniably intelligent, but somewhat blinkered
by his smug self-satisfaction. "I don't like that man. One of his eyes
applauds the other like a pair of castanets," Anna de Noailles remarked
caustically after he had interrupted the poetess in the middle of one
of her socialist tirades. "You forget: you are a woman of the world,"
he admonished her. "So that is what they're going to put after my
name in the encyclopedia then? 'Anna de Noailles: woman of the
world'?" The countess was furious.

Mrs. Keppel observed La Rochefoucauld's flutterings over Violet
without enthusiasm: after all, he wasn't yet divorced from Alice Cocéa,
his actress wife. As though butter would not melt in her mouth, she
discussed English marriage customs with the count: when a widow
remarried, she could not expect a penny from her parents — she had
to make do with what was left of her dowry. "I wonder how much
Violet still has," she dropped casually. "She's *such* a child." The
count's calls on Violet began to dwindle immediately. Later, Stanislas
de La Rochefoucauld married a charming woman from his own set,
but he demonstrated less than consummate tact in extolling the virtues
of his first wife in front of his second. One day at lunch he said: "It's
extraordinary, but when I married Alice a lot of people thought I
would become an actor." "And now, dear Stanislas," said Violet, "now
that you've married a lady, do people expect you to become a gentleman?" In the notes she gathered for the French version of her memoirs, Violet described him in a way that might have pleased his
ancestor, the author of the *Maximes:* "I don't like his character, but
I admire his faults."

Among Violet's escorts were a couple of very Proustian young men
of confirmed bachelor propensities. One, Comte Jean de Gaigneron,

a close friend of Harold Nicolson's, was brisk, catty, and heir to the elegance of his mother's many relations. Proust found him congenial, but the count found Proust a compromising acquaintance. And there was Comte Louis de Lasteyrie, who in complete contrast was the soul of amiability. But like the Comte de Gaigneron, he detested hearing Proust's name mentioned. If somebody did bring up the forbidden subject, he would raise his long white hands to heaven and sigh: "*Not* our sort; I've never understood why my cousin Marie de Rohan could bring herself to receive him." Perhaps he had read the letter in which Proust finds in him a resemblance to Léon Blum, the Lasteyries' bête noire, and calls him "Lolotte," a nickname the count had imagined reserved to a few intimates. He also had the misfortune of seeing this name attached to the hero of *La Fleur des Pois*. Not far from St. Loup Lolotte owned a gloomy medieval chateau crammed with the venerable relics of a daughter of Louis Philippe to whom his mother had been maid of honor. Its library housed the papers and portraits of his detested great-grandfather, that frightful demagogue, the Marquis de Lafayette. Ten years after the war the house, La Grange, was taken over by a cousin of de Lasteyrie's, Comte René de Chambrun, who brushed away the cobwebs and displayed its treasures to advantage, turning La Grange into a fascinating place to visit. From time to time Violet would suggest marriage to Monsieur de Gaigneron or Monsieur de Lasteyrie, throwing them into something approaching panic, sharpened by a pang or two of regret, since neither had much money.

I don't think Violet ever proposed to Comte Louis Gautier-Vignal, another of Proust's friends, but she often asked him to St. Loup because of his urbane conversation, his wide reading, and extensive, almost erudite, acquaintance with the ins and outs of society — all of which adapted him to every variety of guest. A handsome man, he liked to display his profile. Once when Anna de Noailles saw him enter a drawing room with his three equally imposing sisters, she asked: "Who is that family of unicorns?"

It must be said that in general there was a Proustian side to most of the visitors to St. Loup. A close friend from *The Guermantes Way* was Princesse Lucien Murat, born Marie de Rohan-Chabot. Witty, spirited, and extraordinarily badly dressed, for years she pursued a liaison with an ambassador, Comte Charles de Chambrun, like Louis de Lasteyrie a descendant of Lafayette's. Their relationship was the image of the affair between the Marquise de Villeparisis and Monsieur de Norpois in Proust. Wilde was right, Violet reflected: life *does* imitate art. Violet always called Marie Murat "my cousin," since through the Keppels she shared with her a common ancestor in Louise de Kerouaille.

Among the couples younger than herself in this same circle, Violet was particularly close during the thirties to the Duc and Duchesse d'Harcourt, the Charles de Noailles, and the Jean-Louis de Faucigny-Lucinges. No longer simply a young Englishwoman living in Paris, she had become French enough to gain entrée to the châteaux, which put up much higher barriers to the outside world than did Paris drawing rooms. She became a part of that large family called the *gratin,* remaining enough of a foreigner so that escapades which might have slightly tarnished the reputation of a Frenchwoman could be laid to her English eccentricities. For between the wars she took one lover after another, a fact she made no attempt to hide. If a man attracted her, she did not wait for him to make the first move; she would take the initiative herself. It is not surprising that Catherine the Great was one of her favorite fantasy roles. Thus she had a number of affairs but no lasting relationships. Quickly bored, or overly romantic, and more often than not dissatisfied, she accepted male homage, experimented, but rarely renewed the experience.

Perhaps these lovers were camouflage for loves of another order pursued much more discreetly. In her old age Violet would, sometimes, talk about only one of her old lovers, probably because he had been a prime minister, and she talked about him without emotion. Paul Reynaud had indeed been much too shrewd and meticulous to remain a pleasant memory for Violet. She met him through Gaston Palewski, his private secretary. Reynaud was something of a snob, and since he aimed at cutting an international figure, he felt the chic thing to do would be to take an English aristocrat for a mistress. He was a man of narrow horizons who should never have left his post as minister of finance. Small and foppish, he looked somehow Chinese. Women found him attractive, but he was caught between the twin jealousies of his wife and the formidably scheming Madame de Portes. "You have two wives," Violet told him. "It's time you had a mistress." She must have found their relationship more socially diverting than sensual. She met politicians and diplomats, and she was sure that the fate of Europe hung in the balance at her lunch table. She was an honored guest at the entertainments held for the visiting George VI and Queen Elizabeth in 1938, but it seems likely that she would have been invited in any case. In fact, during her stint as political hostess, Violet acquired among people who didn't know her a reputation as a spy from the upper echelons of British intelligence. Even today, her old neighbors at St. Loup, who seldom ever had more than a glimpse of her, are prone to mysterious mutterings about "the intelligence service" when they talk about her. Another legend, this one a favorite of people who like to claim inside knowledge of the social scene, holds that Violet's real name was Dreyfus — easily Anglicized, of course, to Trefusis.

In the elegant and eclectic group that surrounded Violet in the thirties there were no lesbians. She would even make fun of lesbian affairs when they were conducted solely for social-climbing purposes. Much later, Violet used to tell a story about a very beautiful and very rich American woman, with a penchant for her own sex exclusively, who tried to seduce Misia Sert. But Misia was in love with nobody but her husband. The American finally arranged a rendezvous with Misia, threw herself at her, and initiated a series of bold maneuvers, eventually suggesting even more complicated positions. Misia looked at her coolly for a long moment: "Is that all you know how to do, then, Miss W—?"

Violet's mistrust of ambiguous situations cut her off from some fascinating people. She visited Natalie Barney's salon, where she might have met Gide, Joyce, or Pound, only once. She used to tell about the time Gertrude Stein made overtures to her in a bookshop, and invented a little pastiche: "A pose is a pose is a pose is a pose." Violet had conceived a positive distaste for Sapphic circles and the sleazy success she might have enjoyed after her love affair with Vita. The "old pal" attitude of people she would never have dreamed of seeing socially, the familiarity bred by shared inclinations, if not shared pleasures, were enough to rule out any faintly equivocal woman from Violet's circle of friends. She was nevertheless tempted to get to know a certain Madame X, a member of the *grande bourgeoisie,* who was said to be wildly amusing, and who entertained constantly in her elegant house. It was perhaps this latter consideration that persuaded Violet to accept an invitation there. But Madame X's companion lived in the house too, a lady of the same age, sixty or so, and consumed with social ambition. A large dinner was held at which Madame X, eager to shine, launched on a series of stories, each more scandalous than the next, despite desperate signals from her friend. Eventually there was a lull, suddenly filled by Violet's stage whisper to Henri Sauguet: "The lady is not very funny." Madame X's friend rushed from the room in tears. To save what was left of the evening, Reynaldo Hahn, an old friend of the household, volunteered to sing, and proceeded to do so in his tremulous voice. Years later, Violet turned the dinner party into an amusing story. She was never more at the top of her form than after some social catastrophe which all at once managed to expose pretentiousness, vulgarity, or greed.

Nearing forty, Violet suddenly aged. Nora Auric's portrait of her in 1933, when she was thirty-nine, shows quite a different woman from that in Jacques Émile Blanche's portrait made eight years earlier. She is pale, the lines of her face are more drawn, her expression curiously contradictory: the eyes sad, the mouth malicious. The painter had captured Violet's ambiguity precisely: gay in society, melancholy in private, incapable of close attachments, flitting from one distraction to another. She also began to develop an exaggerated sense of her own importance. Yet it would be a mistake to think of Violet, even during the Roaring Twenties, as a character from Paul Morand or Scott Fitzgerald. She of course followed fashion to the letter and adored dancing, but her attitudes were really those of the preceding generation. She had always been a gourmet, and food began to claim more and more of her attention. The excellence of her table had a lot to do with her adoption by Paris society. And like a three-star restaurant, she had her specialities. The most remarkable was her seven-hour leg of mutton, a recipe Colette gave her. The mutton, a pig's foot, vegetables, and herbs are simmered overnight in an earthenware casserole. The next day, the mutton should be tender enough to be eaten with a spoon. Another speciality was her madeleine stuffed with marrow and served with a truffle sauce.

She never drove; she always had a chauffeur. And she never traveled anywhere without a maid to dress and undress her. Appearances counted now, and they were scrupulously respected. Nevertheless, weekends at St. Loup were more relaxed. As the years passed she put jealousy behind her and delighted in welcoming women younger than herself — as long as they were pretty and intelligent. Among them were Elisabeth de Breteuil, previously Princesse Chachàvadzé; Minou de Montgomery, who married General Béthouart; a very pretty American, Bettina Jones, whose husband, Gaston Bergery, founded a leftist political party for society people; and most delightful of all, the Duchesse d'Ayen, the first woman of her class to take a job — with *Vogue*, to be sure, but a job. Between marriages, Louise de Vilmorin came too. And so for nearly fifteen years, St. Loup was known as one of the most amusing houses within easy reach of Paris. Violet's guest book is filled with the signatures of the great and the famous, with a sprinkling of the kind of forgotten name which suddenly prompts one to reminisce: "Ah yes, she was so lovely!" or "He was so amusing!" In France, only a foreigner could have made such a mixture work. St. Loup was indeed a house worthy of its guardian spirit, Marcel Proust.

# 10. *Europe*

DENYS TREFUSIS also came under the spell of St. Loup; the tower provided a welcome haven between trips to Russia. In 1928 he came back from the last of these missions — after a brush with the police and a hairbreadth escape — with his health completely undermined. Though he was able to draw up a long and distinguished report on conditions in the Soviet Union, he was past recall, and died in the summer of 1929. Violet seldom spoke about her husband in later years, perhaps out of remorse, but here is how she remembered him in *Don't Look Round:*

> All through the winter he coughed, a small undramatic cough, as quietly persistent as Scottish drizzle. Let it not be supposed that the cough was allowed in any way to interfere with the routine of his life. He continued to go to bed as late as ever, sometimes even neglecting to take an overcoat on the wildest winter night; precautions were not for him, I could not but admire his lordliness. Then, what was bound to happen, happened. The cough got suddenly worse, he was X-rayed. Galloping consumption was the diagnosis. He was taken to the American Hospital in Neuilly, where for months he languished, with the sudden spurts of optimism characteristic of his disease. One of the people whose visits he seemed to enjoy most was Madame de Polignac. I can only suppose they talked about music, as I was not encouraged to be present . . .
>
> I have known many remarkable men, I have never known a braver, a more prodigal. He had all the ballad-like qualities I most admire, I, all the defects it was most difficult for him to condone. Nevertheless, there was a great link between us, we both loved poetry, France, travel, being insatiably interested in foreign countries. We were both Euro-

peans in the fullest sense of the term. The same things made us laugh, we quarrelled a lot, loved not a little. We were more to be envied than pitied.

That Violet should have been so profoundly saddened by the death of a husband, who, when all was said and done, made little impression on her life, is one more paradox in a life filled with them. That she did suffer is undeniable; a letter she wrote to Cyril Connolly on September 20, 1929, is proof enough of that:

DEAR CYRIL

Many things have happened since I saw you last. By now you doubtless know that Denys — my husband — is dead. He died nearly three weeks ago — and since I have been living in a sort of mist. I see people, but they all seem alike, and flat, without relief — I dislike seeing people because they interfere with my thoughts. My life is going through a series of revisions — *"du débris du palais je bâtis ma chaumière."* D. was a curiously *sumptuous* element in my life, like a tapestry brought out on fête days, precious because intermittent. I never got tired of him, he had all the freshness of a chance encounter. More than anyone I know he liked to live dangerously, his life was spent in impossible crusades. Russia was his Holy Land. His attitude towards life and towards death was magnificently condescending. If I am stunned I am also dazzled — *"épatée"* in the fullest sense of the word like when you hear a very difficult piece brilliantly executed. I am so glad you are coming to spend the winter in Paris. I long to talk to you about this and many other things — your letter was perhaps the most intelligent one I received about my book excepting one from Colette. I hate fulsome praise and all you say is helpful. I am writing hard at present with the fervour born of unhappiness . . .

Through Denys, Violet had acquired an affection, tinged with nostalgia, for Eastern Europe and a way of life that had vanished from the West long ago, a way of life which Russia had more recently snuffed out brutally. The Polish aristocracy kept their immense estates until the Second World War, however, filling their enormous chateaux with guests right up until the end. In 1925 Denys and Violet were invited to Lançut by Count Alfred Potocki:

Though awed by its size, we were not, I am sorry to say, impressed by the beauty of the place. It was a typical Austrian *Schloss* with bulbous pepper pots and rococo flourishes. What was staggering were its contents . . .

Here foregathered the *élite* of four or five middle-European countries: Roumanians, who stood out for their perfect mastery of the French language, their Oriental standard of flattery and their taste for power (this especially applied to the women), which was only equalled by their thirst for intrigue; Hungarians, handsome bores; Viennese, graceful, anglophile, frivolous; Poles, chivalrous, heroic, with here and there a woman of outstanding beauty and vivacity, central Europeans all, with a background of great rivers and jagged fir trees, resonant with languages richly incomprehensible and mutually aggressive, furred, frogged, feudal, the envious onlookers of the East!

Countess Betka came of princely Viennese stock; her mother had been a famous beauty, and her father one of the crack shots of Europe. She was persona grata at the surviving courts of Europe; was wafted, without inquiry, without comment, from embassy to embassy. Most ambassadors were either distant cousins, or hopeful candidates to the shooting parties at Lançut. Great men abounded in her ancestry. Shorn of prestige, bereft of legend, Metternich was merely *der alte Clemens,* the not-too-faithful husband of Tante Mélanie; Talleyrand, also a connection of the ubiquitous Potocki, was spoken of as a testy, though diverting cripple, chiefly to be remembered for his excellent cuisine and his amusing, though equivocal correspondence with his niece, the Duchesse de Dino.*

For a daughter of Mrs. Keppel a role of international grande dame came naturally. The race died out after the last war, but as long as there still existed a network of courts, as long as ambassadors were more than figureheads, these political Muses held, if not the reins of real power, positions of exceptional prestige at the least. And there were the Geneva *"précieuses,"* those women who hovered over League of Nations society. The most famous of these political ladies was Violet's friend Princesse Marthe Bibesco, a fine-looking woman who had affairs with both Europe's royalty and smartest politicians.

For a while, Hungary also loomed large in Violet's life; perhaps she

* *Don't Look Round.*

believed she could discover there some of the vanishing qualities she so regretted. For a few seasons she took a small baroque palace in the old part of Budapest:

In Budapest, I fell in love again, or perhaps it would be more accurate to say that love was "wished" on me by the décor, the cold (always, in my experience, an aphrodisiac), the environment. It appealed to the comic opera strain in my make-up that I have never entirely succeeded in quashing: when I was not being Wittelsbach, I was being Offenbach.

Love, or its understudy, is a tribute exacted by Budapest of the unwary foreigner. Look at me — and love. It was all too easy; every conceivable "aid" to love was available, proffered. Shakos, tzardas, spurs, gypsy bands, twirled moustaches.

The Hungarians, how good looking! They would be photographed standing behind rows of game, pheasants, hares, partridges, stags, wild boar. Game. That's what they were: game for anything. Then the excitement of the Danube, those bloated waters which had witnessed the death of Attila, the Scourge of God! At night you could hear the clink of ice block meeting ice block like the moves of some gigantic game of chess . . .

No wonder I fell in love with Horthy Estvan, the Regent's son. He had eyebrows like swallows' wings, and the figure of a Caucasian dancer. No wonder I took a rococo house in Buda, which might have belonged to the Rosenkavalier, with its china stoves and convex balconies.

Night after night, the tziganes would bend over us, "milking" their violins; night after night, we would dance in beautifully organised *boîtes* with revolving floors, cubicles for two. Up and down outside, the detectives would pace, up and down, for Horthy's escapade with an Englishwoman was not approved of. It was lovely while it lasted.

Poor Pishta! His plane was shot down over Russia in 1942. I never saw him again.*

Another close Hungarian friend, Count Palffy, a Don Juan with a marriage mania who had been wedded to some of the world's most aristocratic and beautiful women, decided finally to settle for brains — and asked the hand of Louise de Vilmorin. Violet ran into the engaged couple on the Orient Express, where Palffy drew her aside: "Tell me, Violet, I understand that Louise has had an affair or two." "Louise!

---

* *Don't Look Round.*

But my dear, Louise is an angel!" Violet protested. Reassured, Palffy went back to his berth resolved to marry Louise after all. "What a super guy you are!" she whispered to Violet on the station platform when they pulled into Budapest. Perhaps Violet did not find this virile compliment entirely to her liking, for somewhere behind the friendly façade she bore Louise a grudge. Once after the war Violet was busy autographing her memoirs for charity when Louise showed up to buy a copy. Violet set about inscribing the flyleaf at some length. With a smile, Louise picked up the book and began to read what Violet had written; all at once, her smile froze, her eyebrows shot up, and slamming the book shut she turned on her heel and left without a word. No one ever found out what Violet had put there, but in any case, the incident seems not to have cast any lasting shadow over their friendship.

In 1936 Violet went on a cruise to Russia, where she was amazed to see that Nicholas II had lived in middle-class stuffiness which reminded her of nothing so much as a Kensington drawing room. She had already gathered from the Tsarina's letters the impression of a sentimental governess, and she found it easy to remain as indifferent to the fate of so commonplace a royal couple as she was to the Fabergé menagerie which surrounded them. Her sympathies lay with Catherine the Great. But she enjoyed the palaces and vistas of Tsarskoje Selo, and her brief tour resulted in a harvest of observations still valid today. She turned them into a series of articles for *Le Temps,* the predecessor of *Le Monde.* The newspaper's publisher, Jacques Chastenet, was a great friend of Violet's, and it was he who suggested that on her next trip to Italy she might like to meet Mussolini. But for some time there had been another reason for visiting Italy:

In 1927 my parents had bought the Villa dell'Ombrellino in Florence. What amused my mother was turning a house that was practically a lost cause, into a thing of beauty . . .

My mother had excellent taste; she felt not the need of privacy. She liked large handsome rooms, leading out of each other, *salons en enfilade,* geometrical Chippendale chairs, uncompromising Régence settees, perspectives, statues. For a woman, her taste was grandly objective. She had a horror of knick-knacks. When she first settled in Italy she had only one Italian sentence: *"Bisogna begonia"* . . . Well, *"bisogna begonia"* worked marvels.*

Naturally, Mrs. Keppel reigned over Florentine society with a charm which conquered even that most ironical member of the English colony, Harold Acton, who included a portrait of both the Keppels in his *More Memoirs of an Aesthete:*

> Mrs George Keppel came and went with the seasons since she had bought l'Ombrellino, her villa on Bellosguardo. The house was gloomy in spite of its splendid view, but Mrs Keppel brightened it with gay furniture and filled it with titled guests. Here none could compete with her glamour as a hostess . . .
>
> The Colonel spent much of his leisure compiling booklets of contemporary dates for his sight-seeing guests. Naturally he acted as cicerone to the prettiest débutantes — "such a little cutie," he said fondly of more than one. To a certain extent he shared his wife's aura. A rival guide once pointed him out to a group of inquisitive tourists as *"i'ultimo amante della regina Vittoria"* — Queen Victoria's last paramour.

The colonel had another hobby, photography, and his thick album of l'Ombrellino photographs provides both a history of taste and a panorama of what people were starting to call the "international set." In the early years of his picture-taking, house-party groups follow Edwardian traditions, each with its nucleus of visiting Greek royalty from the Villa Sparta on the other side of town. These groups give way to *Tatler*-style snapshots: Chips Channon and his Guinness in-laws; the exiled queen of Spain; the Infanta Béatrice and her Scottish terrier; the McKenna cousins; Emily Yznanga, an old maid who knew "absolutely everybody"; those old friends of King Edward VII, Lord Stavordale and Mrs. Hwfa Williams, taken "informally" on the terrace, glass in hand; and that lion of Florentine society, Carlo Placci, friend of Gabriele d'Annunzio and Bernard Berenson. But there is no glimpse of Berenson; the pope of I Tatti found Mrs. Keppel's kingdom a frivolous place, though he admired Mrs. Keppel herself. Things went, however, from bad to worse. Mrs. Keppel took it into her head

* *Don't Look Round.*

once too often to pack guests she didn't know quite what to do with off to I Tatti. Berenson wrote her a note: delighted as he always was to see *her,* he could do without her guests. She replied: "Dear Mr Berenson, I shall always be delighted to see your guests, but *you* need no longer take the trouble to come to l'Ombrellino." In the good old tradition of the Guelph-Ghibelline feud — which still divided the Florentines — the rift between the two villas was never bridged.

The most renowned of the "artists" invited to l'Ombrellino was certainly Winston Churchill. Lady Churchill recalled in a letter written to Violet in 1952 how her husband had set up his easel on the terrace, tempted by the sublime view, but after a few unproductive attempts retired to the kitchen garden, where things went much more smoothly. Intellectuals of the style welcomed at I Tatti were rarely invited, except for friends like Raymond Mortimer or Lord Berners, that composer straight from Firbank. Another Firbankian guest was the eccentric millionaire Evan Morgan (Lord Tredegar). And there was Monsignor Vay de Vaya, the Hungarian prelate who undoubtedly inspired Firbank's Cardinal Pirelli. His violet silk capes were made for him, people said, at Worth. Later, the colonel's photographs went through an early Beaton phase: debutantes photographed against the light; the Duchesse d'Harcourt in profile *à la Marie Antoinette;* the loveliest women of Florentine society — Ginoris, Guicciardinis, Antinoris — against a mass of flowers or at the base of an antique statue; now and again the Princesse de Polignac in a white scarf and a rope of pearls; Violet strangely resembling Count Raben (a Dane said to be a son of Edward VII); Violet with a group of French friends. Violet looks out of these photographs with an air both vivacious and preoccupied. But Mrs. Keppel is always regally erect beneath her abundant white hair, cigarette holder at the ready. Who, though, are "Vera" and "Zita"? "Peggy"? "Daisy"?

In his review of *Portrait of a Marriage* Cyril Connolly recalled the first time he met Violet:

> She never had a very good figure, her attractiveness centered on her voice which was low and quite bewitching, equally at home in French and

English and seldom rising above a husky murmur; her mouth was wide and sensual, her nose rather large, her eyes magnificent and working in close support of her smile to produce an ironical, rather mocking expression. She was an excellent friend.

I first met her in Florence in 1927. I had been taken to stay with Berenson by his brother-in-law Logan Pearsall Smith, she was at her mother's villa, the Ombrellino. We both discovered that we didn't like Florence and cared only for France, which made us conspirators. Violet was older than I, one of the first sophisticated married women I was to meet.

Violet usually sat with a long cigarette-holder in one hand, a short skirt revealing her elegant crossed legs as in the Blanche portrait, while puns and epigrams bubbled forth in what was really a continuous bilingual word-play. I knew nothing of her role as a queen in Gomorrah, she was more like a literary elder sister. Her husband, Denys Trefusis, I liked immediately, he was charming, graceful, and rather dashing, like so many of the men who had returned from the war.

It was, then, ten years after this meeting with Cyril, during the spring following her trip to Russia, Violet's interview with Il Duce was arranged. It was a time when relations between England and Italy were at a low ebb indeed. Violet has left us a witty record of the meeting that reveals both her anxiety to hew to the role of vital international go-between and the fact that she was the first to laugh at it. Once ushered into the dictator's august presence, a comic mishap shattered the ice:

A dreadful thing happened. My foremost foot skidded! I fell, scattering the contents of my bag, lipstick, cigarettes, bills, compact, love letters.

What could Mussolini, who prided himself on his "way" with women, do but help me pick them up? We met on all fours, face to face, under the writing table.

Before she left, Violet asked a favor of the Italian dictator in a purple-dipped scene straight from d'Annunzio:

. . . "Will you show me the balcony from which you harangue the people?"

"*Venite pure.*" He rose; he was a little taller than I, more brawny than fat, with massive shoulders and too short legs. He was meanly, cheaply dressed in a suit that looked ready-made. He stepped out on the balcony. Rome, reared on martyr's bones and pestilence, its paws sunk in sepulchres, lay couchant, carnivorous, like a superb lion, at our feet. The invading hordes had passed through Rome like so many grasshoppers, all they got was a flick of that tawny tail.

His arm swept the great, raucous city. *"Che bellezza . . ."* Then: "It is not easy to create beauty, where there is so much already . . . *Che bellezza,"* he repeated, and this time his tone was wistful, envious. He had mastered many things, his country, colonies, conferences, languages, strategies. Beauty was more elusive. Beauty had outstripped him. Not for nothing was he a Latin. Beauty had made him doubt.*

But no place was so propitious to her role-playing as the Château de Chimay, in the Belgian Ardennes. By turns the Duchesse de Dino, privy to the last days of the Holy Roman Empire, and Offenbach's Grande Duchesse de Gerolstein, she adored visiting this little principality and its superb old prince, Joseph de Caraman-Chimay, whose new wife, Gilone, was a friend of Violet's.

Two celebrated beauties held sway at Chimay in the nineteenth century, Madame Tallien, the friend of Josephine de Beauharnais', twice married, twice divorced, who finally settled down as a model princess with the first Prince de Caraman-Chimay. To amuse her a theater was built, where the current princess organizes excellent music festivals. And then there was that millionaire Mae West, Clara Ward, the old prince's first wife, who ended up married to the stationmaster of the funicular railway at Mount Vesuvius and the inspiration for the song "Funiculi, Funicula" — after a scantily clad career at the Folies Bergère and an elopement with a handsome Gypsy violinist from Maxim's. And, of course, Comtesse Elisabeth Greffulhe, one of the models for the Princesse de Guermantes, was born at Chimay. Well into her old age, Violet would come back from Chimay full of stories, some of them romantic, some outrageously funny. One of these always went down well over coffee ("There are during-dinner stories and after-dinner stories," Violet believed). An atmosphere of thrift pervaded Chimay, and one day the Princesse said to Violet, "Haven't you noticed the great improvement in the bathroom?" "Uh

* *Don't Look Round.*

— no," she replied. "Well, you know, Violet," the Princesse went on, "how impressed I've always been to see that you provide guests with a choice of toilet papers, so I've decided to follow your example. Now you can choose between the *Figaro* and the *Libre Belgique!*"

With a premonition of dark days to come, the Princesse de Chimay had bought a small chateau in the Dordogne, and it was there that Violet was to shelter in the June 1940 exodus from Paris. In her prewar round of chateaux and capitals, Violet recalls a Paul Morand heroine: insatiably inquisitive, frequently amused, rarely happy. She couldn't abide solitude, and there is little doubt that her literary career suffered because of it. She would have had to share that solitude, however, with her regrets over the collapse of her affair with Vita, over their failure to achieve something lasting together. In photographs taken of Violet in the twenties, as in the Jacques Émile Blanche portrait, there is the same "wistfulness of exiles" in her face that Walter Pater noted in Botticelli's faces. The social round, however amusing, fascinating, or flattering, was only a makeshift for what she had had to give up. But suppose she had managed to live with Vita in sublime solitude: she would still have had the air of an exile from a world in which she was made to shine. It is not necessary to put much faith in astrology to observe that Violet, like everyone born under the sign of Gemini, had two sides to her personality: that she lived in an ambiguity from which arose all those contradictory and chaotic aspects of her behavior which the friends who loved her often found so trying.

# 11. *The War*

IN SEPTEMBER 1939 Violet joined the ambulance brigade, a somewhat quixotic gesture in view of the fact that she didn't know how to drive, and, if she had, would never have found her squeamish sensibilities up to administering the slightest injection. Still, it was chic to join this particular division of the Red Cross, and a number of women she knew belonged — some of them with rather equivocal reputations.

The debacle of May 1940 found Violet at St. Loup, directly on the path the invading tanks would take unhindered on their drive from the east. Violet shut up the house, hid her silver with friends, and drove off to the hideaway Princesse de Chimay had established in the Dordogne. Meanwhile, the Keppels left Italy for Dax, near Bayonne. Parents and daughter eventually reached Bayonne together, where Violet decided that their best avenue to escape lay through Spain. The frontier, however, was besieged by thousands of refugees. Fortunately, Violet knew the Spanish ambassador, who was by then, like the French government, installed at Bordeaux. This contact enabled her to obtain a visa after a great deal of difficulty that she amusingly recounted in *Don't Look Round*.

She made her way to Saint-Jean-de-Luz, where she found Colonel and Mrs. Keppel in excellent spirits, a Royal Navy troopship standing in the harbor to embark English refugees, and the visas for Spain suddenly rendered useless. For three days English governesses and retired couples filed aboard ship, joined by hundreds of Polish soldiers. Violet had time to reflect on her last visit to the little resort town, twenty-one years before, with Denys. Naturally, Mrs. Keppel was im-

mediately recognized as the ship's most illustrious passenger and given
the only available private cabin: the captain's. She would go below to
the engine room every morning carrying a jug to be filled with hot
water for the colonel's morning shave. Dodging enemy planes and
submarines, the ship eventually deposited its passengers safely in England.

The imperturbable Keppels first went to Sonia in Hampshire, then
to the Ritz, where friends welcomed them as calmly as though they
had simply come as usual for the London Season. This understatement
on the part of her compatriots saved Violet from a breakdown: "People
were very kind, they forebore from questioning me; it was as though
I were in mourning for an unmentionable relation." Not surprisingly,
the first person Violet telephoned was Vita. Vita was comfortably
settled at Sissinghurst, busy with her garden and her latest book, and
concerned above all with letting Harold get on unhindered with the
delicate business of reconciling British interests with those of the Free
French. Did Violet entertain the idea of renewing her love affair?
If she did, she was turned down categorically. A certain panic is
discernible in Vita's letters at the prospect of coping with Violet. The
preoccupations of Vita's first letters to her refugee friend were taken
up later at greater and more affectionate length: "You are an unexploded bomb to me. I don't want you to explode. I don't want you
to disrupt my life." But in closing, Vita returned to her earlier
brusqueness: "This letter will anger you. I don't care if it does since
I know that no anger will ever destroy the love that exists between us."

In the letters that follow, it is true that affection subdues caution,
but eventually Vita wrote: "I don't want to get involved with you
again. I really dislike the complications and intrigues your life entails.
They bore me." Despite her prudent resolutions, Vita was certainly
tempted to return to the days of her youth with Violet, and Violet,
in letters now lost, must have exerted all her charms, since Vita's
replies are couched in increasingly endearing terms. To be near her
friend, Violet suggested that they write a book together based on the
story of their love. But Vita wrote that she had already thought of
such a book, and should it be written, she would undertake it on her
own. A decade earlier Vita had published one of her best novels, *All*

*Passion Spent,* about a passionate woman who attains the serenity of age. Vita hadn't quite achieved this serenity herself, but contrary to what Violet thought, she was a good deal less under the sway of passion than she used to be. In the first year after her return to England, Violet was a siren who might have lured Vita-Ulysses to her destruction. Vita wanted at all costs to avoid being alone with her: "I only wish that I could trust myself (and you) to come and stay with you."

Harold's role was that of the sailors who lashed Ulysses to the mast to prevent his throwing himself overboard in answer to the siren's call. He was on his best behavior, not only wiser and more patient than Vita, but also a much better strategist. His tack was to keep repeating, "Poor, poor Violet!" Anyone turned into an object of pity is already far less to be feared. And he made a point of seeing Violet often. Their love of France forged a new link between them. He would put himself at her disposal in small ways: he had his secretary, for instance, type the manuscript of Violet's last novel, *Pirates at Play.* In short, he succeeded in defusing the situation by becoming her friend. Which is not to say that Violet's imagination, which so frequently deteriorated into pure chaos, did not sometimes grate on this eminently reasonable man. "A *mythomane,*" he would sigh from time to time, using the French expression in preference to "pathological liar." He told me once: "Sometimes Violet reminds me of my mother-in-law. She was a very amusing woman but totally devoid of humor. Her comic sense was based on farce, on mimicry and caricature." In fact, Violet possessed a good deal of humor and delighted in laughing at herself, but this was a quality she did not extend to her fantasies. Cut off from the international life they both thrived on, Violet and Harold meeting in imperiled London talked about Jean Cocteau, Marthe Bibesco, Marcel Proust — or rather Proust's characters and their real-life originals. Another common link they found was their enthusiasm for *grande cuisine.*

Violet, terrified of bombing raids, left London in September 1940, returning only to see her parents, who were then installed at the Ritz for good. Beneath the lobby's potted palms, or deep in the cellar bomb shelter, Mrs. Keppel would welcome and comfort Violet, and,

as usual, keep her abreast of the latest gossip. She had decided to
ignore the existence of the bombs, and settled down to await total
victory. To complain, she felt, was in the worst possible taste. It
was, of course, comforting to know that Violet was in Somerset in
the capable hands of an old friend, Dorothy Heneage. Mrs. Heneage,
fifteen years Violet's senior, was also a friend of the Nicolsons. Before
the First World War, she had been considered a little "fast." One
of her eccentricities consisted in leaping — like Nijinsky — from her
garden into her drawing room. With the years, she was seized by a
pathological fear of infection and took incredible precautions against
any sort of physical contaminations, though in other ways she relaxed,
taking on, as Violet noted, the air and physique of a "motherly
hedgehog":

> To this day, I suspect she did it on purpose, weighing herself each week
> with a wink and a chuckle, impishly assessing the potentialities of this
> visa to a quiet life, sated with sighs and scenes, adulation and flattery.
> At the age of, say, fifty, she must have deliberately given *carte blanche*
> to encroaching fat, to poaching fat. "Ouf," no doubt, was the exclama-
> tion suscitated by the comfortable reflection in her looking-glass.
>
> Besides, there was Coker Court which took the place of everything. It
> became her life work, her *raison d'être,* religion. In its way, it was
> perfect. It was beautifully situated, on an eminence overlooking two
> lovely counties, Somerset and Dorset. The house itself was partly
> Tudor, partly Georgian, partly taciturn, partly gregarious. There was
> a great hall with a Jacobean screen of a gloomy richness, dark angular
> furniture, Persian rugs, the colour of bruised peaches. A great bowl
> of agate, like a round of beef, dominated the room. Set on a kind of
> pedestal, lit from the inside, it resembled some profane Gargantuan
> grail.
>
> A turn to the right, and a few steps, brought you into a different
> world, a world of Georgian green walls, elegant fireplaces, parquet
> floors, Coromandel screens. The six or seven members of a chubby,
> delightful Georgian family, who, one felt, still wished for company,
> were hung about the room; over one was suspended the viol which
> figured in the portrait . . .
>
> I have always loved the English countryside, its drowsy, hypnotic
> charm. It was a taste I had never been able to indulge in to the full.

It was like a cool hand on my brow. I loved the gracious, deliberate rooms through which no one hurried; the only things which were ever changed were the flowers. I loved the smell of pot-pourri, and Floris bath essence that clung to the passages; most of all, I loved the carillon high up in the clock tower; its chilly chimes were like a courtly aerial minuet.*

Later Violet rented an Elizabethan manor in a nearby village. She moved in, brightening it with furniture borrowed from Mrs. Heneage. There she renewed her St. Loup existence; she found and trained a cook and began entertaining on the weekends:

French friends began to arrive, Palewski, General Catroux, Hervé Alphand [later ambassador in Washington]. Once again, my equanimity was in tatters. They poured down to Somerset where we evoked the happy past. *"Je ne me suis pas consolé, bien que mon coeur s'en soit allé."*

General Catroux's arrival never failed to cause a small stir on the local platform. Romantically handsome, he would be dressed as a full General (*Général de Corps d'Armée*) with a kind of *brassière* of ribbons. I used to enjoy lunching with him at Claridges, with two magnificent Spahi sentinels guarding the door. He won all hearts with his elegance, tact, unfailing courtesy, in the most trying circumstances. I had known him when he was Resident in Morocco, which is the French equivalent to being Viceroy of India. Since then, he had been Governor of Indochina; he had not hesitated to sacrifice his career to his patriotism, and was one of the first to place himself [though infinitely superior in age and rank] at the disposal of General de Gaulle . . .

In connivance with Dorothy, I had persuaded my parents to spend several months at Coker Court, which made me very happy. Papa was quite content to potter in the garden, but Mama had the spirit of a pioneer. In a few days the village was at her feet. She had provided spring-mattresses for the crippled, wireless sets for the lonely, ear-trumpets for the deaf, gossip for all and sundry.†

The Princesse de Polignac had also taken refuge in London, and came to stay with Violet two or three times. One of her final pleasures in

* *Don't Look Round.*
† *Don't Look Round.*

life (she died in London during the war) was to publish a fragment of her autobiography in *Horizon*. There were usually a number of English guests: Leslie Hore-Belisha, Lord Berners, Raymond Mortimer — who provided yet another reminder of Paris:

> There is a lot of Cocteau in Raymond, a Cocteau more stabilised, less iridescent, perhaps, a Cocteau with a good solid eighteenth-century background, more humane, less narcissistic. Raymond is a frightening person to those who do not know him, and even more frightening to those who do. Twitching with impatience, he listens to your pedestrian story, on the look-out, nevertheless, for anything which could possibly enliven its tempo, anything worth retaining, or reporting. I know no greater reward than Raymond's laugh, when, for once in a way, you have said something not too stupid.
>
> In spite of his intransigence, he is the kindest, most understanding of men, one to whom I would not hesitate to confess any crime — provided it were not a dull one.*

When people heard that the witty Lord Berners had spent several weekends at Violet's, a practical joker inserted an announcement linking their names in the "Forthcoming Marriages" column of *The Times*. Violet laughed delightedly when she heard about it. Later she told Gerald, "All sorts of people have rung up to congratulate me. What about you?" He reflected a moment, and replied coolly: "Not one."

Vita, however, never came down to Somerset, and Violet, hindered first by the Blitz, then by her move into the West Coker Manor House, was unable to come to Sissinghurst until August 1941. Sissinghurst immediately summoned up visions of St. Loup. Through Vita, Violet met Mrs. Clive, the owner of Brympton d'Evercy, a Tudor house set in a splendid garden, about whom she told the amusing anecdote of a distinguished Frenchwoman that she took to Brympton. The lady, on the usual assumption that all people who live in the country are oafs, exclaimed, recognizing the product of a French eighteenth-century *ébéniste*, "In France we call that a *console Régence*." "So do we, madame!" rapped the chatelaine of Brympton.

Violet fascinated the neighbors, and nearly won the heart of the local vicar. Every Sunday she would sit in the front pew, where her

* *Don't Look Round.*

short skirts and shapely legs would bring blushes to the clergyman's cheeks. Some parishioners still claim that she cast a spell over him. In 1942 Violet met someone who for the rest of her life, despite the occasional falling-out, was to remain her closest friend: Betty Richards. Betty had just lost her pilot husband, Nigel, who people said was the handsomest man in England (he was the original of a character in Cyril Connolly's novel, *The Rock Pool*). Betty had spent a good deal of time in Paris, where she'd even worked as a mannequin for Coco Chanel. Unfortunately her looks were gone, but there remained a brilliant wit and a tendency to dramatize: "Hedda Gabler by Rowlandson," Violet once summed her up. Betty, like Vita, spoke perfect French — and found her household routine disrupted by Violet's chaotic habits. She liked to repeat a story Violet eventually told on herself in her memoirs. Two porters at the Ritz were discussing the hotel's guests: "Well, we've 'ad V1, we've 'ad V2, we've 'eard of VD, but in my opinion, V.T. is the worst of the lot!"

And this is what Violet had to say about Betty:

Betty Richards owned a charming little house just over the Dorset border. It had all the attributes of the nursery rhyme, chubbiness, cosiness, a certain primness: *parva sed apta*. Most suitably, Betty collected china, rustic Bow, ornate Chelsea; the small stylised groups further emphasised the primness of the house; its desire to act as an object lesson to unruly guests.

Betty herself would follow you about with an ash tray, a duster, a feather broom. It was nerve-racking. The only incongruous object in the house was Betty herself. Just under six foot tall, blonde, decorative, muscular, the *belle* in the china shop.

Nobody was funnier than she, her farce was her fortune. The possessor of a magnificent, not unpedantic, vocabulary, the tiny house resounded with the rich roll of her rhetoric, jokes as *cocasse* as they were penetrating, tumbling over each other in baroque profusion.

"I'm having Violet to lunch to-morrow, just we three," a mutual friend once telephoned; "there are eggs, and a duck, that should be sufficient?"

"Surely you realise that Violet is a *one* duck woman?" was Betty's only comment.*

* *Don't Look Round.*

A few years later, Betty married another friend of Violet's, Colonel Bill Batten. Earlier, she had rejected Eddy Sackville-West, Vita's cousin, an exceptional man but one whose health was fragile. Betty hadn't wanted to take up the career of companion to an invalid, even at Knole. At Yeovil, however, Betty was both a model lady of the manor and a confirmed eccentric. She was always a faithful admirer of Violet's without taking her too seriously, and she built up a fund of funny stories about her. Both women liked to laugh, and any misunderstanding usually ended in gales of laughter. Betty, a decade younger than Violet, died six months before her.

The countryside wasn't able to detain Violet indefinitely. Despite her horror of bombs, she began going up to London more often and for longer stretches. At the Ritz, Mrs. Keppel's apartment had a room for the colonel and another for her brother, Archibald Edmonstone. Her parties were still the most amusing in London, distinguished by the presence of ambassadors and cabinet members, particularly a Keppel cousin, Archie Sinclair, Secretary of State for Air. Sometimes Winston Churchill would attend. When Violet was there, Cyril Connolly, Harold Nicolson, and Robin McDouall came. Violet loved talking about food to Robin, the author of several books on gastronomy, and she loved his invitations to dine. Mrs. Keppel asked him: "Tell me, Mr. McDouall, are you really so rich that you can take Violet to such expensive restaurants?" To these gatherings, Princesse Callimachi brought that element of the Orient Express which Violet missed so much. Violet published a book of reminiscences of France, a somewhat helter-skelter affair but full of excellent sketches. She wrote short stories for *Horizon,* and frequently broadcast for Radio Free France. At Lady Cunard's, she could recapture a little of the Paris she missed.

Lady Cunard lived in the Dorchester and there, despite the bombing, she entertained all the most fascinating people of the moment. Writers, politicians, and diplomats alike would meet in her rooms, always accompanied by the most beautiful women. The war was never mentioned and somehow she managed to recapture the gaiety of peacetime, but she was now handicapped by old age and insomnia as well as rationing. Her sleepless nights were passed with books and endless

Proustian dialogues on the telephone that only finished when the other
party finally fell asleep.

> Tony Gandarillas was her favourite confidant (also mine). Small,
> dapper, international, he had the prestige and power of a Figaro —
> Figaro ci! Figaro là! He was in the "wings" of every intrigue, in the
> prompter's box of every social dilemma. Neither the mighty or the
> flighty could dispense with his advice. Mischievous, inventive, he would
> speed from one to the other, bringing a delectable eighteenth-century
> element into the dullest lives, suggesting screens where there were
> doors, masks where there were spectacles. No woman in her senses
> would ever be without him. Neither was I.*

It is surprising that Violet did not give more space in her memoirs
to Tony — Don Antonio Gandarillas — one of her oldest friends:
they certainly spent enough time on the telephone. This faintly simian
little Chilean, no stranger to the delights of opium, was able to trans-
form the most mundane piece of gossip into something exciting; he
could describe a party as an absolute paradise — or a veritable hell —
depending on his whim. He lived in one of the prettiest houses in
Cheyne Walk, hung with family portraits by Boldini and Sargent
and ornamented by some marvelous Chinese screens left to him by the
infatuated Sargent. He was also a great friend of the Sitwells, and in
Cheyne Walk Violet met some of the newest and brightest of the
upcoming young writers: Peter Quennell, James Pope-Hennessy.
Tony was an intimate of Cecil Beaton's and, dressed as a German
baroness, he posed for photographs in Beaton's volume of imaginary
memoirs, My Royal Past. His house was usually full of Frenchmen,
for he had kept an apartment in Paris before the war, to which he
returned immediately after the war's end. In Paris, his set included
Christian Bérard and Étienne de Beaumont; he was a friend of Picasso's
because his aunt, Madame Errazuriz, had been the first woman collector
to buy his paintings.

Then, at last, on the morning of Violet's birthday, June 6, 1944,
came the exciting news:

* Don't Look Round.

. . . my old maid burst into my bedroom: "Madam! It's started! They've landed!" At last! Great joy is as annihilating as great pain. Knocked out, inarticulate, beyond tears, beyond speech, I lay flooded, drunk with gratitude that pulsed through my brain like the reverberating chords of a mighty organ . . . An assortment of disconnected objects suddenly appeared before my eyes, in surrealist juxtaposition, the blue letter boxes of Paris, the undulating Art Nouveau lettering of the Métro stations, the thick blue cups of the P.L.M., the black alpaca sleeves of the *employées des Postes,* the blue blouses of the porters, the little girls with gold rings in their prematurely pierced ears, the concierge's crocheted shawl, her fat sated cat; *"Cordon, s.v.p."* I heard the clang of the *porte-cochère,* the imprecations and hootings of the taxi chauffeurs, the shuffling of small black larvae carrying other people's dresses in the *maisons de couture.* It was too good to be true. I was back in France.

A year was to elapse before I returned there in the flesh; a year of preparation, readjustment.*

But in October 1944, she at last received the necessary visa with a note from Gaston Palewski, then chief of staff for General de Gaulle: "My dear friend, naturally your presence is part of Paris. Respectfully yours . . ."

Mrs. Keppel had a surprise a few months later, initially a shock but welcome nevertheless. It was delivered to her by a young friend on leave from the army in Italy, Hamish Erskine:

"Mrs Keppel, Mrs. Keppel," he exulted, "I can't wait to tell you that the Villa is safe, everything is intact, even the Chinese pagodas!"

This was altogether too much. My mother disliked being taken by surprise; besides, by then, my parents, by mutual consent, had "buried" the Villa. It was exactly as though they had decently mourned a relation for years, only to be told now that the relation was alive and kicking.

"Those, my dear Hamish," my mother returned with hauteur, "those were the *common pagodas!"* . . .

Of course, as soon as this wonderful piece of news had been properly assimilated, they were overcome with joy. The curtain we had thought

* *Don't Look Round.*

drawn for ever, parted: Florence, a terrace overlooking the town, orange and lemon trees in tubs, the air vibrates with a jangle-tangle of bells . . .*

These four years of what Violet called "exile" had served to bring her closer to England and old friends. She had the comfort of finding out that at least Vita still loved her, even if it was a love that drew the line at sharing her life. For the "right" people, her name no longer held overtones of scandal. She had become a "character," someone who would be forgiven anything as long as it was consistent with her reputation as an eccentric. Something Queen Mary said summed up the opinion of society. Violet had gone with Mrs. Keppel to call on the Queen Mother at Badminton. During tea, the regal old lady observed Violet but rarely spoke to her. Then, as her guests curtsied their farewells, she boomed approvingly: "Very good, Violet. You hold yourself as straight as ever!"

* *Don't Look Round.*

# 12. *Time Regained*

PART FOUR of Violet's memoirs is called "Paris Reconquered," though there was little enough reconquering for her to do. She effortlessly slipped back into place among her French friends in a city that had come through the war largely unscathed. Lady Diana Cooper, the new British ambassador's wife, began inviting everyone to the embassy. In that rarefied world where society took precedence over politics, people deeply compromised by the Occupation rubbed elbows with the most fashionable adherents to the new regime, resentments and fears discarded. At the Duff Coopers' it was enough to be charming to be forgiven, but since some kind of scapegoat was needed, the choice fell on the guileless André Maurois, who had had the misfortune to rally to Marshal Pétain in New York. Generally speaking, Louise de Vilmorin intimated to Violet, collaboration had been more chic than the Resistance. Louise reigned over the embassy parties with Jean Cocteau, whom Violet approached to ask: "But how *did* our friends spend the war?" The poet smiled at her: "Like caged birds caught in a fire."

The darling of the embassy crowd was a huge bearded personage who contrived to look like Henry VIII and a retired diva at the same time: Christian Bérard. "Bébé" Bérard was an outstanding theater designer, and if social frivolities — and drugs — had not dragged him from his easel so often, he would have become a great painter. As it was, his imagination was a match for Violet's fantasies, and his craving for the extraordinary prevented him from ever admitting that Violet was not the daughter of the most fashionable of kings, a king that, fresh from the barber's chair, he in fact happened to resemble. It was Bébé Bérard who dressed Violet as Queen Victoria for one of

Étienne de Beaumont's balls, and since Violet had just broken her leg, she was a Victoria confined to a Bath chair — propelled by her gillie, John Brown, the sturdy Danish husband of the Princesse Radziwill. Some of the English guests were shocked; the French found the resemblance spectacular. Decidedly, not much had changed in Violet's four-year exile. The Comte de Beaumont was giving his fancy-dress balls again, and Marie-Louise Bousquet began to hold open house every Thursday in her little flat on the Place du Palais Bourbon. Violet would go there to meet Marie-Louise's collection of young painters and writers, most of whom turned out to be Americans and scarcely to Violet's taste. Entering fully into her role as Victoria, she watched grandly once as a miniature Truman Capote entered the room, cradling in the folds of a red shawl a proportionately miniature dog. "We are not amused," she breathed. Violet *was* amused, somewhat reluctantly, by Marie-Louise's zest for life: you never knew what to expect from this *Parigotte* — this Paris cockney.

Another Englishwoman made her entrance into Paris society about this time: Nancy Mitford, a dozen years Violet's junior, who took a ravishing flat on the ground floor of a house in the Rue Monsieur; its front windows gave onto a verandah and cobbled courtyard, the rear onto a tree-filled garden. Violet had known Nancy in London when she was working at the Heywood Hill bookshop in Curzon Street, and she decided to launch her. She began by introducing her to people she already knew. Daisy Fellowes, back in town herself, also began introducing the charming novelist into Paris society. And Lady Diana Cooper continued her own series of introductions, completely unaware that she was not alone in doing so. The feeling of these years in Paris at the end of the forties is captured to perfection in Miss Mitford's Paris novel, *The Blessing.* It was a time of lavish parties. Arturo Lopez, a Chilean with a Louis XIV complex, entertained in a Trianon at Neuilly, Philippe de Rothschild gave a huge ball at the Château de Grosbois, and a fashionable Portuguese decorator held a party on the Seine. Marie-Laure de Noailles reopened her immense house on the Place des États-Unis to give concerts and balls that were more or less · fancy-dress. One of them re-created a village fête, and Violet was a sensation as the lady of the manor with her immense hat and parasol.

Violet Trefusis
at the age of five, 1899.

Violet and Mrs. Keppel,
one of Violet's favorite
photographs.

Croquis
pour
Papa

A drawing of Violet's father made by her for Philippe Jullian when he was illustrating *Don't Look Round*, 1950.

A group picture taken c. 1899, probably on a visit to the Prince of Wales's Own Civil Service Rifles, of which Lord Albemarle (in light uniform) was C.O. Mrs. Keppel is seated second from left with her hand on Violet's shoulder. The Prince of Wales, later King Edward VII, stands behind Mrs. Keppel.

King Edward VII and Mrs. Keppel watch an unidentified golfer
and her caddy on the links at Cannes.

At the age of nine, Violet
dressed as a bacchante.
This photograph was taken
at Gopsall, the country house
of Lord and Lady Howe,
where the Keppel family
was spending Christmas holidays.

Violet posed for this portrait
by Ambrose McEvoy when
she was twenty-three.

Vita Sackville-West in 1924.

⋯t drew this sketch of herself holding
⋯ Vita, dressed in a man's suit. She
⋯d that Vita would use it on the
⋯t of her novel *Challenge*.

This fanciful sketch from Violet's pen
was sent to Vita. It depicts Sir Basil
Zaharoff and Violet at Deauville and is
entitled "If V. accepts Sir Basil's offer."

Violet and her husband, Denys Trefusis.

A portrait of Violet
by Jacques Émile Blanche,
painted in 1926, which
she gave to Philippe Jullian.

A portrait of Violet
by Nora Auric, 1932.

Violet and her sister, Sonia, on the steps of the
Villa de l'Ombrellino, c. 1932.

Colonel Keppel took this group photograph of the Greek royal family at l'Ombrellino. Mrs. Keppel is seated, second from left, with Violet and Sonia in front.

On the terrace at l'Ombrellino: Queen Sophia of Greece with Lady Londonderry.

The Queen of Spain and party are shown around l'Ombrellino by Colonel George Keppel.

Violet sketched the writer Rebecca West in the late 1920s.

Nearly thirty years, 1938 and 1965, separate these two photographs of Violet with Sir Osbert Sitwell. The later photograph was taken during a luncheon on the terrace of l'Ombrellino shortly before Sir Osbert's death.

A sketch of John Phillips
by Violet Trefusis, 1965.
All her life Violet delighted
in making drawings
of her friends.

La Tour in Saint Loup de Naud,
Violet's country home in France.

The next year, she came as Lady Hester Stanhope in her self-imposed Middle Eastern exile. Guests at this ball came dressed as famous writers, artists, or composers — Harold Acton as William Beckford, Peter Glenville as Byron, Lady Diana Cooper as Lady Blessington, Pamela Churchill as Titania. Violet wanted to bring along a friend whom Marie-Laure found insufferable. Tall and rather horse-faced, he didn't have much trouble in passing himself off as a camel, an appropriate mount for the eccentric Lady Hester. But Marie-Laure outwitted Violet: all steeds to be tethered at the door, she decreed.

As the years went by, Violet was intimidated by Marie-Laure. Intelligent and fun-loving to a degree that often far overstepped the bounds of propriety, she could inspire alarm. But she had a soft spot for Violet, who like herself had stood up to scandal. Less forbidding than Princesse de Polignac, she had taken the Princesse's place in Violet's life, and Violet loved lunching in the magnificent mansion of the Place des États-Unis. These occasions were faintly bohemian and populated with lots of good-looking young people when Marie-Laure was in charge, very Faubourg-Saint-Germain when Vicomte de Noailles arranged things. In both cases, the guests were virtually all extraordinarily intelligent.

Violet came back to St. Loup to find her house in need of a good cleaning but otherwise intact. It was her wardrobe that had suffered most, since the house had served as a rest home for SS troops whose parties had featured fashion parades starring Violet's Schiaparellis, Patous, and Chanels, modeled by hulking blond Germans in a preview of Visconti's *The Damned.* But once Violet had reclaimed her silver, wiped the walls clean of their dubious graffiti, and restored order in the kitchen, St. Loup weekends began where they left off — and if after the wartime hiatus the new dignity which sat on some of the guests lent a more formal air to Violet's gatherings, they were no less fascinating. Among the signatures that ornament the St. Loup guest book for those immediate postwar years are those of the Duke and Duchess of Windsor, Prince Paul of Yugoslavia, General Georges Catroux, General Béthouart, Christian Dior, Pierre Balmain.

Violet was not eager to have her guests add sketches or witty remarks; she felt about this much as did the old Duc de Gramont, who warned one of his guests, "No philosophising, Monsieur Proust!" One Sunday she made the mistake of inviting a political hostess who looked more like a Balkan madame in her "country" clothes of black satin and chunky gold jewelry. That the lady was an intimate of Pope John XXIII's (in those days the Papal Nuncio in Paris) suggests both the Pontiff's innocence and lack of discernment. Seizing the pen as though inspired, she put all her bulk into scrawling "Plunged in a sea of Violets" in French across a page of the visitors' book, running the words together with scabrous intent: *"PlongéedansunemerdeViolettes."* Her hostess paled, and there were sputters of ill-concealed laughter. Hardly had the political lady turned her back when Violet ripped the page out — with a pang of regret since several ambassadors had signed the other side. One afternoon Edmonde Charles-Roux, the editor of French *Vogue,* came to a large lunch party at St. Loup. She glanced at the guests and smiled at Violet: "If I'd known it was all to be so elegant, I'd have brought a photographer with me!" Violet Trefusis' connections netted her a supply of aristocratic guests, including Denys' relations, Prince and Princess George of Denmark. Fenella Trefusis, Denys' sister, had married the brother of the present Queen Mother, then still Queen, and was therefore fair game for a chambermaid of Violet's who was a famous Mrs. Malaprop. Instead of addressing Violet's sister-in-law as "Mrs. Bowes-Lyon," she insisted on calling her "Madame Boeuf-Lion."

Henri Sauguet was a perennial favorite, with a spontaneity which broke through the crustiest reserve. Everyone was talking about his ballet *Les Forains* in those days. If Bébé Bérard was there, the pair treated the guests to a veritable commedia dell'arte, and by the time coffee came round, a charade was under way involving the guests' borrowed hats and coats. There were always a number of English on hand, including Nancy Mitford and a breathtaking creature married to a Frenchman, Doodie Costa de Beauregard, as amusing as she was lovely. Sometimes Betty Batten would come, and Violet began to tremble for fear that her forthright tongue would come up with something to shock her French friends. One afternoon Mrs. Batten sat next to a writer better known for his looks than his novels. Not once during lunch did he address a word to her. When dessert was brought in, she turned to him and said: "Of course, I'm neither young nor pretty, but I *am* terribly rich. Perhaps you've made a mistake ignoring me." The table exploded into loud laughter, since the novelist's love affairs were not always conducted in a completely disinterested fashion. If there were usually several English guests, there was rarely an American, though a fairly frequent appearance was put in by the corpulent Eddy Waterman, a rich gentleman who may always have had "his nose in his glass and his foot in his mouth," as Jacques de Lacretelle put it, but who also, Jacques added, "had his heart in the right place."

At Violet's first Paris party after the war, her guests — who ranged from the Duke of Alba to Léonor Fini — packed themselves into her pied-à-terre behind the church of Sainte Clotilde, not far from the Chamber of Deputies. The heat was unbearable. "Nothing like a breath of fresh air!" cried the ancient Mademoiselle Le Chevrel as she strode briskly into the drawing room. On the same occasion, somebody who saw her kiss the English ambassador commented maliciously that two years earlier, in occupied Paris, she would have hesitated at displaying so much affection. "Oh well, nothing's to be done about it, I've always swayed whichever way the wind is blowing and everybody knows it," she answered.

No new recruit to St. Loup was lovelier than Isabelle de Broglie (Marquise de la Moussaye), Princesse de Polignac's favorite niece. She was a *précieuse* in the best sense of the word, and the author of a widely acclaimed novel, *Maldonne*. Denise Bourdet came often, a widow now (Edouard had died in 1945), and if she overawed Violet a little, Violet was happy to defer to her in literary matters. Denise was still beautiful, and despite her dogmatic manner, she had a sense of humor. Mademoiselle Le Chevrel was one of the people whom Violet welcomed most enthusiastically; it was she who had introduced the Yousoupoffs as the Rasputins. Her salon was celebrated, and until her dying breath she went everywhere. Sometimes the old spinster would confide in Violet: at seventy, she told her that she had begun an affair with a lady novelist somewhat her senior. "What can I do? *Le bon Dieu* has allowed me one last fling," she simpered, much to Violet's delight, for that sort of thing was very much behind her now. There was nothing in her life any longer in conversation or dress to suggest the fact that she had once loved other women, or, more precisely, one other woman. On the other hand, she made no attempt to hide her stream of male lovers. One was a handsome Italian called Guido Sommi Picenardi, Marchese de Calvatone, with whom she embarked on an affair in 1946. He would have been quite content to marry Violet, but she could never get used to the castle in which she would have had to spend six months of every year.

I was staying with an Italian friend, on approval. He thought I might conceivably suit him as a wife. Guido owned a magnificent castle near Cremona. We had agreed to give it a trial. It was understood that we should live *en tête à tête* for a fortnight: no breath of the outside world was to be allowed to impinge on our intimacy.

We had much in common: a far-fetched, sometimes ferocious, sense of humour; a paradoxical, rococo imagination; an immediate response to beauty in any form. In fun, we would call one another Klingsor and Kundry. He had a fanatical love for his home, I for mine. True, he was no modern character. "You remind me of that sanguinary, superb, pious, depraved lyrical *condottiere*, Sigismondo Malatesta," I would tease him.*

Guido sadly realized that Violet missed Paris, her friends, and the social round on which she doted. Violet claimed that the castle was "jealous," that it tried to rid itself of her, even preventing her from sleeping. In short, the experiment was discontinued, and it is perhaps a great pity that Violet never married her Guido — who not only possessed good looks and intelligence, but loved her for herself.

Violet's acute aesthetic sense included a feeling for physical dignity; she used to say that "when you can no longer display yourself in a night dress, it's time to give up love." And she would add, "It's not easy!" But like Elizabeth I, with whom she began to confuse herself from time to time, Violet could not do without suitors:

In 1948, I met a man who came to count for a great deal in my life, Rolphe de Faucigny-Lucinge.

The main obstacle was my taste for smart society and smart people. Rolphe's friends might be dentists or hairdressers. He undoubtedly

* *Don't Look Round.*

thought that they would be unwelcome at my dinner table, and in this he was only half wrong. Yet we continued to play with the idea, and spent long months together in Florence or at Saint Loup. Had I had a villa on the Côte d'Azur instead of in Florence, the marriage would certainly have come about.*

Coming as a kind of consolation prize, in 1950 Violet received the medal of the Légion d'Honneur. A diplomat friend, Jacques Dumaine, then Chief of Protocol, brought the decoration to her at St. Loup: "I had wanted my gesture to remain discreet, but how could it, more than fulfilling as it did the childlike aspirations of a very complex woman? Violet, blushing in astonishment, scarlet with joy, immediately displayed the Légion d'Honneur as though it were a geranium. At least I had the amused feeling of having given pleasure." Also present at this impromptu ceremony were the Italian ambassador and his Russian wife, an elegant Swedish diplomat and his wife, and Lolette de Lasteyrie, more stooped and petulant than ever. Nancy Mitford, whom I myself brought along in my car, turned out to be the life and soul of the party.

As a token of her gratitude, Violet sent General de Gaulle an *Almanach Royale* of 1780 which had once belonged to an ancestor of his; by accident, she had run across it in her library. In his well-bred way, the general thanked Violet in a long, friendly letter in which he recalled that this de Gaulle, his great-great-grandfather, had been a member of the chancellery of the pre-Revolutionary Parliament of Paris, then procurator of that Parliament. Later, the Princesse Radziwill gave a large party to celebrate the event, and in front of an audience bristling with Academicians, ambassadors, and duchesses, General Catroux officially bestowed the medal on Violet.

Her English friends didn't take the honor very seriously. One evening at a dinner party one of them ventured that "Violet got the Légion d'Honneur for all the work she's done for French letters." "I never knew she ever joined a Resistance movement," growled her sister, Sonia. Just then, she and Violet were not on the best of terms.

Christian Dior, a great friend, ruled the fashion world in revival of

* *Triple Violette.*

luxury after wartime austerity. Dior's look suited Violet, whose figure remained small-waisted if at the same time stately. By degrees, yet remaining completely up to the minute, she gave the impression of returning to the styles of the happiest period of her life, her childhood. She got out her tiaras, put aigrettes into her short, curly, salt-and-pepper hair. She was turning into an Edwardian grande dame. She never realized how much life had changed, that her friends no longer kept quite so many servants as she did. When she went to stay with anyone, she always brought along a maid or two and her chauffeur — which hardly simplified matters for her hosts. She especially liked staying in embassy residences, where she quickly sowed chaos, blocking the telephone lines, engaging the attachés in endless talk: surely that was what they were there for. Despite her habits, her friends the Massiglis adored having her to stay in London. One morning, Violet found a shopping list Odette Massigli had left for her secretary. Violet added: "And *No Orchids for Miss Blandish.*" The embassy staff spent an entire morning trying to find out who Miss Blandish was, and what flowers to send since she didn't like orchids. Violet's trips to England, where rationing was still the order of the day, took on an expeditionary quality. She would conceal hams in her lingerie and hang them in the bathroom of her hotel suite; customs officers would discover Camemberts in her shoe boxes, foie gras in her hats.

In the spring of 1947, Violet's life was overshadowed by the death of her mother at l'Ombrellino, aged seventy-eight. She has told the story of it movingly in *Don't Look Round:*

When I reached the Villa, my father was waiting for me in the hall. His eyes were full of tears. "She is very ill," he said, "the specialist will be here at any moment." Something comparable to a landslide took place in me. Things just toppled over and collapsed without a sound. Where there had been plans and perspectives, monuments and temples and terraces, there was nothing now but an aching void, full of surprise.

I was not allowed to see her that day. The following morning, long before I was really awake, I was conscious of an odious presence in my room, in my brain. It had come to stay.

The specialist had diagnosed sclerosis of the liver. It had been coming on for a long time and now it seemed unlikely she would recover. She might live for weeks, for months. "Is she in pain?" I questioned with anguish.

"Not for the present. The pain will come later" . . .

The terrible routine of illness set in. As the Spring waxed, she waned. Day after day, she lay patiently waiting to be read to, or told small stories about the day's happenings. The contrast between the Spring and her hushed room was almost unbearable. Whenever we came into her room she contrived a smile, sometimes a joke. She missed England, her friends; the beauty of her surroundings did not atone for the smoky cosiness of her beloved London. "Look, darling, at the view from your window." I would try to comfort. "Surely you love Nature?"

"Yes, the nature of the Ritz," she managed to tease. The state of tension in which I lived, was conducive to many things, including boils. An enormous one appeared on my nose. "Look," Mama pointed to it, "Pierpont Morgan without the money!"

My poor father, who had a weak heart, was never off the stairs. Rejuvenated by his selfless devotion, he was more like a desolate fiancé than an aged husband.

Mrs. Keppel was buried under the cypresses of the Protestant cemetery in Florence.

Two months later, my father died also. He did not wish to survive her. Always the most courteous of men, it was as though he were loath to keep her waiting.

Puzzled and homeless, he was like a man in a foreign town without an interpreter. It would have been uncharitable to wish to prolong his life. He went willingly to a secret assignation . . .

What has happened to me since is but a post scriptum. It really doesn't count. Any little success I may have had is dedicated to her. Success is a cul-de-sac, it leads to no lasting satisfaction, it is the smart substitute for happiness.

In his memoirs, Jacques Dumaine summed up what Mrs. Keppel meant to his compatriots:

The aged Mrs Keppel, Violet Trefusis's mother, died lingeringly in Florence. The English watched their last Edwardian bastion crumble, a fortress of good spirits, with an optimistic bent for intrigue and cynicism. She had outlived all the contemporaries of her renown as the beloved of Edward VII.

Violet kept the use of l'Ombrellino, but her sister decided to sell the furnishings, and the splendors of Grosvenor Street found their way back to London: the tapestries, the Louis XV furniture, the lacquer screens, and the famous pair of pagodas from the Brighton Pavilion, a gift from Edward VII. Violet found herself alone in the vast, half-empty house. She set about improving a décor to suit those theatrical suites of room upon room, and every year she managed to furnish one or two completely.

The impact of Mrs. Keppel's death was aggravated by an accident in 1950 which further aged Violet. Attending the first night of the Ballet des Champs-Elysées with Rolphe de Faucigny-Lucinge, she was jostled, fell on the stairs, and broke her thighbone. The fracture was never properly set, and Violet often suffered from it. For the rest of her life she limped slightly and used a cane, but her carriage remained ramrod-straight. It was then that she decided to make herself over into one of those wonderful old ladies who have always reigned over Paris society, and she quite naturally fell into line behind her forerunners, the dowagers who entertained Horace Walpole on his visits to Paris and whom he described meticulously in his letters home. Like Walpole, Violet might have murmured as she passed the Hôtel de Carnavalet, "Ave Marie de Rabutin-Chantal." For the Marquise de Sévigné had become her model, and if there were no longer a court, there was the *Tout Paris,* whose doings Violet chronicled with the same verve la Sévigné had displayed in her own letters nearly 300 years earlier.

When a member of the British royal family came to Paris, Violet bustled about as though she were responsible for the whole thing. She arrived late to lunch the day of an Opéra gala: "I'm dead! I spent the whole morning trying on tiaras." However, she regained the suppleness of her girlhood when the time came to curtsy. On Queen Elizabeth's first visit to Paris, somebody reported seeing Violet in the grocery shop at the corner of her street showing local housewives how to curtsy. That one of her cousins was married to the Duke of Norfolk's sisters, that a relation was Princess of Denmark, and that a few old friends had become dukes all lent a certain substance to her flights of fantasy — which were undoubtedly much easier to launch in Paris than in London.

# 13. *Florence*

THE DEATHS of Violet's parents had left her at something of a loss now that she was into her fifties, but she was able to take a sensible view of the onrush of old age in a passage from *Triple Violette:*

> After the deaths of my parents, to my great astonishment, I went on living. They had been the staff of my youth; while they were alive, I was able to preserve the illusion that I was still young. I was fifty, well preserved, abundantly supplied with the goods of this world. But, insidiously, indifference began to harden the tissues of my heart, deprived now of the stimulant of Mama . . . At fifty, old age is in its infancy; it needs several more years to get into its stride. Standing on tiptoe, I can just see into the sixties: those elegant women, with plenty of fight still left in them, staving off the encroachments of fat or emaciation, secretly envious of their daughters and their youthful swains, hiding their passports as though they were pieces of incriminating evidence, and in their moral poverty, too frightened to let themselves go grey as they keep feverishly abreast of the latest fashionable novel, wait impatiently for the next opening night, the next chic concert.

Violet's English memoirs can be judged from the excerpts included in this book: *Don't Look Round* is a delightful work, unfailingly vivacious. As a prologue, she inserted C. P. Cavafy's "Ithaka," a poetic allegory of that imagined Greece which illuminated her adolescence: "Ithaka has given you your lovely journey."

Published in 1952, when Violet was fifty-eight, *Don't Look Round* enjoyed a brilliant success. Harold Nicolson reviewed it for the *Spectator.* He had one or two reservations: "After all," he observed, "this is the world of the Ritz" (a criticism echoed two decades later by some left-wing critics of Nigel Nicolson's *Portrait of a Marriage*). Soon after Harold's review appeared, Violet came to London. She wreaked a playful revenge on him by inviting him to lunch — at the not so fashionable Hotel Rembrandt in Kensington. "I presume, dear Harold," she wrote, "that the atmosphere of the Ritz doesn't agree with you."

But before she settled down to the serious task of getting her memoirs ready for publication, she had had to proceed with the task of refurbishing l'Ombrellino; it was this that helped rescue her from her despondency after the deaths of Colonel and Mrs. Keppel. She decided to spend the best part of every spring and autumn — April and May, September and October — in Florence. The villa was well worth the effort Violet spent on it. Its terraces on the hill of Bellosguardo dominated the Arno and the city beyond; Violet used to say that "it is one of those views that inspires the most remarkable people to the most banal imagery." Once the famous view led to a farcical misunderstanding involving a celebrated Hungarian actress, the widow of an Italian diplomat, who arrived at l'Ombrellino after nightfall. The next morning there was a cry from the garden followed by shouts, sighs, and moans. Violet's guests ran to the windows in full expectation that despite her venerability, Señora Cerutti had been chased and captured by one of the gardeners with the most voluptuous consequences. But no: she had simply discovered the panorama below. Another unsettling aspect of l'Ombrellino was its profusion of flowers. They were massed in vases strewn through the galleries, sitting rooms, and bedrooms — lilies in the spring, tuberoses at the end of the summer — where their heady scents reminded some of the older guests of a line from the nineteenth-century poet Albert Samina: *"Une odeur de péché rode dans la maison":* "An odour of sin steals through the house." But such languors never managed to overpower Violet's guests, and life at l'Ombrellino was distinguished by its *bon ton.*

In 1951, Harold and Vita came to spend a few days there. Alerted to their imminent arrival by a friend, Bernard Berenson kept telephoning from I Tatti to insure a meeting with this fascinating couple. He left messages and invitations with Violet's staff, but Violet was not included. With all the aplomb of her mother, she sent B.B. a note: "Dear Mr Berenson, The next time I receive distinguished or titled guests, I shall let you know the precise time of their arrival, so that my servants need not be disturbed by your telephone calls. A tit for Tatti." The visit was a great success.

The Nicolsons had been introduced to St. Loup not long after the war. Vita had immediately fallen under the tower's spell, and Harold wrote a charming thank you to Violet:

Sissinghurst Castle
October 1 1950

My dear Violet,
We got back last night in blustering rain and dark. We had an easy journey and Vita was not at all tired. I spent the time in the train writing a *Spectator* article in which I have dragged in Saint Loup, rather incidentally, rather deliberately but in a way I hope which will cause you pleasure. I really felt the charm of Saint Loup and I hope in your sort of way.

It was then that Violet conceived the idea of leaving St. Loup to her friend, a notion which led to a slightly embarrassing exchange of letters — a correspondence which nevertheless reawakened memories of their love. Vita finally accepted the legacy, but it is debatable that Violet ever thought to have her will changed. Violet's trips to England now always included a visit to Sissinghurst. And there too the old magic revived, now purified of all passion. Vita acknowledged as much in a number of moving letters written at this time.

In September 1952 Vita returned to Florence on her own, with less happy results. Vita was tired; Violet was engaged on an intense round of social activity. There was a large lunch for the Duff Coopers, which Vita found amusing enough, but she often preferred staying in her room when Italians came to lunch. And they, obviously, wondered who on earth this elderly and badly dressed Englishwoman could possibly be. I was at l'Ombrellino that September, and once in a while I would accompany Vita as she revisited, more in sorrow than with pleasure, the Florence of her adolescence, the Florence she had known with Violet and on her honeymoon with Harold, the Florence of her affair with Geoffrey Scott. She never talked about her interlude with Scott, but *Portrait of a Marriage* outlines the progress of her disenchantment with the author of *The Architecture of Humanism:* how it grew as his love for her deepened. Among the guests that September were Comte Jean de Gaigneron, Harold's old friend; Prince Rolphe de Faucigny-Lucinge; and a charming young relation of Violet's, Catherine Sinclair. As long as the party's harmony was not disturbed by outsiders, everyone was in excellent spirits — and even Vita agreed one day to take part in an elaborate hoax.

A French acquaintance called Pierre Guérin, usually referred to as "Présentez-moi-donc" ("Why-don't-you-introduce-me"), invited himself over for a drink and obviously intended to stay for dinner. Violet improvised a scenario into which we all entered immediately. Vita began by absently wandering across the far end of the drawing room two or three times without paying the slightest attention to the rest of us. "That's the Princess Royal," Violet whispered to Guérin. "We mustn't disturb her." Dazzled with excitement at the idea of meeting royalty, "Présentez-moi-donc" entrenched himself even more firmly. A quarter of an hour passed. The butler entered discreetly to inform Violet that the Princess Royal wished to dine. "I'm sorry we can't ask you to stay, Monsieur Guérin," Violet apologized, "but unless one has been introduced to Her Royal Highness, it's impossible to be seated at table with her." None of this, however, inhibited Guérin from telling everyone in Paris how he had dined with the daughter of George V in the house of Edward VII's daughter.

A day or so later, Violet decided that she wanted to be alone with Rolphe and announced to the rest of us: "You're all invited to lunch near Lucca with the Marchese Carlo Torrigiani." And before we knew it, Vita, Jean de Gaigneron, and myself were virtually pushed into Violet's car. An hour later it pulled up before a sumptuous baroque villa, where the Marchese welcomed us with extreme courtesy. He showed us the grounds, offered us an aperitif — and it suddenly dawned on him that Violet expected him to give us lunch. Simultaneously, Vita realized that he had not known we were coming. "I'm sorry lunch is so late," our involuntary host apologized, "but there's a new cook." And he vanished tactfully into the kitchen for a moment or two with the result that we lunched late indeed but excellently, and Vita, with consummate delicacy, let the Marchese know that she had not been taken in by Violet's *combinazione* without blaming her in the least, or aggravating our host's embarrassment by seeming at all taken aback. Until we said goodbye, she had spoken only French, but her grateful farewell was delivered in flawless Italian.

Vita was extremely put out, and once we were back in the car, she let off steam: "Violet is still twelve years old! She was a wonderful little girl, the absolute soul of intelligence and fun, but she's never grown up. Her chaotic life, all that immense waste of talent, boils down to that. This sort of escapade no longer amuses me in any way whatsoever!"

She never went back to l'Ombrellino. Vita retreated into the eccentric solitude of her tower at Sissinghurst; Violet displayed her eccentricities in the harsh light of society. Sometimes Violet would drop a barbed reference to Vita: "She means to write a novel about her Alsatian — how sad!" Violet found English sentimentality about animals almost incomprehensible. When Harold was knighted, Violet sighed: "The poor darling! She's going to have to call herself Lady Nicolson, like some small-town mayor's wife." On other occasions, she deplored the fact that Vita kept on writing those gardening articles instead of devoting her talent to poetry.

When I visited Sissinghurst in the next few years Vita would always inquire about Violet and her social round with the aloofness a soul that had found salvation might employ in speaking of another soul forever lost in worldly revels. There could be no doubt about it: their autumnal honeymoon was over. From then on Violet willed St. Loup to so many friends in succession that Nancy Mitford suggested they form a union.

In their later years, the Nicolsons frequently went on long cruises. At every port Vita would drop Violet a postcard, or sometimes an amusing letter about life on board ship. The last letter Violet received from Harold came shortly after Vita's death in 1962. It accompanied the Doge's ring that Violet had cajoled from Sir Joseph Duveen: it had been her first gift to Vita. Harold's letter is affectionate and generous, but on reading these lines one is inclined to reflect that a well-turned epitaph needn't adhere strictly to the truth:

Sissinghurst Castle
July 1 mean August 5 1962

My dearest Violet,

I think Vita would have liked you to have a book of hers as well as the ring. You were her best and oldest friend and she thought much about you and admired your work. These long and deep affections are the best thing in the world and I am grateful to you for your long and devoted and amused affection for her. I am glad indeed that she had so happy a life and you were a large part in it.

Things will never be the same to me again. But one cannot expect such happiness to continue for ever and the day will come when I shall be able to look back on the last fifty years with gratitude instead of torturing regret.

Your loving,
HAROLD

But Violet probably found another letter, in the trembling hand of Sir Osbert Sitwell, even more moving: "I know her death will have brought back to you many occasions," he consoled her. Little by little, the Sitwells were replacing the Nicolsons in Violet's mind if not her heart. There were several reasons for this. Sir Osbert was a better writer, and he was an aesthete; he retained an impudence and panache that Vita had lost; he was a neighbor, and Violet was enchanted by his castle, Montegufoni. "Let snobs and Americans pay court to Berenson; I have the Sitwells."

Montegufoni was a masterful blending of the medieval and the baroque, the ancient fortress of the Acciaiuoli, the Dukes of Athens, which jutted up from the roadside twenty or so kilometers outside Florence. It was one of the last citadels of the aesthetic movement in Tuscany, much as the elderly writer toiling at his autobiography was the last representative of an aristocracy passionately concerned with poetry and painting. At Montegufoni the atmosphere was grandiose, heraldic, with a sense of melancholic decay. Perhaps Sir Osbert might have been a little surprised to find himself included in the front rank of Violet's ex-fiancés, but no — he knew her too well.

Violet's gift for caricature inspired a repertory of monologues in the style of Ruth Draper; it's too bad they were never recorded. There was the American senator's widow, Mrs. Van den Pusch, making her assault on Paris society; there was the French tourist, torn between thrift and culture in Venice; there was the handsome Italian picking up a pretty foreigner; there was the Harrods shop assistant, totally indifferent to her customers' wants; there was a selection of French and English friends. Her imitation of a distinguished and self-satisfied Frenchman who refuses to be impressed by Italian palaces, Italian titles, or Italian cooking was a masterpiece. He summed up his visit to the Uffizi: *"Pas mal de bonnes choses, mais beaucoup de croûtes"* — "A few good things, but an awful lot of junk."

L'Ombrellino was completely restored to its former splendor by 1955, and Violet began to spend more and more time in Florence. She could keep her friends to herself more easily there than at St. Loup. Christian Dior was a frequent visitor; he shared her taste for beautiful things and *grande cuisine.* And there were the Duc and Duchesse d'Harcourt; the Princesse Alyette de Croy, whose laughter would ricochet through the house and out onto the terraces; Gaston Palewski, in those days ambassador in Rome; Denise Bourdet; the Massiglis; even the famous Socialist leader François Mitterrand — who, in no way averse to the luxuries of l'Ombrellino, came to see Violet while he was in Florence studying the history of the Medicis. Violet thought him very intelligent and good looking. Sabine de Bonneval's high spirits quickly broke the ice at these house parties if the guests were strangers to one another, or not entirely in sympathy with Violet's whims. Cecil Beaton's visit, for instance, was ruined when he saw how Violet had retouched his photographs of her with pencil strokes as vaguely applied as the lipstick Violet resorted to without benefit of the looking glass. One afternoon Cecil called the other guests into his room and announced solemnly: "Let's face it, our hostess is completely dotty!" L'Ombrellino was something of a French ambassadorial outpost in Tuscany, the way St. Loup at Sunday lunch turned into an annex of the British Embassy in Paris.

It was about this time that Violet's "fiancés" began to be replaced by a succession of "nephews." I was one of the first: in favor and out, then in again. A friend of mine, the playwright Jean-Pierre Grédy, diverted Violet for several seasons, then the English writer Quentin Crewe. Later, Lady Diana Cooper's son, Lord Norwich, joined the string of honorary nephews.

The Duc d'Harcourt composed a pastiche of Proust's pastiche of Saint-Simon's *Mémoires,* which amusingly reflected life at l'Ombrellino, particularly Violet's rejuvenation every time a "royalty" appeared on the horizon, when despite cane and limp she was able "to execute a surprising curtsey."

Violet set up a system of protocol lightened by gales of laughter. One of her rules was that she should come into the drawing room last, like a sovereign. From the far end of the gallery her guests would hear the tap-tap of cane on marble and the flutterings of her maid, Madame Alice: "Madame has forgotten her bag! And the compact! Where is her compact!" Then Violet would appear, supported on the arm of a "nephew." After dinner she would summon her guests one by one in order of precedence to take their place on the sofa beside her. But anyone who failed to amuse her, no matter his rank, was not detained long. She was torn between the need to impress and the desire to enjoy herself. Laughter won out almost every time, thank heaven: she was always the first to laugh at her fancies. She simply wanted her friends to join in her charades, a requirement anyone too pompous or staid found hard to comply with.

Since 1946, Violet's maid, Madame Alice, had been a perpetual presence in the background of all Violet's entertaining. Alice to her mistress, Madame Alice to guests, Madame to the other servants, she was Proust's cousin, Violet claimed, since she had been born near Chartres into a family called Amiot, like the novelist's Aunt Amiot, the original of "Aunt Léonie." The pretty and flirtatious Alice had been the mistress of a grand duke not long after the Russian Revolution, but to divert the suspicions of the duchess, whose maid she was, the duke married her off to a muzhik who spoke nothing but Russian and made a once-a-week appearance to clean the silver. Alice was Violet's treasurer, confidante, dresser, and intermediary with the other servants, who detested her. Small, mischievous, with a kind of provincial chic, she deplored her mistress's eccentricities. Yet neither scenes nor tears could tear her from Violet, and she was desolate if separated from her. Violet always thought that her friends and servants might show more affection for her if she told them what she meant to leave them. One day she went through a list of what she intended to leave to Alice. Then she asked her, "What about you, Alice? What are you going to leave me?" "My health, madame," she replied.

Alice was slightly older than Violet and preceded her in death by a year. Her replacement was more austere, and a frown from Marie expressed disapproval far more effectively than Alice's nagging. L'Ombrellino also contained a chauffeur, a cook, a butler, and a miscellany of other servants. Violet loaded her motorcar as though it were a camel, never budging without a retinue of servants and an incalculable number of parcels which Madame Alice used to count and recount until she was hopelessly confused.

One reason French guests liked to stay at l'Ombrellino was the likelihood of receiving invitations to other Florentine villas, the Queen of Rumania's Villa Sparta, for instance, where the clocks were stopped somewhere around 1912, with its László portraits, furniture as immovable as monuments, tables smothered in silver-framed photographs and enormous China-blue hydrangeas. Or Harold Acton's villa, La Pietra, where this Anglo-American, a Florentine by way of Oxford and Peking, lived with his eternally lovely mother. Acton, an expert on the Italian rococo, was renowned for his almost Chinese courtesy, and he was occasionally bemused by Violet's whims. He adopted a policy of not introducing the most brilliant of his guests to l'Ombrellino. In Florence, rivalries flourished from villa to villa and palace to palace, but without these factions and cabals, Florentine society might have been a trifle dull. Violet entertained members of all camps, and if some of these Italians made fun of her, they eagerly accepted her invitations and entertained her in return. In short, in their fashion, the Florentines liked and appreciated Violet. Her friends included the superb Duchessa Visconti, to whom Violet willed an enormous emerald originally given to Mrs. Keppel by the Shah of Persia; the Nicolini; the Gondi; the Antinori; the Catalani-Gonzaga; the Corsini; the Ricasoli; the Guidi, and the Capponi. An English friend, Lady Enid Browne, who lived on the quay of the Arno, was there to remind her of the world of her childhood. "Enid is the daughter of *due conti*," Violet would tell her amazed Italian friends, and then explain that her father was the Earl of Chesterfield and Stanhope.

Violet was a kind and generous woman behind the façade of social backbiting, but she found it impossible to forgive anyone who defended himself against her fantasies. This was the fate that befell Carlos de Beistegui, despite the facts that he was an old friend and that she admired his flair for interior decoration. She had gone of course (as a Scottish chatelaine) to de Beistegui's famous ball in the Palazzo Labia, but it was a party she recalled without much enthusiasm. She used to tell a story about de Beistegui in the days when he was the uncrowned king of Venetian society. She was staying with a friend whose little house had just been expensively done over. Violet invited "Charlie" to come for a drink, and the two women waited for his verdict. Without a word, he surveyed the drawing room, the dining room, and even poked into the bedrooms. In one of these he took the braid-trimmed border of a curtain between thumb and forefinger: "Ravishing!" Later, Violet and I invented a new disease called Beisteguitis: its victims set themselves up in surroundings more luxurious than they could afford and went bankrupt planting gardens and giving balls. Alas, Carlos de Beistegui eventually suffered a mild stroke, but its effect was precisely the opposite to what might have been expected: it loosened his tongue. He would suddenly launch now into the exposition of long-forgotten truths. One day at l'Ombrellino, he interrupted a darkly ambiguous monologue of Violet's on Edward VII. "You're boring us, Violet. Everybody knows you were born four years before your mother met the Prince of Wales." From that moment, Violet's "sumptuous" friend, the "last of the Maecenases," was changed forever into a "grotesque old dodderer" and "a third-rate decorator."

Violet's fantasies were always constructed about a core of irrefutable fact, as I found out during a visit to l'Ombrellino in 1960. One day Violet came to lunch looking like the cat that ate the canary: *"Mes chèrs amis,* rather tiresome but the Duke of Windsor's just sent word that he's arriving tomorrow. I do hope he'll be on his own and not stay too long, but he's a childhood friend: I simply can't say I won't see him." "Did he telephone?" somebody asked, slightly surprised but hardly incensed that so eminent a personage should give such short notice. Violet brandished a slip of blue paper: "He sent a telegram: 'Arrive Florence tomorrow. Love. David.'" "Chère Violet," I was obliged to say, "I have good news for you: the telegram's for me. It's from my friend David Carritt." I had been expecting David to come through Florence. From that day on, however, Violet was firmly persuaded that David Carritt, one of England's foremost art historians, was a bad influence on me. She refused to receive him — until she heard that he had identified a painting belonging to one of her relations as a Watteau.

It was around this time too that the Italian government awarded Violet the Order of Commendatore. Since this is an honor almost never conferred on women, it led to a multitude of small misunderstandings. She was on the invitation lists to official functions, for instance, as a man, and when she traveled by train, porters refused to deliver *il Commendatore*'s luggage to a woman's compartment.

And now that she was a Commendatore, oughtn't she to be raised from Chevalier of the Légion d'Honneur to Commandeur? She invited a good friend of Nancy Mitford's, a man highly placed in the government, to come to an exquisite lunch. Coffee was served in a rococo silver *cafetière* which the knowledgeable minister immediately praised. *"Chèr ami,"* Violet bubbled. "You *do* have superb taste. Yes, it is a lovely thing; it was made by Paul Lamerie. The day I'm made Commandeur I'll give it to you!" The minister was the first to find Violet's "bribe" hilariously naive, but when he repeated the story to Nancy, she was furious. The man was scrupulously honest, however, and the affair was more comic than scandalous. Violet was never elevated to Commandeur, but she left the *cafetière* to the minister in her will — and a piece of jewelry to Nancy!

# 14. *All Passion Spent*

ONE OF VIOLET'S most touching characteristics, though it bothered some of her more solemn friends, was that she was never able to apply her clear-sightedness to an analysis of her own behavior, which in certain respects was precisely that of the women she derided. This conscious absurdity, this illogical need to carry out all the implications of a chosen role, is characteristic of eccentricity. Violet's impersonation of a Paris dowager was endowed with a wholly English flair. Eccentricity is an impertinence which can flower fully only in an aristocratic society. It is also, in old age, a screen which serves rather admirably to conceal the heartache and loneliness of this time of life, and it can sometimes even turn its infirmities into assets. Violet's cane, for instance, served as the crowning touch to her role as a dowager.

Slow and hesitant as she was in later life, she could still summon up amazing energy on the right occasion. When Princess Margaret honored a ball at the British Embassy, Violet plowed her way through to the Princess's side in a trice, and began an animated conversation. Someone whispered, "That woman is an absolute miracle of snobbery!" Perhaps it was Nancy Mitford, whom Violet had once snubbed for permitting herself a somewhat caustic observation about the Princess. Nancy, a brilliant novelist and outstanding historian, had many virtues, but patience was not one: her reaction to Violet's Lamerie *cafetière* "bribe" showed that. Violet's relationship with Paris's most celebrated Englishwoman had its ups and downs. Nancy refused to take Violet seriously, and the fact that she had met a number of her friends through Violet didn't commit her to taking Violet's advice on how to succeed in Paris. Violet could never see that Nancy had not come to Paris to conquer society (an achievement for which she was well equipped) but to be near a close French friend and to live a life free of material worry, easier then to do in France than in England. She saw the people she wanted to see, not those she was expected to see. Outside of a few intimates, society was for Nancy a play put on for her amusement. It was not long before Violet was cast in a farcical role whose final performance was awaited unsparingly.

A fairly long period of frost set in around 1955, when Princesse Dolly Radziwill, a friend of Violet's who had become Nancy's best friend, commissioned her portrait from still another friend of Violet's, Derek Hill. The painter turned the Princesse's ravaged elegance to marvelous account, producing a Boldini with overtones of Goya. Princesse Radziwill, rather more accustomed to László's portraits, was not pleased. She invited her friends to a portrait-burning; later, Nancy claimed that she was the one who gave the picture its final kick into the fireplace. Hill retaliated wittily by sending Nancy a catalogue of his latest exhibition — and a box of matches. At the same exhibition, Violet bought his sketch for the vanished portrait — which didn't help matters along with Nancy. But Nancy herself unwittingly upset her French friends by claiming in one of her books that Marie Antoinette was a traitor whose fate was well deserved. The Faubourg Saint-Germain recoiled in horror before this act of treason, and Violet hung a Union Jack at half-mast outside the window of her Paris flat.

Nancy may sometimes have been a trifle harsh when faced with the childish antics of her compatriot, but another English writer living in Paris was much more indulgent: Lesley Blanch, that lovely voyager through the Arabian Nights who embodied so many characteristics of the women she portrayed in *The Wilder Shores of Love*. She enjoyed Violet's stories, delighted in her flights of fancy, and treated her as something of a princess; Scheherazade, perhaps? Both women were romantic, both were gourmets. When age and illness forced Violet to alter her diet, Lesley made her a charming little picture book full of delicious suggestions for dishes she could eat with impunity. And she embroidered for her one of her famous cushions with which she filled her own apartment, each a reminder of some important place or person in her life.

Violet knew all the women in Paris who still maintained salons, but she became especially friendly with the most intelligent of them, Jeanine Delpech, a good friend of Lesley's and Nancy's too. She frequented the congenial and unorthodox salon of Emily Faure-Dujarric, where she met Ionesco and Marcel Jouhandeau, as well as a host of younger writers.

The lunches Gérard and Hervé Mille gave in their house in the Rue de Varenne were a particular delight because Violet's hosts knew how to respect her fantasies and laugh at them at the same time. And in the Rue de Varenne, Violet called the conversational tune — unless the notoriously garrulous Coco Chanel was there!

Marie-Laure de Noailles continued to exert her fascination over Violet, and she could, if necessary, revenge herself by reminding her that she was descended from the Marquis de Sade. Marie-Laure treated Violet like a very precocious little girl who had to be told from time to time to stand in the corner. Violet still went off to the Place des États-Unis in suspense: whom would she find this time? A crowd of geniuses or a handful of dull supernumeraries? In any case, at Marie-Laure's she would be at the heart of Paris, in the one drawing room in the city where there was always something of note going on. Marie-Laure's was the only house in Paris where Violet sometimes seemed out of place, dazzled or scandalized as she was by this sample of bohemian Paris.

Violet was unendingly inquisitive, and she would nearly always accept invitations from people she hardly knew, even at the risk of having to leave in a hurry, never to return, if she were bored, or didn't like the cooking or the way they'd arranged the furniture. In her old age, a friend reproached her for dining at the house of an American woman married to a Frenchman everyone called "the self-made duke." Violet explained: "It's perfectly natural to get invitations from people I've always known, but so flattering to be asked by people I don't know. It shows that they've heard of me." When a penniless "nephew" or "fiancé" invited Violet to lunch in his garret with a few friends, she was delightful company, and the next day her host would receive a dozen porcelain plates as an incentive to renew the invitation.

Just as good-hearted, if somewhat ridiculous, was Baroness Le

Monaco, who typified international café society. She was a tiny, gaudy old lady who owed her success to the way she had once stood up to Princesse Colonna. "Who are you?" demanded the haughty Levantine, faced with the American baroness. "Princess, I'm just a little nobody from nowhere," she twanged, a reply that launched her on a career as a clown which lasted until her dying breath — exhaled, in what Violet found was a fitting farewell for a socialite, as her guests dined in her Roman palazzo in the room beneath her deathbed.

Fortunately, you could not really take Violet seriously when she would say, "You mustn't forget that I'm a very conventional old lady." Of course, she scrupulously observed all the rules: precedence at table, the right clothes for every occasion. She would carefully choose ties as presents for her "nephews," for if conversation could be relaxed, dress always had to be correct. She played the Faubourg Saint-Germain dowager to perfection, but always with a wink to her intimates. One of the role's requisites was getting her bachelor friends married off at all costs. Having given up her "fiancés," she made up for it by making matches for her "nephews." I still think somewhat ruefully of all the splendid catches Violet landed for me that I never pursued. One day, dressed to the nines, she went so far as to pay a call on the mother of a woman I knew to explain that here was a young man with a future and that the happy couple could have l'Ombrellino for their honeymoon. "But, madame, you forget! My daughter is already married — and a Catholic!" the horrified mother expostulated.

In 1958 Violet moved into a wing of a mansion in the Rue de Cherche-Midi, which had once belonged to the Duc de Saint-Simon. There she had a vast drawing room, a dining room, a conservatory, and two bedrooms lit by lofty small-paned windows. Marble busts rested on gilt consoles; Louis XV chairs were upholstered in needlepoint; Empire Aubusson rugs covered the floors, eighteenth-century portraits the walls. The effect was very Faubourg Saint-Germain. Violet's own room seemed somehow Venetian with its hangings of flowered red-and-gold damask. She liked calling herself "a *déclassée* woman who lives exclusively in *classé* houses."

Several times a week Violet gave lunch to friends. The cuisine she offered them was always superb, but perhaps the most extraordinary aspect of these lunches was the dishes on which they were served. There was a service in Meissen for state occasions; another in blue-and-white Tournai for more intimate gatherings. Her dessert plates were Chinese export porcelain or Delft; the centerpiece, Capo di Monte. The extraordinary silverware, or rather, silver-gilt, had the monogram of Catherine the Great; cut and gilt Venetian crystal turned even the simplest luncheon into a gala occasion. Never was Violet more brilliant than when she sat at the head of a table of carefully chosen guests: she knew just how to display each to advantage. In no time at all the talk would rise far above the usual chitchat. There would be a writer or two, perhaps an Englishman passing through Paris, the latest fashionable young couple, some witty women friends, a politician or a diplomat. After coffee, Violet never missed taking one of the latter aside for a serious talk in the "China worries me" vein Proust attributed to the Duchesse de Guermantes. In the sixties, lunches like these may have been something of an anachronism, but they were unfailingly charming and frequently fascinating.

Violet read avidly in French and English, historical works in preference to fiction, and applied her extraordinary memory to everything she read. She could quote hundreds of lines from poems in either language; she had a weakness for puns in both languages too. When I got together with a few friends to produce a *Dictionary of Snobs,* Violet not only contributed an excellent chapter on Italian snobs, but provided a flood of inspiration on English and French provincial snobbery. "Your nonsense is my nonsense," she told me one day, adapting Charles II's remark to the Earl of Rochester. Nevertheless, now that she had become so preoccupied with decorum, she bridled at anything in print which she felt was in the least scandalous. I published a novel that was in fact more preposterous than indelicate, but she warned me in some consternation, "You have put back your admittance to the Académie by five years!" Nothing about her now betrayed that she had ever been capable of rebellious or scandalous behavior herself. People had heard some vague story of an affair with Vita Sackville-West, but the publication of *Portrait of a Marriage* in 1973 left Violet's French friends aghast.

What dreams now haunted this old woman whom splendid surroundings and her own wit could not always save from sadness? What imagined lives did she pursue in the long nights of insomnia beneath the damask hangings in the Rue de Cherche-Midi? What memories was she fleeing during her dinners and parties? Regret that she had not been born Empress of Russia or Madame de Sévigné or even Virginia Woolf was mingled with the pain of a lost love before which all other loves paled into insignificance. At l'Ombrellino she wandered beneath the cypresses like an exiled queen who could entrust her confidences only to the statues lining the terraces. At St. Loup, she climbed the tower to make sure all was in order in those charming rooms which sheltered charming friends but never, alas, the valiant lover, the sublime poetess, the Prince Charming for whom she had longed. What did it matter: like the lacquered chests, the tapestried screens, the Venetian looking glasses, her faithful friends were part of the décor, walk-ons in the plays of the imagination in which Violet took the leading roles. With the onset of age, insomnia, and illness, these roles became harder for her audience to follow, despite the fact that now they were rehearsed again and again. They concealed the real Violet behind a clown's make-up applied by a blind man. Her friends suffered as they watched; now, a perusal of one of her finest letters, written in May 1920* reveals that Violet had always lived in a poetic, irrational world: that in her latter days far from being a woman who lived in the past, she was a kind of fairy, mustering her remaining charms to exert them on a society which believed her only insofar as it expected miracles of *mondanité*. She worked her spells well enough, however, to keep a few faithful friends at her side between the parties and the dinners.

In her old age Violet began to think more kindly of her native England. She would go to stay at the London Ritz, where she could enter Mrs. Keppel's world, unspoiled and eternal. The chill between Violet and her sister did not last, and she enjoyed weekends at Sonia's Hampshire house, where life went on as she had known it in childhood. At heart, the sisters admired each other for the virtues they did not share, and there were many things they both found amusing despite the fact that Sonia's gift for order and organization intimidated Violet

* Letter No. 33.

a little, and Violet's vagueness bothered Sonia. But Violet's friends
were welcome at Hall Place: old friends like Rebecca West or Harold
Nicolson, much diminished by Vita's death in 1962. Robin McDouall
would arrive, and he and Violet would spend days comparing recipes
and vintages. She made new friends, a rare occurrence past sixty.
But her outgoing quirkiness charmed people nostalgic for Edwardian
times; she had become a historical personage. Eccentric in France,
in England she was a "character," someone able to impose her fantasies
on the fabric of everyday life the way a star is able to tailor her roles
to her personality. She made a friend of the Hogarthian Lord Kinross,
an avid traveler, a talented writer, and a bon vivant. She liked him for
his independence and his fund of good talk; in London, Patrick would
plan amusing little dinners for her in his house in Little Venice.

And at the last, a final, loyal beau let her feel once more that she
was irresistible. His name was Frank Ashton-Gwatkin. He had
begun his diplomatic career in Japan, continuing it under the aegis of
Neville Chamberlain as far as Berchtesgaden. Erudite, amply stocked
with anecdotes about the mighty of this world, and with plenty of
time on his hands, he had all the qualities of an indispensable traveling
companion. And as Violet's guest, he was able to restore order in an
occasionally chaotic household. Violet's charm lightened Frank's
old age; Frank's generosity, wit, and devotion helped Violet forget her
infirmities. In this mood, she returned to England and Scotland with
pleasure in 1962. Some of the letters she wrote to Frank during her
journey signal this revival of her youthful spirits.

But from 1963 onward, Violet's health declined rapidly. It was her
custom to give a dinner for fifty or so in the conservatory of St. Loup
every July 14. In 1963 the weather was perfect; the park was hung
with Japanese lanterns, and the moon hovered between the church
tower and the tower of St. Loup. It was all like the setting for a play
by Edmond Rostand, and the party was a spellbinding success. After
the last guest had gone, Violet imprudently decided to close one of
the tall windows. She fell — and, for the second time, broke her hip
on the tile floor. A series of painful treatments and operations turned
her in a few months into an aged invalid. Frank Ashton-Gwatkin and
John Nova Phillips, a young American she had met in Florence some

years earlier, took turns escorting Violet when she traveled. She
wanted to see Spain again; she wanted to visit Turkey, where her
admirer Jean Ostrorog entertained her in his *yali* on the banks of the
Bosphorus. In Florence and Paris, despite her fatigue, she continued to
entertain. Her new friends made her feel that she was still somebody to
reckon with, and for their sake, she revived all the old charm.

John Phillips introduced her to his friend Peggy Guggenheim; unexpectedly, the two women felt an immediate sympathy for each other.
It would not have been surprising if Violet had felt a little lost among
the Ernsts and Picassos of Peggy's Venetian palace-museum, or if
Peggy had felt a little bored among the *principessas* and *contessas* at
l'Ombrellino. But for each there was the charm of novelty, and both
had a preference for the world of fantasy. I took Baroness Blixen
(Isak Dinesen) to see Violet on the baroness's last visit to Paris before
her death in 1962. These aristocrats understood each other immediately. One might have thought them birds of some species so ancient
that it had lost the energy to fly.

Approaching seventy, Violet looked eighty. Young people meeting
her for the first time sometimes saw her as a Queen of Spades, the
clouded and chimerical survivor of a vanished era. To some, she gave
the impression that she drank, but Violet had never been a drinker;
it was simply that, unable to sleep, she had begun taking sleeping
pills on top of powerful painkillers. With a single glass of champagne,
she could appear completely befuddled. In fact she shared a French
prejudice against hard drinking. One English friend of long standing,
elderly now but still beautiful, arrived at l'Ombrellino for a visit.
Before dinner she managed to imbibe a fair number of bloody marys.
Violet began to worry about what the rest of the evening was going
to be like, so she warned her gently, "Darling, I'm so glad to see that
you've stopped drinking." Her distinguished friend screamed with
laughter: "But, darling, can't you see I'm completely *tight?*"

Some of Violet's last parties were given at l'Ombrellino. There was
a dinner to honor her old friend Artur Rubinstein when he came to
stay with the Boissevains. And on the day that Florence was declared
twin city to Edinburgh, she gave a particularly grand lunch at which
a superb kilted Scot piped the guests into the dining room, recalling

the Scottish holidays of her childhood. She presided between the Duke of Bedford and the Lord Mayor of Edinburgh, and down the center of the table glittered an enormous silver-gilt sturgeon that had belonged — of course! — to Peter the Great. But now there was little spirit left in such occasions. Violet entertained like a faded star who feels that she owes her public one last performance, then another, until her audience finishes by looking on this incredible effort of love and art as a demonstration of courage.

None of the festivities in the closing years of her life was more heartbreaking than the party she gave to see in the New Year of 1967. L'Ombrellino was filled with congenial friends, including Ambassador and Madame Louis Roché, who would have liked nothing better than to spend a quiet evening at home with their suffering friend. But every night of their visit, Violet organized a dinner somewhere or other, and her guests found themselves hard put to keep up, even when these evenings out involved agreeable people in beautiful houses. New Year's Eve at l'Ombrellino climaxed this dizzying series of brilliant evenings. Violet's leg pained her terribly, and, pushed to the brink of despair by her insomnia, she tried one contradictory and consciousness-dulling remedy after another in search of relief. Everyone who was there would obviously have preferred staying home, and it was only Monsieur Roché's gracious presence of mind which managed to give the gathering a veneer of gaiety. This was stripped away immediately with the first glimpse of Violet. Glittering with diamonds, preposterously rouged, her eyes wandering vaguely, she came in supported on the arm of a butler straight out of Charles Addams. The party drifted into the dining room, where the dimly flickering light of guttering candles transformed the company into a band of phantoms that hovered over the table and the silver-gilt sturgeon. With a faintly malevolent air, Violet sat erect on a sort of bishop's throne, motionless, silent, neither eating nor drinking. Suddenly she spoke: "I'm alone . . . so all alone . . ." There was no question of amiable protest; no one answers back to the Commendatore's statue. But as Violet herself became aware of the unsettling cast of her remark, she made a lightning switch from King Lear to the Grande Duchesse de Gerolstein, and, clapping her hands, decreed: "Dance, *mes amis,* dance!

Music!" A record player was brought in and somebody put the sound track of *Never on Sunday* on the turntable. Between courses, the younger guests improvised a dance more macabre than Greek in the dining room shadows. After coffee, everyone felt that the New Year couldn't come too soon.

The beginning of 1970 was another sad time. In a single month Violet watched three old friends disappear: first Louise de Vilmorin, next Tony Gandarillas, finally, Marie-Laure de Noailles. A little later it was the turn of Madame Alice, then Betty Batten. In the autumn of 1971, Violet returned to Paris ravaged by a stomach ailment and almost incapable of walking. Yet exerting incredible will power, she invited her friends to lunch almost daily, as though entertaining again might somehow prolong her life from day to day. As she put it to her doctor, giving a new twist to Madame du Barry's remark, "One more lunch, Mr. Executioner!" Violet would preside despite everything, so weak that her guests wondered whether she would survive until dessert. But she was always impeccably dressed and quick to relish the latest gossip. Her courage could sometimes become embarrassing as when instead of bons mots she proposed her own epitaph: *"Ci-gît l'immodeste Violette. Croyez bien qu'elle se regrette"* — "Here lies the unblushing Violet. Don't think she doesn't regret it." The macabre rhyme is impossible to reproduce in English.

Violet left the Rue de Cherche-Midi for l'Ombrellino on December 24, 1971. The last two months of her life were cruel, and the immense villa surrounded by statues, empty fountains, and dead flowers was indeed the perfect setting for the death agony of someone who had never liked doing things halfway. Seen from the road, sequestered among the cypresses, the villa recalled Arnold Böcklin's "Island of the Dead." The French consul general, the Vicomte de Dampierre, came often with his kindhearted Spanish wife, reminders of the two countries Violet had loved most. Her English friends were especially loyal and these included, in addition to Lady Enid Browne, an old Bellosguardo neighbor, Nancy Pearson, a novelist especially interested in the Stuart Pretenders. Sir Harold Acton frequently used to buy Violet the latest books. She in turn presented him with a Chinese court robe, which Mrs. Keppel had brought back from Peking. When one reads what

Sir Harold has written about Violet in his biography of Nancy Mitford, one can only compare him with another Florentine, Dante, who never forgave the slightest offense. One of the last visitors was François Mitterrand, who later wrote two very moving pages about Violet in his memoirs. She rarely left the spacious bedroom hung with Mrs. Keppel's eighteenth-century Chinese wallpapers. Her devoted Marie did what she could to help Violet through the ordeal of these last days and Lady Enid Browne was the most loyal of friends. John Phillips and Frank Ashton-Gwatkin took turns by her bedside through January and February and until, unable to digest food, Violet literally died of starvation on March 1.

Violet was cremated according to her wishes. Most of her ashes are buried close to her parents' tomb in the Protestant cemetery near Florence; the remainder have been sealed in the ancient ruins near the Monk's Refectory below the tower at St. Loup. A marker indicates the spot: "Violet Trefusis 1894–1972, English by Birth, French at Heart" ("Violet Trefusis 1894–1972, *Anglaise de naissance, Française de coeur*"). She had given St. Loup to John Phillips; the apartment in the Rue de Cherche-Midi was left to her nurse (who sold it to Andy Warhol: its elegant eighteenth-century *boiserie* must now echo gatherings of quite another kind). Violet remembered all her old and faithful friends — with checks, jewelry, silver. The apparently raddled old lady forgot no one. L'Ombrellino was hers to use only as long as she lived, and her family sold it after her death.

Three months after Violet's death, Prince Jean-Louis de Faucigny-Lucinge organized a memorial service in the British Embassy church (since demolished, alas), which reunited Violet's friends with the ambassador's wife, Lady Soames, and Lord Ashcombe at their head. Her friend since prewar days, Jacques Chastenet of *Le Temps,* now a member of the Académie Française, delivered the eulogy; her composer friend Henri Sauguet played the organ. The affair was as she would have wished it: an elegant and not unhappy tribute in keeping with the epitaph she finally chose:

*She Withdrew.*

# THE LETTERS

Selected and Edited by John Phillips

# 15. *Introduction to the Correspondence*

FORTUNATELY for those interested in Violet Trefusis, Vita kept everything. Among her papers at Sissinghurst Castle was found a mound of "Violetiana," hundreds of letters, mostly in their original envelopes. The postmarks helped to determine dates.

Chronologically the papers begin with Violet's precocious journal, written in a round childish hand in 1905, when she was eleven, during her first visit to Paris with her Aunt Jessie. The journal is adorned with Violet's pen illustrations including those of the Dôme of Les Invalides and of Buffalo Bill, whom she saw at a Wild West show in Paris. At a later date, Violet annotated this journal, commenting on her "greed for iced lemonade and chocolate éclairs."

Then follows the group of Ceylon letters written in 1910–1911. Violet, aged sixteen, is writing to her "Princesse Lointaine," inspired by the exotic beauty of the tropics. These letters are a self-conscious exercise, delightful and revealing in their childish sophistication.

But the great mass of the letters are those written during the years of the *"grande passion,"* from 1918–1921: more than five hundred, ranging from those scribbled in pencil on scraps, frequently impossible to decipher, to those on fine paper with splendid letterheads. The latter are often brilliant, witty, and very beautiful; they are I believe in the tradition of the best English letterwriters. Above all, the reader feels keenly the sincerity and intensity of Violet's passion for Vita, an all-consuming passion which all but destroyed her. In a sense, it did destroy her: the youthful Violet whose idealism burned with a pure bright flame was transformed into a *femme de lettres* and *femme du monde,* who would embrace and conquer — supreme irony — the society which she had thought to reject, the society which was her heritage. She was to pass much of her life amid its pompous façades. But always, there remained in the shadows glimmerings of the "other Violet," an ephemeral, fanciful creature.

As for Vita's letters to Violet during these years, we know that they were burned by Denys Trefusis. A letter from Violet records:

> "He has done you a good turn by burning every single one of your letters — the ones that were either in his or my father's possession and the ones that were in my writing table drawer. He has read them all so he can have no illusions left."*

It is inevitable to speculate about the lost letters. While Violet often complains about Vita's not writing, we can imagine that Vita's letters, if not always so long or so passionate as desired, were of a quality to content Violet. As in a game of tennis, the balls had to be returned, and Vita's letters, while reflecting a less ardent nature, did, we can assume, succeed in reassuring Violet of her love. But by 1920 the mood has changed and Violet's increasing despair is apparent. That this despair was justified can be confirmed by reading Vita's autobiographical manuscript, published in *Portrait of a Marriage.* Vita has changed. Violet remains constant, consumed by her love, suffering and alone. Desperately she clings to her dreams as Vita slips away. Not a quick and clean break, however, because Vita vacillates, reluctant to give up Violet. And so the correspondence fades away with Violet's pathetic letters, written in 1921, including those to the intermediary, her friend, Margaret (Pat) Dansey, who appears to have betrayed her trust.

The scene shifts from Vita's tower of Sissinghurst to Violet's tower at St. Loup de Naud. In 1972 following Violet's death, I found at St. Loup some forty letters written by Vita during the forties and fifties. The first group were written after the fall of France to Violet, who had just returned to England.

Vita's letters are of exceptional interest, revealing that her love for

* July 26, 1919.

Violet had remained and that, above all, she feared the revival of that intense passion. Her emotional stress is vividly reflected by the calligraphy of these pages when at times the usually neat, precise script is transformed into a violent scrawl by a shaking hand. "You are the unexploded bomb," she writes, at the moment when German bombs are peppering Kent and invasion appears imminent.

To begin to read this selection of letters we must return to the world of 1910; it is the same century, but with what a difference. Britannia still rules the seas and the sun never sets on the British Empire. King Edward has just died and his beloved, the beautiful Mrs. Keppel, with her lovely daughters are wafted away to Ceylon. From Sir Thomas Lipton's tea plantation Violet, aged sixteen, writes to Vita at Knole — in French, of course.

The Ceylon letters make me think of William Beckford: two anachronistic personages, they had not a little in common. Both were precociously gifted, exotic, *enfants gâtés,* who became involved in scandals which shocked society, and both were, in a sense, crushed by society. Violet and Beckford: they belong to the very small group of English authors who could write effortlessly in flawless French. They were both born "collectors," though Violet was a pauper compared with Beckford. Most important, for both Fantasy mattered far more than the so-called Reality. They battled and half succeeded in ignoring the "realities" of mundane existence so that their worlds of fantasy might triumph.

Both were, in one word, *aesthetes.* And here, I believe, is the essential key to Violet. Even her unique *grande passion,* her love for Vita, was for her — as her letters reveal — an aspect of her quest for an Ideal Beauty. Shades of Walter Pater! Shades of Plato!

I shall always remember the intensity with which on several occasions, she summed it up for my benefit: "Nothing but the Best shall content my soul."

# 16. *Violet to Vita (1910–1921)*

Colombo, Ceylon
December 1910

To my incomparable sister
    Of the velvet eyes,
The mother-of-pearl skin,
    The ebony hair,

The pomegranate lips,
    The clove like breath,
By the inspiration of Dawn,
    Greetings and Prosperity.

I write to you beneath a bewildering swaying of gigantic bamboo trees, at the far end of a garden which ought to belong to the *Thousand and One Nights,* or, if you prefer, this resembles El Dorado.

Do you like orchids? I adore them.

You would have the same feelings if you could see them as I do at this moment: meaning, in clusters, purpled, narcotic, with here and there some shameful misalliance as is suitable for plebian orchids.

Haven't I a talent for descriptions, darling? But I think you will not expect anything better when I tell you that it is 90 degrees in the shade and my poor aching body is in a complete state of collapse, both moral and physical.

Would that I were the daughter of a sea-wolf, to go roving with only slippers on my feet, a necklace, and that's all!!!

I am becoming incoherent; I'd better stop.

1. Written on three different days but all included in the same envelope. The letters from Ceylon were written in French.

Beneath a blazing tropical midday sky, the road to Maradane is reduced to powder: . . . on each side arises the unexpected; foliage in turn sombre, sparkling, or brilliant. The heat is such that the slightest movement is exhausting. At a distance in a cloud of dust, one perceives the great weary oxen with their bloodshot eyes and backs slashed by blows. Alongside, gleaming black, the ox drivers.

Everywhere reflections, everywhere light, and then, from time to time, a coconut falls, slowly, with a dull sound, on the brown earth.

A land of an absolute repose, of an absolute beauty, a rich land, an unbelievable land, bursting forth with all fruits and spices — the purity of a vermilion land, enamoured of light, drunk by sunshine.

POSTSCRIPT: What do you say about my oriental style? As for me, I am stunned by it! *I flatter myself I am the possessor of one of the most adaptable natures in existence.*

Dambatenne[1] at 5000 feet,
200 feet from the sun.
4 December 1910.

I am giddy, the dizziness of heights.

I feel tiny, so tiny . . . you have no idea . . . from one moment to the next it seems that I should be swallowed up. All the surrounding mountains conspire to crush me with their weight. Immense shaggy rocks are heaped up pell-mell around the house. The view is superb. 2000 feet below us smiling hills with delicate sylvan slopes can be perceived.

You see it, the stump of Adam's Peak[2] in the distant haze. Nearby it's the jungle, then, the sea. Here and there the lagoons — girded by banana trees, pomegranate cactus, camphor trees, eucalyptus, and nutmeg trees — smoke in the sun like enormous tubs.

1. Sir Thomas Lipton lent Mrs. Keppel a bungalow in the midst of his tea plantation.
2. Adam's Peak. The most remarkable mountain of Ceylon (7360 feet), a striking pyramid on whose rocky summit is a celebrated depression shaped like a huge footprint. The Buddhists have identified the footprint as that of Buddha, the Hindus as Shiva, the Muslims as Adam, and the Portuguese conquerors attributed it to Saint Thomas the Apostle.

Unnecessary to tell you that I am of a sovereign laziness and that nothing less than a monsoon would make me abandon my divan. All of this is understood.

How far away is England! Vita mia!

How is it possible that you are not here?

It occurred to me several times during my sojourn, to ask myself, in effect, why you don't make any effort to come here, in spite of everything, in spite of everything??? I shouldn't wish to be in your place for an empire! This is not so bad, it seems to me, for a person who is double-faced.

*Now for the little matter-of-fact information you love*[3]: we will be going perhaps to spend several days towards the end of this month at Nuwara Eliya, but you can write to me here and it will be forwarded.

I had all sorts of adventures on the steamer that I should like to be able to tell you about in person. Among others, one very amusing with a Spanish lady and another with — *ma non importa!*[4] *It will keep.*[5] Enough to tell you that the lady Violetta amused herself madly at the expense of others. Which is perhaps not altogether a good thing, but one pardons youth for many things, especially at 16½. These are what you call puerilities. I call them simply imprudences — which amounts to about the same thing.

Do try not to get married before I return.

Dambatenne
12 December 1910

In vain one looks for some coherence, some telltale blade of grass in the inextricable labyrinth which is your last letter — a labyrinth, alas, which lacks an Ariadne to provide the conducting thread.

But after a brief attempt, I give up guessing! It's too hot to persist. Unless you have become suddenly enamoured of some happy mortal,

3. Written in English.
4. "But no matter."
5. Written in English.

I confess myself incapable of reading between your lines. Oh well, this will arrange itself.

In attentively rereading suddenly a sort of heavy anguish which I can only qualify as apprehension has just made my heart beat rapidly and makes my hand tremble as I write to you . . .

It's trembling and it's sad.

For the first time your extra two years[6] seem to me very real, arrogant, sinister.

But don't believe that I haven't foreseen this moment: often I have imagined myself at this turning.

Oh, for pity sake, tell me that I am wrong, that it is my devilish imagination which overpowers me.

After all, I'm only a girl. I ought to have foreseen that perhaps at your age a masculine liaison would come about. I would be wise to accept this. I feel that I'm about to say improper things. You won't laugh, promise that you won't laugh. For a long time I've asked nothing of you, so grant me this. *It would hurt so.*[7]

Tomorrow we're going to Nuwara Eliya. We plan to spend most of this week in the jungle where these gentlemen-hunters are going to hunt alligators.

I hope terribly that they won't force me to participate. These enormous beasts all bleeding — pouah! It makes one shudder. Then we will go to see the *buried cities*,[8] beginning with Anuradhapura. The jungle makes me tremble. I pray to return intact.

*Violetta*

6. Violet was two years younger than Vita.
7. Written in English.
8. Written in English. "Buried cities" is a reference to the famous ruins of Anuradhapura and Polonnaruwa. Anuradhapura, founded in 437 B.C., was abandoned as a royal residence in the ninth century. The ruins were buried by the jungle and completely deserted until the midnineteenth century. They have since become a famous center for Buddhist pilgrimages and the sacred Bo tree is said to have grown from a branch of the tree under which the Buddha obtained enlightenment. Polonnaruwa was the Singhalese capital from the tenth to twelfth centuries, and is rich in Buddhist art.

LETTER NO. 2

Dambatenne, Ceylon
January 2, 1911

*I am in a strange mood today, Vita mia, I cannot make up my mind whether I am a freak in every possible respect,*[1] or just simply — an unnatural child. Enlighten me by your wisdom and tell me my future, oh pythoness!

*I have had every conceivable thing in the way of adventures these last two years.*[2] Shall I disclose some of the more thrilling for your benefit? You ask nothing better, do you? And it's exactly because I comprehend your curiosity — quite natural really — that I'm determined not to tell.

I have more memories than if I were a thousand years old. A great chest whose drawers are crammed with balance sheets, verses, love letters, with law suits, novels, with locks of hair rolled up amid the receipts — hides fewer memories than my sad brain. It's a pyramid, an immense vault containing more dead than the common grave. I am a cemetery detested by the moon where, as with remorse, drag out long verses, which fasten themselves to my most sacred deaths.[3]

'— *et patati patat,* I could go on reciting for half an hour if this would help to solace my spleen.

Your last missive told me much about your present state. Shall I admit it, not hiding anything, that I've been given much cord to twist again. What a bitch you are! Excuse my language. I employ it on certain occasions *to bury my feelings which are apt to prove too much for me at times.*[4]

Well here's something which I think will make you laugh: imagine, chère amie, that I've brought back an alligator from my jungle expedition — an enormous one such as no longer exists in our times, enormous as the step of a staircase!

This takes your breath away really for once. (I see your scandalised face from here: "What a vulgar outburst!")

1. Written in English.
2. Written in English.
3. Baudelaire.
4. Written in English.

*I killed it with my little rifle and if you are very good[5]* (as you would say), *you shall have a purse made out of it for your birthday present!*

Do you know that you have ceased to be a reality for me? You are so far away that it seems to me you have never existed outside of my dreams. You are a mirage which recedes to the degree that one approaches to it. Speaking about mirages, I saw a very beautiful one in the Suez Canal at the mouth of the Red Sea. I was gazing with distracted eye at the desert which stretches out to infinity, the intense implacable sun gleaming as a furnace, a camel marching with great unequal steps towards the south — when suddenly I recall letting out a loud cry: "See over there, the trees, the water?"

One looks: it seems then that a lake encircled by date trees and leafy shrubs, incredibly blue and seductive, had passed unobserved. Immediately we rush to the maps, snatch up the spectacles, then all together to the Captain, who, high up in his cabin is stretched out in a sultry posture. "What is that lake which glitters in the distance, so blue, so solitary?"

The Captain descends, grumbling, directs his telescope towards the Egyptian shore: "That, ladies, that is quite simply a mirage!" and he returns to his quarters, still shaking with his habitual healthy and vulgar laughter.

Myself, I remain for a long time leaning on the balustrade with dreaming eyes. I seemed to see so many things in this reality which, after all, was only a mirage.

5. Written in English.


LETTER No. 3

(Undated) 1918

My beautiful,

Because there's no getting away from the fact that you are beautiful. I become inarticulate when I look at you — at the splendid ivory column of your neck, of your eyes like smouldering jewels, at your mouth with its voluptuously chiselled lips, palely red, like some fading wine stain.

I may be writing rubbish, but then I am drunk. Drunk with the beauty of my Mitya! All today I was incoherent. I tell you, there is a barbaric splendour about you that conquered not only me, but everyone who saw you. You are made to *conquer,* Mitya, not to be conquered. You were *superb.* You could have the world at your feet. Even my mother, who is not easily impressed, shared my opinion. *You have also changed,* it appears? They said, this evening after you had gone, that you were like a dazzling Gypsy. My sister's words, not mine. A Gypsy potentate, a sovereign — what you will, but still a Gypsy.

They also said they noticed a new exuberance in you, something akin to sheer animal spirits — that never was there before. You may love me, Mitya, but anyone would be *proud* to be loved by you, even if they were to be thrown aside and forgotten — for somebody new.

Everyone is vulgar, petty, "mesquin,"[1] beyond all words, in comparison with you. It would be an unpardonable *impudence* to limit you to one life, one love, one interest. Yours are *all* lives, *all* loves, *all* interests! Beloved, my beautiful, I have shown myself naked to you, mentally, physically and morally.

Good God alive! No one in this earth has as much claim to you as I have. *No one in this world.*

Yours, Lushka

1. Paltry

LETTER NO. 4

June 5, 1918

Mer Dmitri,

I adored the letter you wrote me "from the woods" — the only long letter I have ever had from you. Don't you think you might make a *habit* of such letters? I treasured it up till yesterday afternoon, then *"degusté"*[1] it, slowly and voluptuously.

The description of Julian I thought most adequate.[2] You say it's not like you! It *is* you, word for word, trait for trait. I laughed long and

1. Tasted.
2. Julian is Vita in the novel *Challenge.*

uproariously over the part where you said, all people worshipped him *without his* being conscious. *Signiferait-il que tu commences à t'ap-précier?*[3] Let me think you do, at all events, and I shall not have lived in vain.

I must say I should like either a more *detailed* description of Julian's appearance whereas hitherto you have confided yourself more to the impression it produced on other people. "Julian was tall," let us say, and "flawlessly proportioned." The proposed height of the Greek athlete is alleged to have been 5ft 10in, but Julian surpassed this by at least two inches. Julian's hair was black and silky. Eve found herself wondering what it would feel like to stroke, and promptly did so; she was amazed to feel a sensation akin to pain shoot up her fingers and lodge itself definitely in the region of her heart. However she was de-termined to analyse Julian's beauty, feature by feature, and as he lay stretched full-length in the grass, thinking — what! We wondered uneasily — here was an opportunity not to be neglected.

"How graceful he was, how young, how strong! Eve studied the recumbent figure with eyes in which lay something like a grudging caress. Yet she hated herself for finding him beautiful, for beautiful he undoubtedly was. How resentfully she probed those heavily lidded eyes, green in repose, black in anger, even smouldering with some fet-tered impulse. She wondered: will Julian ever let himself go? Will he ever fling all reticence to the winds? Will he know what it is to experience the soul-scarring emotions of love and hatred? Then, abruptly, her gaze fastened itself on his mouth. She was conscious of a slight tremor: — that mouth, nothing if not classical — with its rather full underlip, was not the mouth of austerity, of abstention. No, it was a sensual mouth, and its sensuality was enhanced, not dimin-ished, by the strongly moulded chin, with its cleft in it.

"Eve, often to tease Julian, told him he looked like a Gypsy, but she was later to admit that his wonderful 'apricot' colouring was one of his chief merits. How like a young Hermes he was, pagan, impersonal, indifferent . . . and a wave of unaccountable despondency swept over her. She felt very futile and inexperienced."

How will that do? I haven't written carefully, but it's more or less

3. Does this signify that you are beginning to appreciate yourself?

what I want to convey. I'll write it over again properly, if you like. It's too wonderful, writing about you . . . Darling, I adore you. You're getting too exciting for words.

LETTER No. 5 (*extract*)

August 14, 1918

Oh Mitya, I want to see you. I want to hear your voice. I want to put my hand on your shoulder and cry my heart out. Mitya, Mitya, I have never told you the whole truth. You shall have it now: I have loved you all my life, a long time without knowing, 5 years knowing it as irrevocably as I know it now, loved you as my ideal, my inspiration, my perfection.

Ah, Mitya, and you think it is a flirting fickle thing. And I am telling you the truth, as though I only had another hour of life in which to tell it to you. And the supreme truth is this: *I can never be happy without you.* I am nothing without you. Ah, I want you, my Mitya, my own. I would be quite content to live on terms of purely platonic friendship with you — provided we were *alone* and *together* — for the rest of my days. Now you know everything. You are the *grande passion* of my life. How gladly would I sacrifice *everything* to you — family, friends, fortune, *everything.* What could I care as long as we could be together?

LETTER No. 6

(Probably 1918)
Thursday

It amuses me to continue my indiscreet correspondence with you! Tho' to be accurate, it is not so much indiscreet as speculative and analytical. Still, I don't see why it should be a one-sided affair — in other words, why you should not answer the letters I write to you, when I *should* be writing others most imperatively concerning my personal welfare? But then, as you know, I have few scruples, and (thank god) no responsibilities!

In the generous empire of your affections, you must — and surely have! — alloted me one *tiny* province — say, not larger than the republic of San Marino (over which I have sovereign and undisputed sway, untrammelled by any browbeating constitution — where I can have my tiny say in the affairs of your empire, and a tiny voice in the thunder of your parliament?

You play a very strange and important role in my life. You have grown up with me; we have been children together: consequently you are always there, you have always been "there" — you are as immutable as the mountains, as reliable as the seasons! (until this morning!)

Sometimes I feel with you as a wild and wanton child, but nonetheless with an eradicable reverence for your superior wisdom: a fond and foolish child, rifling the world for new and wondrous toys to lay at your feet. A boastful, reckless child, forever on its mettle, because it is being "dared" to accomplish the impossible, to climb the notchless trees, to jump the 7-foot hurdle. I come to you and I say: "See what I've done! So and so, who has the reputation of being the most fascinating man in England, has fallen in love with me!" Or, "To prove to you what I am capable of, I have surpassed all the students of the Slade!" — or a dozen other things equally fond and foolish!

I wonder if our mutual biographers will know how much of my career to attribute to your unconscious influence?

The only real beauty is to be found in the simplest things — nothing elaborate can ever be beautiful. God forgive that real beauty should ever pass me by unrecognized. I was thinking yesterday at the Slade that here was real beauty: dozens of minds all intent on the pursuit of art, all striving to the utmost of their ability to ensnare beauty, and the pursuit of art, however unsuccessful is always beautiful.

Then I saw people in their true perspective and they all seemed vulgar and uninspired and the meanest drawing there was worth more than all their thoughts and endeavours.

The only two things that matter are love and beauty — beauty of character as well. There are some exceedingly unbeautiful things in my character: lies and deceit which are as morally ugly as a squint and a hunchback — just as unsymmetrical and disfiguring. So is gossip and snobbishness and bigotry. They are equivalent to a crooked nose, a harelip, and a receding chin! No, the beautiful, free, godlike things are passion and enterprise, courage and impatience, generosity and forgiveness!

Heaven preserve us from all the sleek and dowdy virtues, such as punctuality, conscientiousness, fidelity and smugness! What great man was ever constant? What great queen was ever faithful? Novelty is the very essence of genius and always will be. If I were to die tomorrow, think how I should have lived!

With this last Swinburnian transport, I must end this letter. Don't you think it is entitled to an answer? If not, this will be the last of the series!!!

V.

LETTER NO. 7 (*extract*)

(Probably 1918)

This afternoon I steeped myself in music *pour revivre,* and to forget (a contradiction in terms). The medium was a pianola, but one excused that, it was so well played . . . O my dear, there is nothing in this world to equal music: *"la raison est trop faible, et trop pauvres les mots."*[1] alas! for her sister arts — they are nowhere in comparison.

I listened to Grieg, elflike, mischievous, imaginative, romantic — so Latin sometimes despite his Norwegian blood . . . You would love Grieg. You would love the *saccadé*[2] rhythm of Anitra's dances, and the grotesque horror of "In der Halle des Bergkonigs." In the fairyland of music, Grieg plays gnome to Debussy's magician . . .

Then I listened to Debussy, and almost reeled to hear the beauty of *La Mer* (so like Irkutsk) and his *Petite Suite* — which is an epitome of XVIII Century gallantry, joyousness, and impudence. O my darling, I could make you love Debussy as much as I do *myself,* only it would

1. "Reason is too weak and words too poor."
2. Abrupt, jerky.

take time. Then with an epicureanism worthy of Marius, I selected Brahms, the wild, the "exultant" the free — *your* musician, par excellence. Indeed I played *you* into everything, or almost everything I heard. But you are *not Debussy.* I think we agreed that Debussy was the McEvoy of music, and you are not McEvoy.

O God, I have just spoken to you on the telephone. I wish you had not rung me up, it was agony hearing your voice. This time last week — it does not bear thinking of.

. . . I think the combined agony of love and music has completely unhinged me! Music has pressed all the beauty out of Heaven, and all the torture out of Hell — everything else is just drab and meaningless.

*Je t'aime.* Please write me pages and pages. I need them so badly.

LETTER No. 8

March 28, 1919

Mitya,

I am so miserable and I realise miserably and despairingly how imperfect are all human relationships, even the most ideal — how incomplete and unsatisfying . . .

The only real joy resides in *things,* not people — people always fall short in the end — no one more than myself. The only real *beauty* is to be found in things, in nature, in the changing seasons, in art, in music, and poetry. Outside these no real beauty exists. Love is the most overrated institution in the universe. The only really happy people are the egoists — who give nothing and receive nothing, or the egoists in art, who live in and for art alone. The more selfish you are, the happier you are. It doesn't pay to be unselfish.

Or if you can't afford to be completely selfish, steep yourself in some occupation and live for it and it alone.

O the ideal, the ideal love, I long for it, Mitya! How I've searched for it all through my life — you don't know — and I shall never find it, because it is not to be found on this earth. The completely and utterly Beautiful that humanity has always groped for and will continue to grope for — in vain.

Music brings one very near, I think!

It is not to be found in someone else. It is to be found in divine fragments — in ourselves. This sounds contrary to what I have just said, but it isn't. I meant complete *Beauty* is not to be found here on earth, but complete Beauty exists *somewhere,* and these fragments of it exist in each one of us, these fragments that go to make up one huge and absolutely perfect mosaic.

Each artist and each poet contributes fragments, but the average person is born and goes through life without even suspecting their existence . . . O Mitya, the waste and the futility . . . What is the good of love? Look at me, what good does it do me? I feel stupid and half dead. O Mitya, I am so unhappy — *phénix je te cherche, et ne trouve point.*[1]

1. Phoenix, I look for you and find you not.

LETTER No. 9

(Undated) 1919

Men tiliche,

I have been talking all the evening about Paris — Paris when we first arrived there — Knoblock's flat[1] — O Mitya! It makes me drunk to remember it, and the hoard of days, weeks and months we had ahead of us.

I shall never forget the mad exhilaration of the nights I spent wandering about with Julian as long as I live! Even Monte Carlo was not better. As good, but not better. It makes my brain reel to remember! The night we went to the Palais Royal and the night we went to *"La Femme et le Pantin"*[2] were the happiest in my life. I was simply drunk with happiness. We were just bohemians, Julian and I, with barely enough to pay for our dinner, free, without a care or a relation in the world. O god! I was happy! I thought it would never come to an end. I was madly, insatiably in love with you.

Julian was a poet *sans sou ni maille*[3]: I was Julian's mistress. One

1. Edward Knoblock, well-known playwright, author of *Kismet.*
2. *The Woman and the Puppet.*
3. Without a penny.

day Julian would write great poetry and make money — but, *en attendant,* we just had enough to live on. I worshipped Julian. The Paris of François Villon, *Louise, La Bohème,* Alfred de Musset, all jumbled up, lay at our feet: we were part of it, essentially.

As much part of it as the hairy concierge and the *camelots* who wear canvas shoes and race down the boulevards nasally screaming, "La Petue! La Presse!" and "La Femme et le Pantin." I lay back in an abandonment of happiness and gave myself up to your scandalously indiscreet caresses, in full view of the whole theater!

Not ladylike perhaps! But then I had never known what it was like to be a lady!

Then we drove back in the dark taxi, and the chauffeur smiled knowingly and sympathetically at you. I'm sure he thought: *"C'est pas souvent qu'ils doivent se payer ça, pauvres petits . . ."*[4] Then the flat, the deserted, unutterably romantic Palais Royal, Julian's impatience, Julian's roughness, Julian's clumsy, fumbling hands . . . My God! I can't bear to think of it!

Mitya . . . Mitya . . . How I adored you! Our life, our blessed bohemian life! It *can't* be at an end! It can't. It *can't.* I love you as feverishly, as passionately as I did then. I love you with a passion that only increases, never diminishes.

As Professor Ross[5] said to me tonight, you are made for passion, your perfectly proportioned body, your heavy-lidded brooding eyes, your frankly sensual mouth and chin. You are made for it and so am I.

I said to Professor Ross that I thought you were one of the most moral people I knew. He spat with derision: "Pah! With that mouth, with that chin. With those antecedents! Tell me another!" (Professor Ross cheered me up considerably while he was here.)

My beautiful, my lovely, I want you so.

These are the best years of your life. Soon you will be thirty. Youngish, but no longer young, then thirty-eight, forty, middle-aged.

What will you have to show for your lost youth, your fading beauty, no longer exuberant and magnetic, but hard and austere and expressionless? You who might have been, who might still be! one of the

---

4. "It's not often that they must pay this [taxi fare], poor kids."
5. Denison Ross.

*greatest* figures of your century — A George Sand, a Catherine of Russia, a Helen of Troy, Sappho!

Listen to my voice, Mitya, for once I'm not thinking only of us. All the sublime, the magnificent figures of history hold out their hands to you. Nature and youth and joy of living, all supremely for you — everybody, even here in London, acknowledges and clamours for the outer manifestations of your tremendous potentialities. You're huge, Mitya, blindingly beautiful and gifted. The world is tiny, Mitya, the world is at your feet.

By the world, I mean the world of Art — the other world doesn't even count. You don't belong to the other world. You *owe* yourself to the world of art, the world of colour, of adventure, of enterprise, of hazard, of free love.

The other world doesn't matter a row of pins. Dozens of immaculate ordinary people will fulfill your functions in the ordinary everyday world. *Nobody* can take the place you would fill in the world of Art.

You know I am speaking the truth — Mitya. I want you for myself, but I *want you also for History.* I want you for *Immortality.*

I want you for History as a person who has written dazzlingly and lived dazzlingly.

> "Come to us, we've waited so long for you.
> We'll make life a wonderful song for you."

Cast aside the drab garments of respectability and convention, my beautiful Bird of Paradise, they become you not. Lead the life Nature intended you to lead. Otherwise, Mitya, you'll be a failure — you, *who* might be among the greatest, the most scintillating and romantic figures of all time, you'll be "Mrs. Nicolson, who has written some charming verse. She is daughter of the — ? Lord Sackville (forgive my ignorance), and often appears in charity matinées."

LETTER NO. 10

March 30, 1919

Men tiliche,

Determined to waste no time, I attacked the object I had in view in the train yesterday — with the most unexpected and deplorable results! I prefer to tell you verbally exactly what I said, but the outcome of it was that "Loge"[1] said he would romandimae[2] on any terms I choose to make, that he would consent to *anything* rather than that I should leave him. He said if I left him he would kill himself. He said I only had to tell him exactly what I wanted and it should be done. He gave me his word of honour as a *gentleman, never* to do anything that should displease me — you know in what sense I mean. What *am* I to do? What can I say?? There is only one thing to be done, that is to run away without saying anything to anybody.

Wretched Loge! He cares for me drivelingly — his one *chic* was that I thought he didn't!

Men tiliche, you must not be angry with me because I am going to have another try today. I swear that I am doing everything in my power — *ce n'était déjà pas mal*[3] what I achieved in the train? . . .

I have just got a letter from him confirming in writing all that he said yesterday. I will show it to you. Mitya, it is all so dreadful.

The last time I was here there was the dazzling possibility of going abroad — the grey skies and dead leaves didn't matter then. I knew I would soon be leaving them behind for ever. And I return here after four months and nothing has changed: there are still the grey skies and dead leaves . . .

The crows are cawing in the naked fields and there is winter everywhere, harsh and unrelenting — without and within.

I say to myself: Have I dreamed? And for a second I see almost sapphire blue skies, great luscious palms, houses of a dazzling whiteness, our fig-coloured sea, and the flippant, *bariolé*[4] and delirious crowds? . . .

1. Denys Trefusis.
2. Violet and Vita's word, signifying to marry.
3. Already it's not bad.
4. Gaudy, variegated.

(Is it possible that I have left such a place for this?)

It is snowing outside, insolently, shamelessly . . . An icy wind goes shrieking through the house . . . The doors slam and the windows rattle . . . I shut my eyes: it begins again, like the echo of a far-distant tune . . . I see orange groves and orchards almost in full bloom, swarthy Italian workmen singing hoarsely and jubilantly with brown throats and little coral amulets on their watchchains . . . I see women in summer clothes and children in absurd hats . . . And everywhere, the sun, the sun, the sun! Everything stupid and drenched and drowned in sunlight! . . . Something burst suddenly and sickeningly, and I realise with a grasp of pain how happy I was in this place, and worst of all, I see you, Mitya, beautiful and exuberant, glowing with youth and health and happiness . . .

Lushi! *Lush!* Why don't you answer when I speak to you? Come and give me a kiss at once! No, not like that! . . . A proper kiss! What do you *mean* by not kissing me when I tell you to? And all the time a voice is singing — but so far away I can hardly catch the words . . . Yes, I can . . . just! . . . And I think that's all that remains of the happiest moments of my life . . .

LETTER NO. 11

April 27, 1919

I have read your letter once again — your letter written in the same handwriting as when you were fourteen, and I was twelve . . .

The same beloved handwriting that thrilled me even as a child. Almost blinded by tears, I seemed to see all the letters you had ever written me — those when you were fourteen were shy and tender and confiding. At 16, alas! they had already begun to be indifferent, cautious, and undemonstrative: but there were one or two cherished exceptions which I knew by heart almost: at 18 and 19, they were no longer regular, your letters. They were few and far between, hurried and noncommittal, but with a stray sentence here and there which betrayed that *malgré tout,* you had not forgotten . . . They got less and less personal, finally when you were 21, they were social arrangements. Then they ceased . . .

For four long years they ceased . . .

A year ago they began again. The one you wrote me after we had returned from Polperro began: "My darling" . . . I thanked God, and thought to die with gratitude. And since, ah, Mitya! . . . How wonderful they have been! They have been love letters, from *you,* from the same you whom I loved as a child, who wrote to me when you were fourteen — the same little neat, symmetrical writing . . . Practically all my life I have known it: it has grown up with me, with me it went into long skirts and with me put its hair up, figuratively speaking. Familiar and adored.

My God! Mitya! How could I think of losing you forever? Had you only been a friend whom I had known from my childhood upwards, the loss would be well nigh unendurable, but as things are — I am half crazy. I miss you so — and most vivid and most cruel, try as I will, every five minutes or so, I see our journey in France. I remember every detail of it, and it seems I must cry out with pain. It hurts like anything. How do lovers continue to remain apart? How do they stand it?

Always you have been in my life, always my ideal, my inspiration.

"The most beautiful person I have ever known," "the cleverest person I knew," "the dearest." You were as much part of me as my arm or my hand. Does your own hand turn against you? I am being stunned and maimed by blows from my own hand. I am bewildered and terrified. How do I know that it won't kill me? What can I do to abate its blind destructiveness? It is not as though I had known you for a short time. All my life you have been there. I remember your saying the first time I went to C. Malet,[1] "We may be separated for a bit, even for a year, but all through our lives we will always come back to each other."

And you threatened to leave me forever!

What have I done to you, Mitya, except love you? What have I done, except dedicate my whole existence to you?

1. Château Malet, the villa near Monte Carlo Lady Sackville leased.

Darling, I look at your letter again, and I remember the copy book I have got of yours when you were little, and wrote about wrestling with the hall boy in the same writing.

And I think, how could someone whom I knew as a child, who has grown up with me and shared my life do me such a terrible infamy?

I am simply racked with pain. I think of your journey to Paris with *someone else*,[2] the intimacy it implies, and I wish I had never been born. Was there ever happiness in this world? I doubt it. Yet, if anyone was happy, *I* was happy. You made me happy. Isn't it dreadful to realise that with one word you could restore all my happiness. You could raise me from the dead so to speak.

Never was there such power given to human being either to absolutely shatter somebody else's life or to make flawlessly and sublimely happy, not only happy, but successful, splendidly high and generous, and a poet.

That power is in your hands. I neither blame nor reproach you, Mitya. All I ask is a little mercy. Don't come away with me, but oh!, merciful God, *don't leave me*. Don't give me up. Don't drop me. It's not too much to ask.

Have pity.

2. Harold Nicolson.

LETTER NO. 12 (*extract*)

April 30, 1919

O Mitya,

I've been dreaming such beastly dreams about you all night. I need hardly tell you they were jealous ones. I woke up very early and have been reading Rupert Brooke's letters ever since. They're so delicious, Mitya. I make this paragraph personal, from a letter of his to Violet Asquith:

> I suppose you're rushing from lunch party to lunch party, and dance to dance, and opera to political platform. Won't you come and learn how to make a hibiscus wreath for your hair, and sail a canoe, and swim two minutes under water catching turtles, and dive forty feet into a waterfall, and climb a cocoanut palm. It's more worth while.

LETTER NO. 13

May 2, 1919

I've just been to *Ivan*[1] with Loge's adamantine family. I *hate* them, Mitya. I came to that conclusion this evening. I hate their overbred appearances, their academic mind, their musical aloofness and superiority, their inflexible point of view, their incredible *pride,* their extreme reserve and insurmountable indifference, their lack of humour, and — let it be faced! — total absence of any outward manifestation of humanity!

My poor Mitya! and it's what I reproach you for! Apparently, to be human is an extraordinarily rare thing. Being intensely, almost vulgarly human myself, I had never realised it! *They* think it indecent to display any enthusiasm about anything, except music, and then — Oh! Mitya! It's not *our* music! It's things we should never, never like, or understand.

I hate them. I would like to tweak their aristocratic noses. I would like to tear their immaculate clothes from off their backs. I would like to give them penny dreadfuls to read, and make them listen to *Helen of Troy* for 4 hours a day on the gramophone!

I'm trying to find the dominating adjective for them, because they're not exactly *bien,* or prigs — no, certainly not prigs — or old-fashioned — no! It's *aloofness,* that's what it is, sheer artistic aloofness. "Yes, *you* love and hate, but good God! *we* would never dream of doing anything as common as that, and if we did we wouldn't dream to show it for worlds!" That's why I hate them. They were unutterably disgusted because I cried at *Ivan.*

O my sweet, my sweet, how I miss you. How I *longed* for you at the opera.

Do you know what would happen to me if I married one of them? I should dry up. I could never be natural, I could never be emotional, I could never confess I like sensuous things. He has already admitted he thinks my enthusiasms puerile and rather silly! And as they have their root in the innermost depths of my being, you know what it would

---

1. Refers to Glinka's opera *A Life for the Tsar,* about Ivan Susanin, a peasant who sacrifices his own life to save the Tsar.

cost me to suppress them, and to merely say I "liked" a thing when it fills me with rapture. I *hate* them, Mitya, and sometimes I hate *him*. I should be miserable with him. I feel trapped and desperate.

This morning, in despair, I went to see Pat[2] — she is going to try to find a way out. She wasn't in so I followed her to the rooms of Mr Berkeley. I had to go up in a lift like the one at the Windsor Hotel[3] — with ropes. I felt suddenly sick when I remembered that the last time I went up in one was *là-bas, tout là-bas, au beau pays bleu*[4] — and how you loved working it yourself, and how when *I* went up alone, I always found you rather impatiently waiting on the third floor generally in a hurry because you wanted to go to the Casino!

I have succeeded in putting off the romandinado[5] for a fortnight — *c'est toujours ça de gagné*[6] . . . *Tous les jours il se meurt quelque chose en moi.*[7]

2. Pat (Margaret) Dansey, niece of Lord Fitzhardinge of Berkeley Castle.
3. At Monte Carlo.
4. There [Monte Carlo], over there in the beautiful blue land.
5. To marry: Violet sent the following telegram to Vita then in Paris (May 5): MARRIAGE POSTPONED LAST NIGHT TILL BEGINNING JULY SHATTERED BY YOUR LETTER IMPLORE MAKE ALLOWANCES FOR GREAT UNHAPPINESS AND DETESTABLE CHARACTER PLEASE WIRE ON RECEIPT OF THIS SAYING YOU'LL COME BACK NEXT WEEK DON'T READ MY LETTERS — KEPPEL.
6. It's always something gained . . .
7. Every day something in me dies.

LETTER NO. 14 (*extract*)

May 6, 1919

. . . In the evening I read a book called *The Moon and Sixpence* by Somerset Maugham, which I thought quite excellent.

You must read it. I cut a critique of it out of a paper to send you, but I expect it to be lost — irretrievably, by now.

I won't tell you anything about it, except that it is my theory put into practise: namely, that if a man's a great artist, that it doesn't matter *how* he lives his private life, or how many lives he sacrifices to his own egoism, that it is wrong and unnatural to judge such a person by our own (yours, not mine) miserable standard of right and wrong.

Such things simply don't exist for a person of that calibre. Darling, there are several conversations in that book that might be ours — *ni plus ni moins*[1] — between the artist and a person who hasn't really, but tried to assume, the moral being — not that I wish to compare my despicable self with an artist, let alone a great one, but it is the artistic temperament *que y est pour quelque chose*[2] — and I think I may lay claim to a fair share of that.

And the friend talks, and he talks, and he piles it on: "Then, isn't it monstrous to leave her in this fashion after seventeen years of married life without a fault to find with her?"

"Monstrous," says the artist benignly . . .

1. Neither more nor less.
2. Which counts for something.

LETTER NO. 15

May 31, 1919

Darling

Much as I dislike it, I find it my duty to send you extracts from all the papers. You can draw your own conclusions. You might forward it to your Mother.

"She worships the ground he treads on; they mean to have an old-fashioned family? . . ."    HOME CHAT

"They were observed during Tuesday night at the Ritz: neither spoke."    LONDON OPINION

"It is very pleasant to note in these callous times that Major Trefusis and Miss Keppel have decided on a house that contains large well-ventilated nurseries."    BANGKOK BOURGEOIS

"Is there any truth in the rumour that a certain society bride intends to elope on her wedding day with a dark-eyed stranger?"
    "Things We Want to Know," LONDON MAIL

"I was much touched on my way through the park at seein' Miss Keppel (who is, of course, known as 'Birdie' to her friends) in blue gabardine over the dinkiest of pink petties, sittin' hand in hand with her 'future' O

they have exchanged hats — quite a touch of old Hampstead, what,
Betty?"                                              "Letters of Eve," TATLER

"I'm told things don't half hum in London town. Of course, there's no
doubt about it that Miss V .... t K .... l lived with the G .... St. chef
for three years previous to her engagement to Major T ...., and
that she had much difficulty in housing her large and obtrusive family."
Aunt Tiare in "Where Things are Hot"              TAHITI TIMES


LETTER NO. 16

June 12, 1919
(four days before marriage)


I make a resolution: I will write the most mad, obscene, relentless book
that ever startled the world. It shall be more than a book. It shall be
all passion, insanity, drunkenness, filth, sanity, purity, good and evil
that ever fought and struggled in human anguish. It shall be more
than a book. It shall be the eternal strife between Good and Evil. It
shall be Truth.

There can be no genius without truth. Genius *is* truth — truth as it
appears, violent and irresistible and inevitable to the artist. Light has
broken on me. The whole humanity finds its echo in me, bought
through pain. Thank God for my own suffering.

Note: Violet's marriage to Denys Trefusis took place in London on June 16, 1919.
The following group of letters (Nos. 17-23) were written during the month following the wedding when Violet and Denys visited the Basque country.


LETTER NO. 17 (*extract*)

June 23, 1919
Ritz Hotel, Paris

SATURDAY
The most awful thing happened tonight: I went to a play at the
Vaudeville called *"Le Mari, la Femme et L'Amant."*[1] During an en-

1. *The Husband, Wife and Lover.*

tr'acte I was passing a very dark *avant-scène*.[2] I peered inside and saw the two "friends" who used to dance the tango together at Monte Carlo. They were kissing each other. You must remember them? They were inseparable.

I don't know why, that hurts more than anything has ever hurt — to think that we were apart and that they would still be together, O and that they could love each other as much as they like without anyone to say them nay. It kindled a sweet flame of desire in me: why shouldn't I be able to satisfy my passion like most people? Why must it always be quelled and restricted and curtailed? It maddens me: I see red. *Tu m'aimes; tu me dois ça . . .*[3]

SUNDAY

I was so bored at the races. O Mitya, when I am not actively unhappy, I am bored, bored — it is the only respite I get between hours of intense misery, when I think — but you know what I think. Do you know the poem by Sully Prudhomme which ends *"Des débris du palais . . . j'ai bati ma chaumière"*[4] well, that's what they're trying to make me do.

It's as though a voice were saying incessantly: your ideas are too spacious, too wide your horizon, too lofty your ideals. They must be pruned and trimmed and made to fit everyday life! You must be content with ordinary material things: try to be correct, social, affable, smooth: then all will go well with you, but not otherwise. Forget your cruel, overbearing, wild, exacting tyrannical lover. Forget all you have in common. Forget that you might have the most wonderful life in the world together! Forget that you are a poet. Forget that you are an artist. Forget that you are passionate and young and in love! Forget all these things. Try to think only of luncheon parties, clothes, luxury, social successes, flirtations. *Be small.* You who were so unlimited. It is much better: it *pays* to be small.

You who want to dedicate your whole existence to one love, don't do anything so foolish! Split your heart up into little fragments and

2. Stage box.
3. You love me; you owe me that.
4. "From the ruins of the palace . . . I built my thatched cottage."

give each one to a different person. Substitute Deauville for Tahiti, *amourettes* for *Amour,* comfortable dilettantism for Romance, the rue de la Paix for your Petroushkalike fair, Mozart for Wagner.

I can't. I can't. I never shall as long as I live. O give me back my freedom and my *joie de vivre.* I was happy once, so irresponsible and free. What am I now? A heartbroken nonentity, a caged lark with clipped wings. I feel desperate.

Loge gets so much on my nerves I could scream! so does this empty-headed pointless existence, the banality of which is eating into my soul. I counted the number of cigarettes he has smoked today: up til now, he has smoked 19.

LETTER No. 18 (*extract*)

Golf Hotel, St Jean de Luz
July 1919

At last I got a letter from you this morning. I hadn't heard since Friday, I quite agree with all you say about us, darling, but I cannot feel your serenity. How can there be serenity without contentment? How can I be contented? I see nothing but strife ahead of us. But, O! I *do* feel all you say to be true of us. You say you were at Hendaye. When were you at Hendaye and with whom?

Mitya, you don't know to what a pitch I have brought my truthfulness with L. This is the sort of conversation that takes place constantly:

L: What are you thinking about?
Me: V
L: Do you wish V. were here?
Me: Yes
L: (All this actually happened.) You don't care much about being with men, do you?
Me: No, I infinitely prefer women.
L: You are strange, aren't you?
Me: Stranger than you have any idea of.

The above conversation took place word for word last night and it is a typical one. I will *not* lie to L., save in an absolute extremity. I know the truth hurts him frightfully, but I should feel absolutely beneath contempt if I lied to him. I almost think that if he asked me point blank to tell him the whole truth from beginning to end, without omitting a single detail, I should do so. It would kill him, you know what I mean, but he is essentially a person one cannot lie to.

I have never felt the smallest scruple about lying to anyone else. Almost everything I say makes him wince, poor thing, but it is better than the other alternative. I know it is. Darling, you hold different views, don't you? And I know if you could overhear some of our conversations, you would be desperately sorry for Loge.

I will never deceive you, but *you* must never deceive me. *Tu me dois cela.* Don't think it amuses me to see L. writhe in agony sometimes. It does *not* — nothing has ever amused me less, but I know the answer to things he asks me, if it is the truthful one, will hurt terribly, and I know I would be disloyal to *mea* ———— to withhold it or to modify it in any way, so I never hesitate.

Everything is infinitely painful,
*et plus ça va, plus je t'aime.*[1]

O Mitya, you must be straight with H. about me! *You must.* It is *so* despicable to tell lies to someone who cares for one. All the time I have been here I have neither done nor said anything you could possibly have taken exception to. Are you as straight with H?

O darling, I fear not . . . *Accorde moi cela, et je me montrerai si infiniment reconnaissante*[2] . . .

I can't tell you how marvellous the sea is. It is blazing hot and there is a thunderstorm coming from the Spanish coast . . . I can hear the thunder rumbling through the mountain passes.

1. The more it is, the more I love you.
2. Grant me that, and I will show myself so infinitely grateful.

LETTER NO. 19 (*extract*)

Golf Hotel, St Jean de Luz
July 6, 1919

I love the Basques, Mitya, and all the surrounding country. It is utterly unspoilt and the peasants are completely primitive and uneducated and fierce and free. There are bears and wolves in the mountains, not many, but still a few. I am dying to go after them. You couldn't get wolves now, of course, but in remote parts of the Pyrenees, you can sometimes get a bear in the summer. You may think I am inventing, but I will show you a Basque history which confirms all I say. There are quantities of wild bear and chamois, to say nothing of vultures and eagles. The vultures are enormous here, apparently, and are constantly carrying off sheep and goats, etc.

LETTER NO. 20 (*extract*)

Golf Hotel, St Jean de Luz
Friday (July 1919)

What ages letters take from Paris and vice versa. I go for yours every morning. Yesterday morning there were 4, today, but one. Perhaps I shall get another tonight. This morning I went out and bought you a ring. There is a shop here where they sell all the stones they find in the Pyrenees: aquamarines, chrysolites, topaz, garnet, tourmaline, jacinth, etc.

O darling, I do wish you were with me — but no, there was only Loge, silent, taciturn, unresponsive. Sometimes I feel like throwing something at his head. *Il a le don de me mettre en fureur, ce type-là.*[1] He was too insufferable the whole morning.

We spent the entire day arguing. Mitya, *tu ne m'en voudras pas trop,*[2] if I go to San Sebastian (which is only 34 kilometres) for a day or two? There at least I shall be able to get away from Loge as much as I like. Here it is impossible as there are practically no shops and

---

1. He has the gift of putting me into a temper, that fellow.
2. You would not reproach me too much.

there is absolutely nothing to do. I should go mad if I had to stay here another week. I can imagine no more ideal place for an uninterrupted *tête-à-tête* with someone one loved. — hélas.

Darling, how happy we should be here! The Pyrenees would smile instead of frown — and you would love the Basque peasants. They wear berets like the chasseurs *alpins* and they are so good looking *à la manière espagnole:* lean, brown-skinned, blue-eyed, tight-lipped: ascetic-looking men, and women with equally brown skins, flashing white teeth, and delicious hair growing in a peak, low on their foreheads. Half the population speaks nothing but Basque — an entirely uncomprehensible and extremely guttural language of which I only know one rather characteristic morbid little sentence, which you see written over every church door: *"bun guzek dute gizone kolkatzen askenekdak du Hobireat egoitzen,"* — which means: *"Toute heure blesse l'homme, la demain le tue."*[3]

3. "Each hour wounds Man, the last kills him."

LETTER NO. 21

Gr. Hotel Eskualduna
Hendaye,
July 8, 1919

I am alternately miserable, heartbroken, cynical, disillusioned, apathetic, resentful, then miserable again, jealous, despairing, listless — then, my inexorable temperament reasserts itself! All the rest is temporarily swept aside.

LETTER NO. 22 ( *extract* )

Continental Palace,
San Sebastian
( Undated ) July 1919

Here I am in your country, Mitya, and in the country of your language. In the morose, bigoted, recalcitrant country my whole heart goes out to! In the superb, infinitely contemptuous country, that cares not for foreigners, or what foreigners think of her, *qui ne fait jamais de frais,*[1] if you want to get to know her, *she* won't make friendly advances. No, it's up to you! Then, for those who get to know her, what marvellous surprises she has up her sleeve!

You think her cold and disdainful, but wait until she loves you! Then she throws off her austere mantle of bleached sierras and lonely plains. O Mitya! She is no longer cold and indifferent. Her lips are red and smiling. She wears a red carnation in her hair. She holds a fan in her hand. Her feet begin to dance, *malgré elle.*[2] The sierras and bleakness have disappeared. Pomegranates and oranges, and the most passionate landscape in the world have taken their place — Andalucia!

O Mitya, and Spain is so much *you!*

Spain is you, you, you! Proud and silent, and unforthcoming till — you love!

Though I don't know Spain very well, I love Spain *passionately!*

How common Italy looks by the side of Spain. How banal! Just a cocotte . . . A pretty cocotte, I grant you, but no wonder Spain cuts her . . . I miss you so — never have you seemed so vivid. I feel like a person who has gone into a house whilst the owner is absent . . .

1. Who never makes an effort.
2. In spite of herself.


LETTER NO. 23

Ritz Hotel, Paris
July 14, 1919


URGENT

I am back in Paris, which I look upon now as a prison, Mitya. In the Paris that once represented all that was most delicious in life: love, and *joie de vivre,* and freedom.

I shall never forget my joy on arriving in Paris last November: *c'était le comble de tous mes voeux,*[1] to be in Paris, the place I have loved most since I was a child! It was the happiest day of my life.

1. It was the consummation (summit) of all my wishes.

Then the deterioration, the gradual, inexorable deterioration of circumstances began. We were here, but not alone in March . . . Then,
the other day, with the circumstances of November exactly and abomi-
nably reversed. In November we had been together. L. was then a
casual friend, an outsider. He lunched and dined with us — our guest.
The other day, *outwardly,* the positions were reversed. *You* were the
guest, the visitor — O, my God, the irony of it! And now worst of all,
I am in Paris, alone with him.

I doubt if I can get back tomorrow: they say the train is packed.
O God knows, I will move Heaven and Earth to get away from the
mockery of a place, this bitter travesty of all I thought inspired and
beautiful.

Of all the unhappiness that has come upon us, Mitya, I always look
upon Paris as one of the hardest things to bear.

It is such a desecration!

Paris was one of my brightest divinities: Paris could do no wrong
— other places might have feet of clay, but Paris couldn't.

Paris was sacred, and perfection — Mitya, you'll never know, all the
tenderness I have never had for any human being I lavished on Paris.
Paris had always been beautiful in my eyes; last November, she became
sublime.

Paris and Julian . . . Julian and Paris . . . *la vie de Bohème* . . .
not a responsibility in the world . . . I thought then vaguely that
someday I might live here with Julian . . . that we might have a tiny
flat in *le rive gauche* . . . oh! Not at once! An attic to start with.
We would work. I would make Julian happy . . . No sacrifice should
be too great . . . We would be young and poor and desperately in
love with each other . . . artists . . . free.

And now, God forgive you, Mitya! I have lost Julian. I am no
longer an artist, and I have lost my freedom! *C'est un crime ce que tu
as fait là, en plus, au moins.*[2] Put yourself in my place . . .

2. It's a crime what you've done in this.

LETTER NO. 24

Quidenham,[1] Attleborough
August 5, 1919

O God! It does seem strange to be back here! The last time I was here I was seventeen — *que de chose se sont passé depuis lors*[2] . . .

This place brings back all my childhood to me. The days of birds nesting, red Indians, bed at 8:30, hide and seek, Saturday evenings, historical charades (in which Betty always contrived to play the part of Richelieu), endless dressing up, and "consequences" played after tea . . .

Hence a slight soppiness for this grim, austere, un-*gemutlich*[3] house, and a more pronounced soppiness for the generations of stupid, pig-headed, truculent, talented Keppels who have lived here.

Here in my room they look down on me reproachfully: William Anne,[4] fat, and sallow, and Dutch; Elizabeth Caroline, powdered and "pimpante" and Georgian, Augustus,[5] pointing to a beautifully symmetrical fleet on a marcel waved sea. Arnold Joost — the dandy![6] In his curled periwig, begartered robes and red-heeled shoes! And, oh Mitya! In all that stiff and dignified assembly, Louise[7] suddenly thrusts her roguish ringlets, extremely *décolletée* mustard-coloured satin dress, gleaming white shoulders and sensuous red mouth, with its rather prominent under lip (like Mitya's). Her tapering Lely[8]-white (O

1. Keppel family residence, owned by George Keppel's (Violet's father's) elder brother, the Earl of Albemarle, "Uncle Arnold."
2. What a lot has happened since.
3. *Gemiutlich* (German) suggests a cozy homy *petit bourgeois* style. Quidenham was quite the contrary.
4. See p. 10.
5. See p. 10.
6. See p. 10.
7. Louise-Renee de Penacoet de Kerouaille, personage who fascinated Violet and the ancestress through whom she liked to trace her descent from the Medici. Louise (1647–1735) was the Demoiselle d'honneur to Henriette d'Angleterre, Duchesse d'Orleans, and accompanied this princess on a visit to her brother, Charles II, in 1670. She became Charles II's mistress and was created Duchess of Portland. To the English public, she represented the unpopular French alliance. By Charles II, she had a natural son, Charles Lennox, Duke of Richmond. Anne, the daughter of Charles Lennox and Louise, married William Anne Keppel, second Earl of Albemarle.
8. Sir Peter Lely, seventeenth-century portrait painter of the English aristocracy.

darling, for shame!) fingers play luxuriously with a string of grossly
inflated pearls and her grey green eyes look heavy with unexpressed
avowals . . .

> Louise was pretty,
> Louise was witty,
> Louise was a naughty girl!

She alone of all that satire looks friendly and encouraging.

SATURDAY MORNING

I slept very badly, but awoke a few minutes ago with a strange sense
of freshness: it seemed as though all the intervening years since I was
last here had slipped away: for a minute or two I felt marvellously
young and innocent (First signs of grisly kittenhood.) I had never
loved or been loved; had never bothered my head about such things.
It is a lovely spring morning, and with any luck I shall get my lessons
done by 12. Then I shall go bird nesting with Betty. (Oh, I mustn't
forget those bulseps, I promised to get her at the tuck shop in the
village.)

I dare say Uncle Arnold will give us a lump of clay and we can
mess about with it all the afternoon . . .

— Honestly, my thoughts started off quite naturally and spontane-
ously in that direction, — crash! There came the bitter realisation
of all there had been and all there was to be . . .

O! To be able to put the clock back ten years — 15, or not quite 15
— is such a delicious age.

It is so rotten to be getting middle-aged.

I like my Uncle A. I like his massiveness, stupidity, and sheer brute
strength. I like his hooked nose, like an eagle's beak, his inability to
see anyone's point of view but his own. I like his great hairy hands
with a sculptor's fingers, supersensitive for all their thickness. There
is something monumental and splendid about him; something feudal
and unshakable. O God! I know so well the sort of people who appeal
to me: the sort of people I respect and admire. And Heaven knows,
they're different from the sort of people you like. You like wit, flexi-
bility, humour (funnily enough), intelligence, and a certain amount
of mental skittishness, accessibility, sparkle, fizz, and bubble! That

sort of thing amuses me, but doesn't attract me, especially in men.
It is too like myself — I know this is immodest, but more or less true.


LETTER NO. 25

Possingworth Manor,
Blackboys, Sussex
September 9, 1919

I got the most extraordinary lackadaisical letter from you about coming here!  No doubt you will be relieved to hear that D. is here, thus
affording you an excellent pretext for not coming till next Monday . . .

Mitya, I don't know what has come over me suddenly: the most
extraordinary craving for excitement and movement that won't any
longer be gainsaid!

The old incorrigible craving for trains rushing south in the night,
the bustle of frontier stations, the blue-chinned garlic-infested porters,
the rocking, stifling wagon-restaurant, the parched southern landscape,
the sawdust-strewn cafés, the mauve-powered ladies.  And not only
that, Mitya!

I want adventure!  Adventure tremulous beneath *réverbères,* adventure, adventure high-mettled and debonaire in the sun.  Adventure
veiled and elusive in great cathedrals, wanton and provocative in the
[illegible] place, sly and surreptitious in a *baignoire,*[1] flippant and
derisive in the streets, romantic and difficult in the Earth's open places!
I want it!  I want it!  I want to share adventure with you.  I want the
carnival life, the café concert life, the studio life.  I want what M[2]
calls *"le bruyant débraillé."*[3]  I want to prowl the Earth.  I want to
dash my glove in the face of Convention.  I want to fly and sing and
dance and want every kind of new voluptuousness!  But more, fifty
times more than all these things, *man quiero tuti!*[4]

1. Theater box.
2. Violet's governess, "Moiselle."
3. "Noisy licentiousness."
4. Words such as this — Violet and Vita's private language, perhaps derived
from Romany — occur frequently in the letters.  The context suggests "I love you,"
"I want you," or something of the sort.

If you don't feel as I do, leave me alone!

My brain reels when I think of what — *cheringue*[5] could be!

5. Endearment, in private language.

## LETTER NO. 26

(*Letter accompanying Violet's drawing of Eve and Julian*)

Possingworth Manor
September 23, 1919

I have done a rather nice drawing of Eve and Julian. I like the contrasted angles of their bodies — don't lose it, as it has suggested an idea for the cover, which we might work out together on Monday. It is supposed to be a pendant to the one of Lushka with the billionaire![1] Isn't it exactly like Julian? It is so like Julian's length and stoop — more droop than stoop, somehow.

They are under a *réverbère*[2] and in Paris. He is trying to light a cigarette, and she is pulling him back to look at something? Bring it with you when you come . . .

Darling, sorry to be tiresome, but I *do* think the drawing might be adapted for the cover, if it were probably alone in a *décor,* other than a Paris boulevard. I think the dignity and concentration of the tall loose-limbed Julian makes such a good contrast to the waywardness and caprice of the other figure, who resents his being absorbed even in a cigarette!

Darling, please don't misunderstand me: it isn't properly drawn, but it *might* be — however, I'll do it for you when you come . . .

1. See Letter No. 34.
2. Street lamp.

## LETTER NO. 27

(Undated 1919)

O my love,

I am so sad. Another and worse separation is upon us. I feel as though it may kill me. I can't bear to go back to my poor little house deprived of your presence.

The secret of my love for Possingworth[1] is so pathetically easy to guess: it is the nearest approach we have ever had to having a house together.

I always look upon it as "our" house. And now you are going to share another house with somebody else. Your house, your life, your thoughts and your laughter. And you wonder I say it MUST be all or nothing?

Beloved, how could this sort of thing ever have produced itself indefinitely which is what would have happened had I not reached this decision? Each separation during the last three months has brought it nearer. Each time we have been forcibly parted, I have thought: this *can't* go on. O my love, my love, I feel as though my heart was breaking. To think of you separated — mercilessly separated — from me by twenty miles! only twenty miles!

We have been so divinely happy at Possingworth! We take up all our old habits again. That house is haunted by your presence, and the sound of your voice calling me.

O Mitya, no more "Lushi, where *are* you?", no more rushing after me upstairs, no more monopolizing the bath for hours.

My darling, my darling, you must *never never* break or attempt to break your promise to me as it will be the only thing which keeps me alive during this dreadful month.

Besides, I can't seriously believe you would contemplate breaking it after what I did. I have too high an opinion of you to think that. It simply wrings my heart to think of going back to an empty house — empty at least of all our love.

I implore you to impress upon me in every letter that it is the last time we shall be parted. If *ever* I seriously thought you meant to back out of your promise, I should never see you again and I should leave England as soon as possible, never to return. I promise this in all solemnity.

O my love, my love, I have waited so long. If you knew how unhappy I was!

1. Possingworth Manor, Blackboys, Sussex.

If you knew how terribly alien this dreadful and shameful life is to me. It is unworthy of my love for you. You know my views, my striving to be *clean* — well, so far from doing a wicked thing by going away, I look to it as a sort of great purging, an ablution — then *only* shall we be clean, though the means of it be very painful.

It is *not* clean for me to lie and deceive, to live in comfort and luxury (when if the truth were known we would be living on perhaps two pounds a week which we would have to work for cleanly).

It is neither clean nor honest to trick the people we know into believing we are as they are, to let the world (which can know no better till we prove our love exclusively for each other) suppose that I and you are the moral counterparts of women like D — or Maxine Elliott.[2]

It is not clean. It is filthy, abominable. If I didn't think this, I should be beneath contempt.

You say you admire moral courage. It will take tremendous moral courage to disregard the world, fight it eventually, and eventually overcome it. We must fight to prove that Love, no matter wherever it springs, is mightier than anything in the world.

That, and that alone is worthy of us. So instead of lies and deceits, miserable little intrigues, and whispers of scandal, luxury and comfort at the expense of those who would give us nothing if we left them, we would have to brave the world openly and courageously, our love for each other as supreme justification.

I will never fail you, Mitya. You will give me the greatest proof you could give me. I will dedicate my whole existence to your worship.

It is all I live for.

Always your
Lushka

2. Maxine Elliott, actress, born at Rockland, Maine, in 1871. She was celebrated for Shakespearean roles and became proprietor and manager of the Maxine Elliott Theater in New York.

LETTER NO. 28

October 10, 1919

Men tiliche,

You have gone and the sense of autumn has deepened with your going. The very trees have an added ripeness, the wind is more melancholy, the clouds more prophetic . . .

I am overwhelmed by the all-pervading sense of dissolution, finality — the sense of flight — migration of birds, winds, leaves . . . It leaves me lonely. I feel out of place, like a green leaf on a withered stem. I feel that I too must be going . . . The hunter tingles at its bridle, the hound strains at its leash . . . I, too, must be away.

I forgot to tell you, there is a Gypsy caravan not far from here . . . and a blue spiral of smoke curls insidiously around the haggard pines. . . . Also there was a tall girl, with glittering brass earrings, great tawny braids of hair, and a face as brown as a berry. She stood, her arms akimbo, scowling into space . . .

I think I will go and see if I can find them again this afternoon, but like you and everything else, they will have fled!

"Rebellion"[1] will be acclaimed as a work of genius (you have absolutely no conception how good it is). Julian (in the flesh) will be acclaimed as a junior Don Juan, (*hélas*) and I shall by then have developed into a sort of secretary drudge (expected to dust and cook as well) with no higher mission in life than to typewrite your ms. and address your love letters.

Also, you will drink, you will gamble with *my* money. You will sell *my* jewels in order to keep the Mélusines of this world in silk stockings and black onyx wristwatches! *Mais je t'adore, tout admettant que — suis bête!!*[2] At best

Also *man quiero tuti quite dreadfully.* Darling, it suddenly strikes me how terribly affected the beginning of this letter looks. I'm so sorry it just happened like that. It isn't as *voulu*[3] as you might think.

*Je t'aime si passionnément. Je suis tellement à toi.*[4]

1. Name of novel Vita was writing, later changed to *Challenge*.
2. But I adore you, still admitting that — I'm mad!
3. Intended.
4. I love you so passionately. I am so entirely yours.

LETTER NO. 29

(Undated) 1919
Possingworth Manor,
Blackboys, Sussex

You won't get this letter but it must be written.

Yesterday I flew — for the first time.

Before I went up, I thought: I have offended the gods so much and so often that they won't be able to resist this grand, blatant and picturesque opportunity *pour me renverser d'une chiquenanado* (?)[1] They'll say: "There! puny atom, that'll learn you to go messing about among your superiors!" And a little mangled heap would inevitably be the result of so much impudence. So with a wildly beating heart and the absolute conviction that I should be smashed to smithereens, a few minutes later, but not caring much either way, I clambered into the seat behind the pilot. I heard a harsh voice rapping out instructions: "Contact! Release! Contact!" The roar of the engine was such that I felt my head must split: then it was like being whisked up an interminable sky escape in jerks by the Selfridge lift (which is the fastest I know).

I shut my eyes, fearing to look down . . . the engines began to throb rhythmically like a great heart.

Then I looked.

Rip Van Winkle after his hundred years' slumber didn't feel more changed than I! My old self was dead, I knew with complete assurance and indifference — whether it would remain dead was another matter.

Between the spread planes I saw, looking down, a little map dotted with little towns, and a little sea. We were flying back — 3 thousand feet, the pilot told me afterwards — I thought: what a wretched little place the world is! Humanity had been wiped out. So had my humanity, my human relationships — I belonged to another sphere.

I suppose I was near the Gods. Near enough for the *"chiquenando."* Well, why didn't they? I was actually bearding them in their den. Only a few planks and an uncertain engine separated me from an-

---

1. To overthrow me with a flick of the fingers.

nihilation. Really it was cheek. It was doing a *pied de nez* in their faces!

Then the absolute marvel of it swept over me and inundated me with ecstasy. It was so daringly like perfection! It was so surprisingly like the fruit of the forbidden tree. Should I die for having attempted to pluck it. I was between Death and perfection — so near both.

Then I realised that it was the apex of enjoyment, that no sensation could ever rival this one.

If a thing were more perfect, then one would be killed for having forced the gates of Paradise whilst yet living — the Paradise in which only disembodied spirits ever wander unmolested. It seemed to me that I had become suddenly and miraculously purged of all meanness, all smallness of spirit, all deceit, lies, limitless the words had lost their meaning. Perhaps very good people feel like this when they die. I wonder?

Suddenly the pilot shut off his engine. We began to drop, silently.

Never have I felt so impotent. Dropping through limitless space . . . I saw the little map becoming larger, more definite every second. I hated it bitterly. I didn't want to see it.

Damn it, I was no longer a human being. What was the good in bringing me back?

Then — thud, thud! We were down, we were back! The aeroplane was jolting recklessly across the field and I could see two men through my bleared goggles, rushing to our assistance like grooms running to bring in a mettlesome horse!

LETTER NO. 30
[Note: Written the night of the decisive day at Amiens]

February 14, 1920
Hotel Ritz, Paris

My darling beloved,

I am simply dazed and sodden with pain; it seems incredible that I should go on living — how *can* I bear it, how can I bear it?

My God, my God, and happiness was so near. *Nous l'avons effleuré*[1]

1. We got so close to it.

— Mitya, I shall go mad. I know I shall, and we'd gone, we'd gone, we had *got away* — and my darling, my darling, my heart is simply breaking. I can scarcely hold the pen. It's too dreadful, it's too dreadful. If I had thought I was never going to see you again, I would have drowned myself tonight. If you don't write to me I shall still. What is so perfectly *awful* to me is the feeling that our separation is partially due to a misunderstanding. There has NEVER never never in my life been any attempt at what you thought from that person. *Never* —

He said his pride wouldn't allow him to say more, and he particularly doesn't want anyone to know that there has never been anything of that nature and scarcely anything of the other. I loathe having to write this, but what I told you this evening is exactly true down to the minutest detail. O God — if only I — or he — could have explained. I told him I hated him and that I would rather go to St. Moritz[2] than stay alone with him if neither Pat nor Bagnold[3] can come. At the present moment he is sobbing next door.

I told him I was going to write to you all the time, and you to me. I *will* force him to answer your letter. I feel absolutely merciless towards him. He has completely and irrevocably done for himself and he knows it. I told H. to tell you that it was against my will, but now you know more about it than he does, thank God. O Mitya Mitya, Why didn't you give me time to explain? It was even less than you imagine now. You must know, you must know. It kills me to write it, but you *must* know all this.

I am going to try to speak to you on the telephone tomorrow morning. That man has ordered a motor at 11 to go to Toulon — it will take days — but I don't care what I do or where I go. It's Toulon, because I've asked Pat to meet me there. Mitya, Mitya, and you are so near and so supremely unavailable you might be on another continent. Mitya, it is breaking me. I feel I must die.

I don't know where you're going or anything. Try to go somewhere by yourself. I don't know where to write to. You must let me know. O my beloved, my beloved, I feel there has never been sorrow or pain or suffering for me till now.

2. Colonel and Mrs. Keppel were at St. Moritz.
3. Enid Bagnold.

I implore your forgiveness, Mitya, for all the lies and prevarications I have told you. I implore it with the contrition of an absolutely broken heart. Try to forgive me though I have been unpardonable. Whatever I may have done or said to you, I have never loved anyone like I have loved you and I shall never love anyone but you in this life. This world can only hold you, my love, my darling, my most precious beloved. I am dying with longing for you — I can't bear it. I can't. I can't.

O my God, my God, it is morning and you're not with me. The old ache and void has begun again, intensified a thousand fold, and still I feel and still I feel that this sorrow is due to my confounding terms. O Mitya, you must forgive me if I know so incredibly little about the other things, but I should have *killed* him if there had been any attempt at that. How I hate him, how I hate him for being with me when you're not. My only satisfaction is impressing that upon him.

O Mitya, your voice sounded so cold and distant on the telephone. Don't you mind, don't you mind. And you said you loved me so. O Mitya, I can't stand it. I can't. I want you so dreadfully. I am heartbroken.


LETTER NO. 31

March 3, 1920
Bordighera


It is almost unbelievably hot. I have climbed up here by myself, and feel quite exhausted. I am sitting in the shade of the olive groves on the top of a hill. I can't begin to describe how lovely it is: there is a mosaic of wildflowers winding amongst the olive trees and peach blossom everywhere. On the high peaks the snows are melting, leaving only white cornets. The Mediterranean is wrapped in a blue haze and without a ripple.

The olives are shining metal — you know how metallic their leaves look in the sun *"figés"*[1] in a sort of lovely classicism — now — bell

1. Congealed.

from a small mountain campanile stabs the buzzing silence, making an almost perceptible rent which instantly closes up again.

O Mitya, to have you here! You would be drunk with sun and heat and beauty. How can you resist the call of the south? Child of the South, why have you banished yourself! *This* is your décor, not the Weald.

Why persist in burying yourself in primroses when your real place is in an orange grove? (A locust has just "clicked" past me: you know the funny clicking sound they make with their wings?) O God, how I want you. The Riviera has never been so lovely. If you came to me in Italy, I could forgive her. See you I must. If you can't come, I shall get back to England by hook or by crook, *amore, amore mio* . . .

How little I want to see England. How intensely I hate the North!

Damn it all. My great grandmother was a Greek! We don't belong to the North, my dear, I still less than you.

Mitya, for some unknown reason, I remember Via Venezia[2] very vividly. The red bulk of the Duomo silhouetted against my window, and the voice in the street singing:

> *La Spagniola de te saprè*
> *Quant'e dolce la voluttà . . .*[3]

2. Violet and Vita stayed at a hotel in the Via Venezia during a childhood visit to Florence.
3. The Spanish girl knows how to tell you
   How sweet is Voluptuousness.

LETTER No. 32

March 3, 1920

Sometimes it seems so impossible that you shouldn't be coming, that I should be doomed to yet another failure.

Here, *c'est l'appel à l'amour, pur et simple.*[1] Not the pale, diffident English summer, pretty though it is — I know nothing prettier than the English spring. Here it is a great, bold, peremptory flare of brass trumpets. The sea is the colour of lapis, and the sky only a shade lighter. The freesias and mimosas smell offensively sweet. The gardens are ex-

1. It's the call of love, pure and simple.

travagantly pink with blossom. The hills are delirious with anemones, jonquils and hyacinths . . . I go and lie on top of them, look down on all this, and murmur "Mitya!" Then, "Mitya must come." I want you so, Mitya. I am half dead with wanting you. I lie awake for hours at night, longing for you hungrily, hopelessly . . . If you ceased to care for me. I should cease to live . . .

If you won't come here, I shall come to you, but I must see you — *ad ogni prezzo*[2] — even if I can only come for two or three days. Never say I don't love you, if I have to travel across Europe sitting bolt upright, to England which I detest, braving the fury of my Mother, merely to catch a glimpse of you!

You will say, "But that's what you're asking me to do." I retort, but you are going to Florence anyway, and I'm offering you practically a fortnight of certain undisturbed bliss, "in the South, in the Spring, in the Sun" (the one irresistible formula).

Anyhow, if you still refuse to leave your English Weald, I'll come. *Je t'adore* . . .

Lushka

2. At any price.


LETTER NO. 33

May 7, 1920
The Dower House, Sonning-on-Thames

In spite of its dreadful soppiness, I like parts of that play: I liked the part when she hears the voices calling her, didn't you?[1]

I have thought a lot about it. I believe in so many things, Mitya — most of all, I believe quite incorrigibly "In some shy, elusive and wholly delicious 'Other place' " — *I know there is such a place*.

Don't think this is Barrie inspired, it isn't. I have always thought so, and always hinted to you about it. Whether I shall ever get you there or not is another matter, probably not! But I wish I could. One

1. Probably *Mary Rose*.

thing I revel in is my quite remarkably weak grasp on Reality — a little tug, and I should be free for ever, free from what most people term Reality —

My realities are quite different, only they're so *"insaisissable."*[2] They hide in the trees, they lurk in the tiny sibilant wind that steals in through the window and whispers to me as I write. They make music to me when I go for walks by myself, and above all, they are indissolubly mixed up with all "free" things, with the flight of birds, clouds, the wandering of Gypsies. (Mitya, think of the divine people who have been wanderers: Jason, Odysseus, Lavengro, Coeur de Lion, François Villon . . .)

Fauns and fairies are either supposed to be dead or never to have existed — It's a lie! They're not dead. They *do* exist. *Every sort of marvellous thing exists,* only people just don't bother to look for them — and they're the only things worth looking for.

Do you know, Mitya, that my only really solid and unseverable "lien" with this world is *you,* my love for you? I believe if there weren't you I should live more and more in my own world, until finally I withdrew myself inwardly altogether. I'm sure that would happen.

Sometimes I feel so queer, you don't know. Everything people say to me, even everything you say to me, slips off me like water off a duck's back.

And whatever you say and whatever they say, it makes no difference, I mean, about going away, for instance. You trot out your perfectly sane, legitimate and balanced arguments against going and something in myself, as it were, sits on the top of a tree and watches them curiously, amusedly, like a procession of ants . . . They are admirable in their way, but I have got nothing in common with them, and they don't ever come any nearer, or do anything new. I think they're splendid, and so painstaking . . . *et voilà tout.*[3]

It's the very *core* of me that sits at the top of the tree and smiles, though the rest, the intolerably human part of me may be racked by misery at your obtuseness.

2. Unseizable, not to be caught.
3. And that's all.

Don't you see, Mitya, that if you tried for a hundred years to make, say a Fijian, see things from your point of view, you would never succeed. And your trying to make me see is just as futile. I shall just go on playing my own solitary games until you will listen to my point of view, which, in reality, is neither selfish nor immoral, but just DIF-FERENT. In the Middle Ages, when people did things that the community didn't understand they were instantly burned at the stake for being sorcerers and witches.

Because you don't see things as I see them, because you don't really understand, you think I am wicked and immoral and selfish — so I am, according to *your* standards, but not according to my own. According to my own, I am singularly pure, uncontaminated, and high principled. You will laugh, *but it is true.* And you can laugh all your life, but it will still be true.

I am after something which you have just caught a glimpse of, but which is omnipresent with me. I don't know whether I shall ever succeed in making anyone see life as I see it, because it is the side of life they don't and won't see.

I sit at the foot of an invisible altar and am dazzled by its freshness, its richness, and its youth.

LETTER NO. 34

May 25, 1920

Z.[1] has asked me to become his mistress with a house in Paris, a house in the country, and unlimited credit at every bank in Europe — "Gin-evra, *quoi!*

I think it will be terribly inartistic to refuse.

The demand was made with every formality. This was the "business" I had to go to London for yesterday, though I didn't know it was going

1. Sir Basil Zaharoff, the Greek financier, was born in 1850 in Asia Minor and educated in London and Paris. He dominated the great British munitions firm of Vickers and became one of the richest men in Europe. After the First World War he purchased the Casino at Monte Carlo.

to take that form, as in his telegram he merely said he wanted to see me "on business," without specifying.

Well, darling, you always foresaw this, so at any rate it will not be a surprise to you. It is "lift" with a vengeance, isn't it?, to belong to the Richest Man in the World? *On a son petit chic.*

I hope we shan't lose touch with each other altogether: my house will be in the Avenue du Bois, and I shall be at home from 5 to 7 every evening, only you had better telephone first. You will find the telephone number under the name of Mlle Thais de Champagne.

I feel rather like a storm-tossed ship getting into a quiet haven at last, a sunny satiny haven, with gold-flecked waves!!!

After all, we have both always known I was predestined to become Z's mistress — it is merely a question of time. It is very soothing to have hit upon one's real *métier* at last. I shall — or rather we shall — be going to Deauville in August: I hope so much to see you there, my poor Julian — *mais à ton âge on se console vite et tu dénicheras sûrement quelque bonne petite amie à laquelle tu me présenteras.*[2]

Z. always spends the winter at Monte Carlo, at the Hôtel de Paris, so we are certain to meet in the Casino! I shall be so weighted down with pearls that I shall be *méconnaissable mais que veux tu? Faut se couvrir . . .*[3]

Write to me sometimes: I shall often think with regret of the happy times we have spent together. *On s'aimait bien, quoiqu'on n'avait pas trop de pognon?*[4]

I shall always have a soft corner in my heart for you. *Tiens, c'est plus fort que moi: je suis tout en larmes.*[5]

Ta Vielle Louchette

P.S.  *Tu. Tu ne m'en voudras pas. Après tout faut se ranger. Tant qu'on est jeune, passe encore puis quand vient la vieillesse, si on n'a pas placé des petites economies, il n'y a plus qu'à crever en pleine rue. Mais tout de même, ça me fait de la peine de te quitter . . .*

2. But at your age one consoles oneself quickly and surely you will pick up some pretty little friend whom you'll present to me.
3. Unrecognizable but what to do? It's necessary to cover oneself . . .
4. We loved each other a lot, although we were hard up.
5. Well, I'm carried away by it all; I'm all in tears.

*Tu as toujours été un chic type . . . comme je sais que tu es dans la misère, je t'envoie ci-joint un billet de mille . . .*[6]

6. I don't want much, you know. After all, one must arrange one's affairs. When one is young it doesn't matter so much, but when old age arrives, if one hasn't made some small economies, one starves with a smile. But nonetheless it does hurt to leave you . . .

You've always been a "great sport" . . . as I know you're rather hard up, I enclose attached a banknote for one thousand [pounds].

Note: After sending this letter Violet became afraid that Vita might possibly take her seriously, and she sent telegrams explaining that she was not going to accept Z.'s business proposition. In an unhappy letter dated June 3, 1920, she wrote to Vita: "If it weren't for you, I should certainly go to Z. merely for the fun of paying him [Denys] out."

## LETTER No. 35

June 5, 1920
North Mymms Park, Hatfield

Men cheringue,

I am writing to you in bed.

It is too awful that tomorrow I shall be 26! I am dreading it. It is dreadful to be as old as that. I *hate* getting old — *quando io ti camelavo primo*[1] — I was 23 — all the difference in the world.

I adore youth, only not in the same way as you do. For me it is so infinitely shorter-lived. You and I are no longer young, Mitya, and the sooner we realise it, the better. *Ne gaspillons pas le peu qui nous reste . . .*[2]

This is a lovely place, rather like Hurstmonceaux and rather like Montacute. The thing is it really makes my mouth water (for once) — the most gorgeous tapestries, Limoges enamels, and carpets.

*In quanto alla gente, ils m'emmerdent*[3] — and they would you too. You can guess pretty well who they are. Moreover, I feel too ill for words.

I am 26, *passée,* futile, pointless, and — letterless!

1. Combination of Italian and *camelavo* from the secret language: "when I loved you first."
2. Don't let's waste the little that remains (of youth).
3. As for the people they make me sick.

I have had no letters — there may be a post later and I am putting all my faith in that. Nobody has even wished me happy returns of the day, and you needn't have worried about D. giving me a present, because he hasn't, nor did he remember it was my birthday, nor is he going to give me a present. You must think I *want* people to give me presents, but I honestly don't, only, I'm afraid rather childishly and perhaps soppily, I like to be wished many happy returns of the day. *C'est bête, mais que veux tu?*[4]

But I shan't ever again, because after today I want my birthday forgotten, because I am getting too old.

Last night at dinner I talked passionately about ostrich farming, manure, hunting big game, shooting, polo, golf. (I love being thought versatile.) There is only one other person here besides myself who isn't coped in for bridge, and we talk for hours in melancholy undertones for fear of disturbing the bridgites.

*Quelle vie, mon Dieu, quelle vie!*[5] And all the time a little hammer goes on in my brain saying: *"mai più, mai più."*[6] (I shall probably do a rush out of the house like I did at the F's!)

Even the lovely things in this house bring it home to me how life wants simplifying: I have really forbidden myself ever to covet anything of that sort. It's all nonsense: one doesn't really need tapestries and carpets and pictures.

This is what one needs: the person one loves, the sun, freedom. Everything else is entirely superfluous. I really hate the trappings of life; at least I have trained myself to hate them — oh yes, I have! My instinct is all to crave for beauty in all its divers manifestations. I mean indoor — not outdoor — beauty. And I am ruthlessly repressing it, *because it isn't essential.* Therefore I shan't miss the things I shall not be able to have ever in my life. It is perhaps my only form of discipline. It is your anti-Callot[7]–Mrs. Leeds principle extended ad infinitum.

4. It's foolish, but what do you expect?
5. What a life, my God, what a life!
6. "Never again, never again."
7. Presumably Jacques Callot, the seventeenth-century French engraver who ran away with the Gypsies when he was twelve. Mrs. Leeds is unidentified.

(Perhaps the next step will be persuading myself that I don't need any sun?) Whenever I find myself desiring beautiful things, I feel that I ought to live in a quite bare little room with an inkpot and a couple of fountain pens! You'll say — If that's how you feel, why trouble to buy furniture? I know, but the test of its "danger" is whether one is suddenly able to bear to be without anything of the sort. I think I can quite honestly answer in the affirmative.

You see, darling, wanting beautiful things really means wanting money, and one should never never start wanting that: it would be *really* lowering oneself. I have so few qualities that I couldn't bear to diminish those I have. I want passionately to be guiltless of that sort of thing. I want passionately to be hardworking and free, and you know what I want even more than that. There must never be any greed (in the material sense) or insincerity, or shirking, or slovenliness, or snobbishness, in my life . . .

The post has come, bringing only a letter from Clemence Dane, who *did* trouble to write. I *am* so hurt. You took jolly good care to both write and telegraph Harold for his.[8]

8. A letter and gift from Vita arrived a few days later.

## LETTER NO. 36

June 18, 1920

Men cheringue,

I am impatiently waiting for you to ring me up, as you said you would. It is incredible how this place gets on my nerves: I am more restless and nervous here than I have ever been in my life. It is a small place, full of small noises: shrieks of children, babble of sparrows, "honks" of motor bicycle horns on the road. It drives me wild with irritations, so that I can do nothing. Alas, I am feeling very unwell again. (How I loathe the sound of children's voices. There can be nothing shriller, or sillier, or more distracting.) This place is the apotheosis of fussiness.

To think of Berkeley here is like paddling in an inch of too shallow brook, full of bits of glass and ginger beer bottles, and then suddenly to step into a great cool pool of luscious, limpid depths, and water lilies . . . Berkeley, rose pink, unbelievably old and grand and secret.

Berkeley, with hawks building almost in its keep, Berkeley with valerian and fig trees jutting, Berkeley jealously guarded by great trees and a jungle of grasses, Berkeley with a voice singing in its heart, thunder growling round it like an angry watchdog. Was there ever such romance, such colour, such mystery?

I told Pat we had been there. She was miserable and really hurt as I feared she would: I said we had only seen the place from the road. (Though I loved you to love it, I feel guilty of an indelicacy.[1])

Lovely, lovely Berkeley, I shall be faithful to it till I die.

Perhaps I shall be allowed to haunt it?

Some things wake in me such a flood of pure passionate and reverent love . . . Berkeley, the view from the bungalow in Ceylon, Trincomalee, music, forests, mountains . . . These things I worship.

"The purely longed for, longly hoped for thing."

And we go on, you and I, associating with the banal, the trivial, the unbeautiful, the vulgar, the clamourous, the prosaic. O to be free of all but beauty!

Listen, darling: I think we had better go to Gloucester at the end of the week, rather than at the beginning . . . Another thing, I want desperately to go to the ballet with you, and that is only possible if you stay the night in London, as I don't think they are giving any matinées. Couldn't you arrange to stay one night in London at your Mother's house, go to the ballet with me, and we could go away the following day? I have missed you so unutterably since last night. I hate coming back here after you have been here with me. I suppose you are not going to ring me up after all — it is nearly three — why haven't you? You said you would. O, Mitya. You might have done so.

1. Pat Dansey had been Violet's hostess during her previous visits to Berkeley Castle.

LETTER NO. 37

June 24, 1920

I have been walking miles in pursuit of trees and have at length sunk exhausted on a heap of stones without having found any. It is awful, this Tree Quest; it is taking such a hold on me! I have walked past one island, and still further, without any reward.

How I loathe the Thames Valley with its laws and regulations and gates and fences! It is *dreadful*. I wish I could start an anticivilisation league, but that's been thought of before, and nothing came of it.

. . . Anyhow, it's quiet here — no sound, save myriad buzzings and rustlings and twitterings. A walk might be an adventure, not just a mere humdrum logging along an unenterprising path or road, as the case may be. There ought to be pixies and imps and bogies ready to spring out on one, with an occasional Knight in Armour thrown in. There ought to be growls and gleams and glimmerings, and little thatched cottages which recede as you get nearer to them. There ought to be thin blue spirals of smoke curling up from God knows where and birds that can talk like human beings, and human beings that can sing like birds. But there are none of these things — except Berkeley.

O God! How I hate the realities of this world!

But I have a very very distant vision, which never really leaves me. One day I shall be allowed (by the gods) to get right right away — *where* I don't know, perhaps somewhere in the Caucasus — anyhow, hundreds of miles from civilisation and money and trains and people and parties — and there I shall just peel my civilisation off me, layer by layer, till there is nothing left but the impulse to eat and sleep and defend oneself from wild animals. And I shall put up a little tombstone to my discarded intellect and dance a war dance round it, all by myself.[1]

1. The third page of this letter contains a delightful sketch of Violet in the Caucasus attired only in a bikini of flowers, gaily doing a war dance around a little tombstone.

LETTER No. 38

July 2, 1920

I want to write you the most serious letter I have ever written to you in my life.

I know you have cared for me and care for me still, but it is my unshakable conviction that you care not only for me. Heaven forbid that I should blame you for this! I neither blame nor condemn. All I want, all I *beseech* is that you should, *at any cost,* tell me the plain unvarnished truth. I implore you not to treat this part of my letter with your customary evasiveness. If I am to be hurt, hurt me once and for all. Don't toy with me like a cat with a mouse. It is so infinitely crueller than any *coup de grâce* could possibly be.

In the name of our love I appeal to all that is best in you to tell me the *truth* — to be brave and tell me the truth. It is the uncertainty of everything that is torturing me till I am half mad and don't know what I am doing. Make up your mind which it is you want — you can't have both.

This sharing business is revolting for both of us. If you give me up I shall nearly die of it, but I can't stand the uncertainty of our future any longer.

Darling, I want to impress something else on you. There would be no question of "reprisals" on my part. I am telling you this because this is not written in a mean or petty spirit. Don't be a fool and say: you care for someone else — *I don't care a button for anyone but you and never should.*

If you decide you want to give me up, I shall go away by myself or with some disinterested third person as soon as possible, and — I repeat — I shall be utterly heartbroken, but I can't stand this any longer, and no more can you. It is the worst possible thing for both our characters, and brings, as you said, the worst out of each of us.

I want your happiness as well as my own, though I suppose you will not believe it, but O, I do! In cold blood I have been thinking everything over for hours. I know you care for me and if you give me up, I know it won't be because you have ceased to care for me but because you realise the futility of your efforts to free yourself, because you think it wrong to leave H. and the children, and because I make you unhappy. Not a vestige of blame would attach to you.

You think I don't realise your difficulties, *but I do.* That is why I want you to make up your mind to lead a perfectly honest and open life either with your family or with me. You can't do "la navette"[1] any longer. We must have a "situation nette."[2]

There is one thing I will never forgive you: that is if you put any misconstruction on the motives which prompt this letter. I never thought I could be so brave as to write it, because each word I write is torture to me.

I am tired of being a rotten character — tired of being selfish and spiteful and malicious — above all, I am tired of being jealous. It is killing me and making utter beasts of both of us. You will say it is selfish of me to want you to give up everybody for me. It is selfish, but it is honest, and would abolish deceit and jealousy for ever. But on the other hand I see it is wrong to ask you to do this. Therefore I won't ask it of you anymore. If you want to come, you must come of your own accord. I relinquish my rights and pretensions. I abdicate my claims.

You must do whatever you please, go wherever you please, see whomever you please. I shall not interfere.

I shall mind *hideously,* but I must not see you, for you must not know.

You said I gave you no liberty. You have complete liberty. I will neither reproach nor criticize.

You say I am ungenerous. You will no longer be able to say it. I will not do things by halves. O darling, darling, *I want to get back* — I hate wickedness and lies and deceit. I am bitterly sorry for all I have done. I am bitterly repentant. I want to reconquer all I have lost. I want to be good like I was at sixteen. I want most of all to be good to you. If you are unhappy it would be good for you to give me up, even though it would break my heart. It is killing me to write these words. I can hardly see to write them. The tears are pouring down my face — but you owe yourself to your family — if you think it is right, you should give me up.

I know I have always shown myself all that is vile, but I swear to you, all the good in me there used to be isn't dead. I am flinging it at your feet as a not unworthy tribute to our love.

1. A boat that does a shuttle service.
2. A clear situation.

I love you so utterly, you don't know, with such complete surrender.
I have wrestled all last night and all today with my selfishness and
I think I have conquered it at last.

I shall love you till I die, whatever you do.

God bless you and make you happy, and Harold too.

Always, always your
Lushka

LETTER NO. 39

July 10, 1920

I am writing to you in great anguish of mind: please try to understand.

I write to you in the most homeless, friendless condition it is possible for anyone to be in. All the morning I have been making lists of
my things. You know I don't crave a permanent "home," but it is
rather sad to have nowhere to put them. (You charitably said you
would keep them for me, but since I have heard that they may go to G.
Street[1]). I mean nowhere they can remain.

My picture seems to be solitude in hotels — hotels I don't object
to, but I loathe solitude. You, of course, would be miserable with no
house of your own, and faced with my future — mercifully, I mind
that part less.

But what I *do* mind, acutely, devastatingly, is having no friends, no
one who really cares what becomes of me, whether I am happy or
not. You will say that you care: I am sure you do, but life is so
different for you. You are surrounded by people who care for your
comfort and care for your happiness, people who will never fail you.
You are lucky. Do you realise *how* lucky? I wonder . . .

There is nothing permanent in my life, not one person whom I
feel will always sympathize and will always understand. As for you,
darling, you are miles away physically and spiritually. You have been
"reclaimed." H. said you were weak. You *are* weak, darling. I don't
mean in the sense of being soft-hearted; that is surely a most enduring
weakness, and one with which I would never reproach you. *No*, I

1. Grosvenor Street, where the Keppels had their London house.

mean that whoever you are with, *tu te laisses dominer*[2] by that person — sometimes quite subconsciously.

6 months ago it was me, now it is him, and whichever it is, you are temporarily *blind* to the other person. When it was me, you were blind to H.; now it is him, you are blind to me. *Don't misunderstand me:* I don't mean that you are hard and unkind to me; I mean that you are temporarily incapable of entering into my spirit and understanding my sensations . . . The mere fact of your getting angry when I tell you things like this is sufficient proof that you don't understand. For once, won't you show me that you do understand, by not getting angry?

Think to yourself; well, it is thanks to me that she has no friends. I must be *all* her friends; it is thanks to me she feels lonely and desolate. I will see to it that she feels neither.

O darling, darling, I am so abysmally sad. Year succeeds year, and there is no good done, no happiness accomplished. It is the old story of *"La Cigale"* — *"La cigale ayant chanté tout l'été se trouva fort dépourvûe quand la brise fût venue."*[3]

I am *la cigale.* Don't — O don't say to me: *"Vous avez chanté tout l'été? Eh bien, dansez maintenant!"*[4]

2. You let yourself be influenced.
3. "The cicada having sung all summer, finds herself quite destitute when the winter wind comes." (La Fontaine: *Fables, "La Cigale et la fourmi."*)
4. You have sung all summer? Well, dance now.

LETTER-POEM. No. 40

Undated (Probably July 1920)

They have taken my youth,
    They have taken my pride,
And the passionate Truth
    That stalked proud at my side.

They have taken my love,
    They have taken my fire,

The high dreams that I wove
From a fabulous spire.

They have taken my friends,
　They have taken my health,
And, to serve their own ends,
　They have taken my wealth.

They have taken my hope,
　They have taken my knife,
And the draught, and the rope
　Lest I fain take my life.

LETTER No. 41 (*extract*)

August 17, 1920

. . . I played Tchaikovsky's "Symphonie Pathétique" — the one you loved so much — on Pat's pianola. It is surely the most heartbreaking thing that was ever written! Do you remember how we loved it at Monte Carlo? Afterwards we walked by the sea . . . I hadn't heard it since then.

I look at all the things you have given me with a new pang: the powder box, for instance — it was so sweet of you. You chose the one that I had been secretly coveting for ages.

Darling, do you realise that we have never looked upon our three weeks in Italy in the same way? It wasn't the same. Nothing has ever been the same since. We have never been really happy save for the few days at Lincoln. Italy was shadowed, spoilt, by the inevitable separation. *It is only when we have thought that we would never have to leave each other again that we have been completely happy.* (I forgot the brief time between San Remo and Venice. We were happy then, *for the same reason.*)

Before we left Monte Carlo you were mine, darling. I was absolutely convinced that you were going to tell H., and that, whatever he might say, you would return to me . . . Do you remember the day you left me at Cannes? How completely we trusted each other! We were all in all to each other — ah, Mitya, what agony it is to remember! *Don't you see the difference?* You do, you must!

There was little room in your heart for anyone but me. The other claims and affections had faded until they had become mere inopportune ghosts. *C'était moi que tu aimais, moi que tu tenais!*[1] It *was* true, *then,* Mitya, that you cared exclusively for me — you know as well as I do that you can always tell — *"Le coeur a ses raisons que la raison ne connait pas."*[2]

It is because it is so different now, yes, so different, darling. I wish you would be brave and face it as I do — though, mind you, it is you who are different, not I — that sometimes I can hardly bear it, and I feel like . . .

O darling, darling, I have opened my letter again. If only I could put into words what I feel. You are like a person living in a room; you keep your eyes obstinately glued on the things in the room — you daren't look out of the window. If you looked, do you know what you'd see? O, I can't write, I can't express what I feel. It's no use, no use.

1. It was I that you loved, I that you cared about!
2. "The heart has its reasons which Reason knows not."

LETTER No. 42

23 August, 1920
Duntreath Castle
Blanefield, N.B. (Scotland)

The clock has been put back twelve years: I am fourteen, romantic, pedantic, mystery-loving. I haven't got over my stay in Florence: I allude to Verrocchio, Donatello, Cimabue. I am deep in Marjorie Bowen — but I am not too old to surreptitiously enjoy L. T. Meade.

Nana is still one of the most important figures on my horizon: Moiselle is omnipotent. Mama is a remote, sometimes gracious, always stately and beautiful figure in my life. The boys aren't bad fun, only Charlie teases me and pulls my hair. Mrs. Strachen[1] is my only real

1. The wife of the lodge-keeper at Duntreath.

conquest. (She has delicious lemonade in bottles, and she makes drop scones on Sundays.) And Vita — of course, it would be too wonderful if Vita came here. She is so beautiful and clever. (She knows Italian better than me — but I was in Florence longer than she was.) I simply adore Vita, but I don't know if she is really fond of me . . . If only I could find out. But how? If Vita came, we would dress up and perhaps we could do *Le Masque de Fer*[2] again, only I'm such a bad actress . . . Of course, Vita's so clever: there's nothing she can't do.

Look at the way she stumps all the others at Miss Woolf's!!![3]

Though it was a near thing between her and Sibyl Mettersdorf for the prize essay . . .

I wonder if Vita's mother would let her come? How lovely it would be . . . I would scatter rose petals on the carpet . . . (Perhaps there are some tuberoses in the hothouse. I will get my mother to write to hers.)

*Men tiliche,* you have no idea how strange it is being here — finding everything unchanged. You must remember I haven't been here for seven years. It's like coming back to my lost childhood. The illusion is unexpectedly assisted by *men chinday,* who, so far hasn't made a single reference to anything — for which I am infinitely grateful. *Mia Dia* [my uncle] Archie[4] and *Mia Zia* [my aunt] Duckrus[5] (not Iscariot) are most kind and gentle. The other "Zia" is away.

*Man camelo tuti*[6] so superlatively — it seems like an unbroken sequence — I did as a child — I do still. It seems the one thing that must last as long as I last — the one indomitable, the one endurable thing. If only you could be here. It is so lovely and peaceful.

IN BED

I have got the room you had the first time you were here. I have never slept in it for twelve years — and it seems only yesterday. I wonder if I shall hear the owls tonight. It is utterly quiet here — the

2. *The Iron Mask.*
3. School attended by Violet and Vita.
4. Archibald Edmonstone, Mrs. Keppel's brother.
5. Aunt Jessie.
6. I adore you.

mountains are bleakly outlined against the sky and one can just hear the rush of the "burrrrrn" — you know, the place where I used to fish?

O God . . . *Je te tends mes bras, devenus inutiles* . . . *on passerait la nuit bien autrement que la dernière fois.*[7]

Perhaps the spell of the past is in men chinday too, for she has made no allusion . . . It is so easy to forget all that has happened "in between."

I am indelibly stamped with the seal of your personality, *tiro jeli* — It is as abiding as the hills and as defiant.

My darling, I have such a horrid sore throat — apparently — though it's not necessary to connect the two — there is an awful outburst of smallpox in Glasgow, and mio zio[8] thinks perhaps I ought to be vaccinated as I lingered there this morning. I sent you a telegram:

Again and again this awful tide of longing sweeps over me — *man quiero tuti, man quiero tuti.* We could be so happy here. What with my sore throat and missing you, I shan't sleep again tonight.


MONDAY MORNING

I haven't slept — and my throat is much worse — I have no remedies for it with me. I think if it is no better this morning I shall send for the doctor.

When you first came here you had never heard of him . . . *C'etait moi que tu aimais*[9] . . . This place is *not* hostile. It is so friendly and sympathetic and remembering.

Yesterday men chinday, instead of being hard and inquisitorial and menacing, was kind and humourous and gay. She has been gardening such a lot and cutting down so many trees. She is quite brown and sunburnt. She says she has been so happy here away from everybody. She is so attractive like she was yesterday, no one could help loving her — not even you!

She has moments — hours of complete simplicity. She laughs and

7. I hold out to you my arms, become useless . . . one spent the night quite differently than last time.

8. Archibald Edmonstone.

9. It was I whom you loved.

jokes like a girl — in the intervals of locking up the retrievers and doctoring a poor wounded dove that the rats had practically devoured.

Then her manners and her courtesy are so charming. She took me for tea with an old lady who lives near here and several particularly tiresome and offensive neighbors arrived. Men chinday talked to them as if they were the most brilliant and attractive people in the world, teased and chaffed the old lady, admired all her belongings, until her head was completely turned. *Non, il n'y à pas a dire:*[10] I couldn't bear Mama a grudge for anything in the world. Whatever she did, she could always be forgiven. There are some people like that.

There was a nice little man here called Sir Courtauld Thomson, who was quite ludicrously and blatantly in love with her.

Oh! The charmers of this world, what an unfair advantage is given them!

Lushka

10. No, there's nothing to be said.

LETTER NO. 43

August 24, 1920
Duntreath Castle,
Blanefield, N.B. [Scotland]

Men cheringue

I got two letters from you this morning, to my great joy. What a long time they take getting here! I have got the vilest sore throat: it again kept me awake most of last night. Moreover I was vaccinated yesterday morning. If it takes, I shan't be able to go on the 30th . . . but I believe it can be extremely painful.

There is an extraordinary stagnancy about this place: it is very soothing — but this quality belongs preeminently to hills.

I am playing a game with myself: I am still (more or less) fourteen and you are still sixteen in spirit. Darling, how *dreadfully* happy we were before we grew up, you and I! I am terribly against being grown up. It does nobody any good. Hugh[1] always belongs intimately to this place. I can recall him so vividly: a gawky tongue-tied boy of nineteen.

1. Hugh Walpole, whom Violet first met when he was a tutor to one of her cousins during his summer holidays from Cambridge.

(I think the term "boy" is legitimate in this case.) And you — why, you have never left it — the whole place rings with your name.

Darling, it's true, I'm afraid, what you say. You have made a sad muddle of your life. You are neither fish, fowl, nor good red herring. But, while you admit the "martyring" alternative, you don't admit the other — the burning of boats — and — flight! (Surely the more palatable of the two?)

It is more difficult for you to play my game, for you are not alone, whereas I am. It's funny, how, the moment I get away, how gloriously emancipated I feel. I shed certain aspects of my life as easily as a garment . . . I feel so free . . .

*Luz de mi ojos,*[2] last night was magical: the little owls hooted all round the house, like they did . . . The moon rose like a lady of the orient behind a yasmak of cloud, and the steepled black of fir tree made a lovely crest of mystery against the sky . . . It was quiet, quiet . . . only the subdued rush of the stream, and the little owls hooting . . .

I felt so near to you, so closely akin to the trees, and the owls and the earth. Rather like the night when I was "fetched" . . . They are such *friends,* Mitya, — the trees and winds and storms. We understand each other so perfectly. One day I shall disappear in a clap of thunder. Or *l'aquilon rimeur m'emportera sur ses ailes.*[3] (I think this is a quotation.) Oh, at heart, I am clean and chaste and free — like a blade that has never been used.

There is something invulnerable, something inviolate in me, something that will ultimately triumph over everything, and carry me away on its wings of rapture! (Darling, you see how incorrigible is this belief if I can write about it in this idiotic way at 11 o'clock in the morning!!)

Perhaps no one will ever know, perhaps it will never see light, but it is there, it is there, it leaps and throbs and sings, and you are the only person in the world who even suspects its existence . . .

Oh, *je t'aime, je t'aime.*

Lushka

2. Light of my eyes.
3. The laughing north wind will carry me off on his wings.

LETTER NO. 44

August 27, 1920
Duntreath Castle

Mia hermosa

My cousin Eddy (the one who faintly resembles me!) has just arrived from Constantinople. From a rather stocky snub-nosed child, he has turned into a perfect Adonis! He is about six-foot-two, perfectly proportioned, has a deep bass voice (yes, deeper than mine!), almost classical features (the erstwhile snub nose having turned into a Greek one), and a shock of impenetrable auburn hair!!! You never saw such a dream!! I shall get him to sit for me.

The romance of sailors!! I feel he is like a juvenile Lingard.[1] He has had every sort of adventure and skirmish and he is not quite twenty! *Really* young, darling, not fakes young like you and me!

I foresee he is just my sort of person. If I were staying here longer I should certainly "get busy buzzing around" — so it's just as well I'm leaving tomorrow, as little can be accomplished in 24 hours.

Isn't this a bare-faced confession? (Shall I ask him to Holland?)[2] I can see your face getting darker and darker but you deserve to be teased (besides all I have said is quite true) for not having said a single word about Sunday. I don't know where I'm going or anything. You are really maddening, darling.

I am in an impish mood. I shall think of you tomorrow having arty conversations with your flabby host, pompous diplomatic reminiscences at meals, gossip about the latest lion, the latest book, cheap witticisms at the expense of Sibyl Colefax[3] — and you can think of me with my deliciously young, debonair cousin, being shown tame tortoises and a parrot that uses unrepeatable language, a revolver that has been used as a means of defending life, not as an objet d'art in an "old world interior."

Oh darling, don't think I include *you* in that soulful, soulless little set, that miserable intellectual clique — I don't. Mentally, spiritually,

1. Captain Lingard, the hero of Joseph Conrad's *The Rescue, An Outcast of the Islands,* and *Almayer's Folly.*
2. Violet was going to Clingendaal, Holland, where her mother each autumn rented the château of the Baroness Daisy de Brienen.
3. London hostess. Her salon is described in *Don't Look Round.*

and yes, darling, physically!!! (aren't I a tease!!), you tower above them. They are not fit to lick your boots. I should like you never to set eyes on any of them again. They are certainly your friends, but there is nothing big about them, nothing that will live, not a spark of divine fire. As for *living,* they don't know how to live . . .

They live their little padded lives in their little padded houses surrounded by valuable old furniture, the latest thing in poetry, the latest thing in prose. And they go out to expensive luncheons, and they come in to expensive dinners, and they *dare* to criticise, these miserable, flabby, half-alive people, the people who *really* live!

Oh! They take jolly care to protect their little lives, to keep away from any danger zone — Pah, I hate them. I could spit in their faces, I hate them so. I should like to hold them up to ridicule for everyone to jeer at.

When I think that I escaped in the person of G.W.[4] (for goodness sake, don't leave this letter lying about). Thank god for the people, like Julian, and Aubrey, and Maurice — and the bright flower of youth and courage and keenness who perished in the war. Those were the people worth knowing — the people to admire and live up to. I *know* I am right, and in the bottom of your heart, you know I am too. You've only got to look at your own father. He's not exactly thrilling, but there's far more to admire in him than in all the tinselly people you are misled by. Darling, please forgive this outburst. You will because of the truth of what I always tell you . . .

Lushka

4. Presumably Gerald Wellesley, who became Duke of Wellington and remained Violet's dear friend.

## LETTER NO. 45

Undated (October 1920)<br>Clingendaal, Holland

Mitya, I wish you weren't so beautiful! Supposing I had ceased to care for you and had dismissed you, trait by trait — finally there would come the insurmountable stumbling block of your beauty, and I should be as hopelessly inveigled as ever I was!

I dread it, because it is without flaw. Of its "school" quite perfect. You are just as undeniably beautiful as the cathedral in Seville or the "view from the Acropolis." There can be no two opinions about that. You are indomitably, incorrigibly beautiful and I wish to Heaven you weren't because it is the only thing I can't resist.

LETTER NO. 46

October 14, 1920
Clingendaal, Holland

I love nothing in the world but you. Test after test is applied to my love, and test after test is vanquished triumphantly. For you I would commit any crime; for you I would sacrifice any other love. My love for you terrifies and overpowers me.

I am writing this for myself, not for you. I am so hypersensitive where you're concerned that not the slightest inflection of your voice, not the subtlest nuance of your letters, escapes me. I got one yesterday that was cold, almost impersonal. I worried myself almost sick over it.

My love for you is all-engrossing. There is no other love in my life — no other occupation. Everything else is of such mediocre importance compared to you that it is hardly worth mentioning.

You might so easily kill me.

My life is in your hands. If you deceived me in any vital issue, you could kill me.

You must not deceive me. I don't deserve that you should. My whole life is *yours*. I never do anything which does not indirectly concern you. You are never out of my thoughts. You must be ill for it is a crime to deceive the person one loves.

LETTER No. 47

October 19, 1920
Clingendaal, Holland

Do I like your making political and educational speeches? *No!*

I hate it. I think it is to be deplored. You, Mitya, my erstwhile *gitana,*[1] going and mixing yourself up with the "landed classes" and educational reform and such stuff! Pfui! It makes me both angry and sick. For Heaven's sake, leave that to other people. I can't bear it: it is a hideous anachronism and only shows me how false my conception of you must be. Besides, I know who to trace it to!

O God, it is time I came back and took you away from all such stuff. You know how I hate your sense of possession and all that is a part of it. My poor sweet, I know I am stupid and narrow-minded and rude, but oh! I *do* so hate social problems, and education, and feudalism, and possessions and laws and arguments! I realise that such things must be — but they mean less than nothing to me. *Je n'y comprends rien, mais rien de rien,*[2] you whom I sometimes think should be wandering the high roads of the world with no roof over your head and nothing but a bundle to call your own, to go fraternizing with that *galère,*[3] the governing, legislative, disciplinarian *galère* — that is to me sheer anathema. It is treachery, Mitya, treachery to me, to us, to our unfettered plans.

I can't help taking it to heart!! It is like a burglar ogling the housekeeper's wife, or a potential householder splitting a point with a burglar. In either case, it is treachery.

> "The wild hawk to
> The wind-swept sky . . ."

O Mitya, my poor darling, *où diable t'es tu fourrée. Veux-tu bien sortir de là — et vivement!*[4]

"Gypsy, come away!"

1. Gypsy.
2. I don't understand anything of this, anything at all.
3. Gang, or crowd.
4. What in the devil's name have you got yourself mixed up with. You must really get out of this—and quickly.

LETTER NO. 48

1921 (Undated)

Men tilich,

You have gone and I mind as much as though it were for weeks! My silly, inconsequent, banal little room looks sillier and emptier than ever! This room has only one merit: it isn't a "giveaway." It has perhaps one or two clues to the character of its occupant, but nothing vital:

*List of Things to be Taken Away*
The porphyry man
My Tanagra Head of a Greek Matron
The little alabaster bust of the Vestal Virgin
The Persian bowl
The Egyptian beads
The Persian Fish
The Canton Enamel cups
The Persian Picture
Two Pictures of Mitya
AND THAT'S ALL.

It will be as though I had never lived here, so little has my personality impressed itself on this house . . .

LETTER NO. 49

March 18, 1921

These intolerable days of solitude and misery!

The awful monotony of meal after meal alone with Mlle.![1] The horror of never having anyone intelligent or sympathetic to talk to. How lucky you are! How I envy you!

But I know I can't stand it much longer and you will not be able to blame me. This morning I said: "Why don't you go away too?" and you answered blandly, "Why should I?"

Why should you indeed: you have all you want — a lovely place to live in, love, affection, understanding. It is *not fair,* and the sense of

1. Hélène Claissac, Violet's governess ("Moiselle").

the awful unfairness of it all grows daily. How can I *help* feeling bitter? Wouldn't you feel bitter if you were in my place?

Supposing there were no *procès*: then you would be intrinsically intact with all the things that mean most to you: L.B.,[2] H., the children, your books, your animals, all your possessions.

And I. What should I have?

NOTHING

No one who loves me and lives with me, no possessions, no reputation, no hope, nothing.

I ache with the sense of the appalling unfairness. What a triumph and what a proof, that in spite of it all, I still manage to love you above everything!

2. Long Barn, Vita's old house in Kent.

LETTER NO. 50 — *To Pat Dansey*

Clingendaal, The Hague
July 9, 1921

My blessed Misskins

You have GOT to come here. There won't be a soul to disturb us — only Daisy[1] at meals — who has said heaps of charming things about you and would really love you to come. I went into The Hague to see the doctor and various other things. He says my heart is still strained and that I ought not to tire myself. I shall tire myself if I have to keep on begging you to come! You can't refuse, knowing how much pleasure it would give me. It would be too unkind.

Mama goes back to England on the 21st to look after Sonia, who expects the infant at the beginning of August. Poor little thing! I *do* feel so sorry for her: it is terrible to think of what she will have to go through.

It is rather sad to think of my poor house going for absolutely nothing[2] — and the unfortunate things I collected being jolted off to another warehouse — homeless as their mistress. My life has stripped

1. Baroness de Brienen, a friend of Mrs. Keppel's who let Clingendaal to her each year.
2. Violet to Pat Dansey, June 8, 1921: They have sold my house for £200!! I spent nearly £3000 on it . . .

me as stark as one of Hannibal's victims. I have literally nothing in the world. Fate has just flung me down and trampled on me. I feel as though I had been attacked by highwaymen and left bruised, naked and bleeding by the roadside — And Fate gleefully shouts: "There! *Now* let's see what you can do! You had all sorts of other defences, other protections, now you've only got yourself."

"You've got your brain, and as a last resource, you've got your body . . . but *you've got nothing else."* You don't know how exposed I feel. But the only thing I hope and trust I've got: "the love of the highwayman!"

I go for long walks in the woods here by myself. I am so fond of trees. They make me feel less lonely. Trees, wind, and storm. I feel a glorious affinity with all these things . . .

I send you some photographs of this place. Show them to J,[3] also the letter.

3. Julian, i.e., Vita.

LETTER NO. 51 (*extract*)

Clingendaal, The Hague
July 19, 1921

I have nearly finished "Women in Love." Of course, it is quite neurasthenic, hysterical, but there are some beautiful things like jewels in a manure heap. The sex obsession is too disgusting, don't you think? The part where Hermione drops the lapis lazuli bell on "Birkin's" head isn't meant to be funny, but I'm afraid I giggled over it. Also it is quite obvious from the relationship of "Birkin" and "Gerald" what sort of a man Mr. Lawrence is: He gives himself away at every turn.

Darling, you will think me very greedy, but do you think you could send me another novel? There is absolutely *nothing* to read in this house, and reading is practically my only resource. I can't concentrate on anything but novels, so it's no use sending me anything serious . . . My novel progresses very slowly, alas! When I'm feeling particularly despondent I can't write at all. Also I am becoming more and more critical. To think I have been writing it for over two years and it isn't finished yet because I keep on rewriting. I think it's because I couldn't bear to part with it. It is everything to me, inevitably: Lover, Mother, Child, Friend.

O darling, aren't you glad you aren't *me?* It is really something to be thankful for.

Yr. devoted,
L.

LETTER NO. 52 to *Pat Dansey* — forwarded by Pat to Vita

Clingendaal, The Hague
July 23, 1921

Darling,

I am feeling so despondent I really don't know what to do. There seems to be a weight pressing on my shoulders and every day it gets a little heavier. I don't feel well either and that makes it worse. I feel old . . . old, as though everything were over for me, as though I should never be happy again as long as I lived.

I am so conscious of being no longer young. I never forget it for a moment. Also, I suppose one shouldn't mind one's looks beginning to go, but somehow one can't help it. I look ten years older than when you saw me last year. Each day I mercilessly look at myself in the looking glass — and see my chin beginning to sag and my throat getting all wrinkled. Soon I shall be quite plain. I suppose all the suffering I've gone through has helped, and there seems to be nothing to look forward to. You are the only person who cares what becomes of me, outside my family. O Pat! I feel all bruised and crushed. I have been crying all the morning. I feel I am such a trial to everyone, a sort of drag on the family, who are so different. Heaven knows, I am a trial enough to myself. It is so humiliating. I feel such an outcast, a pariah.

It's awful, Pat. It's awful to feel that one had left all one's life behind one, that all that's left is to get older and plainer every day. I'm such a coward. I'm frightened of death too. I shouldn't be if I had been good, but alas! I have not been good.

I think one is only put into this world to be shown the extreme desirability of the other. There must be *some* place where happiness exists, for it certainly doesn't in this world, except in tiny snatches.

I have no spirit, no fighting capacity left — but, O Pat! I *do* believe in another better world.

One of the things I liked in Lawrence's book was where he said that God, seeing man was such a failure, such a falling short of His ideals, would evolve a higher, more beautiful being, destroying the faulty useless man for something nearer perfection. The mestoda, the proto-type of the horse, became extinct because the horse was an *improvement*. It's high time there was an improvement on man.

Again, I liked when Birkin said he wished humanity would become exterminated — the earth which is beautiful would be left purged and clean, "uninterrupted grass with a hare sitting up" — I thought that was such a beautiful phrase, I repeated it over and over again to myself.


LETTER NO. 53 (*extract*)

Ypres, Belgium
September 21, 1921

It is so infinitely worse than I thought it would be: those acres and acres of barren land stuck with lamentable protests of blackened trees like broken antlers . . . At Passchendaele I saw the most desolate sight I have ever seen in my life: a wizened and twisted little hunch-back, sitting on a pile of wire netting, alone in that vast and agony-haunted plain. It was such a terrible illustration of the Godforsakenly grotesque that I shuddered and couldn't look. "How are the mighty fallen" and how good was Osbert's poem[1]: the first thing that leaped to my mind was the last line: "Too late came carelessly Serenity." It couldn't be better said.

How forcibly it makes me realise the sufferings and privations of the wretched men who fought all through the war. Darling, I wish we had come here together . . .

1. Osbert Sitwell's poem "There Fore Is the Name of It called Babel," in *Argonaut and Juggernaut* (London, 1919).

# 17. *Vita to Violet (1940–1950)*

Sissinghurst Castle
September 12, 1940

Darling,

I am really touched by your concern and conversely am glad for you that you should be out of London. I gather from Harold, who has been there all the time and who is not frightened of air raids, that it has been pretty fierce. The actual noise here isn't so bad, as this is a fighting area, which means that they try to drive the German planes into it and then have dogfights over our heads. I daresay this is preferable to A.A. guns at close quarters and it certainly is very exciting to watch. The nuisance is that it makes them "unload" rather vaguely, when the whole of Sissinghurst shakes with the explosion. We have had 2 bombs dropped in the village, ½ a mile away, *mais basta!* These recitals (which are really slightly boastful) become very boring, and there's nothing to be done about it: I couldn't go away and leave *mes gens* behind; besides (don't laugh) I'm the local ambulance driver and thus am rather tired.

I hope we don't get invaded and forcibly evacuated.

No, I never went to Andorra. Do you remember that you and I once tried to go there from Carcassonne and were prevented by snow? Do you remember our garden in Carcassonne with its enormous latch-key? You can't think what nostalgia I get for abroad, Greece, the Sahara, Provence, the Painted Desert.

Am I right in believing that your acquaintance with America is limited to Palm Beach? You should go to Arizona which I prefer to

New Mexico. I think Arizona is perhaps the most beautiful country I have ever seen, and *very* much your cup of tea. But one can't really like America and so I always wished Arizona was elsewhere — in Central Asia for instance. You would agree with me in liking Persia.

(If this letter is slightly disconnected it is because bombers are all over me, the guns are thundering at Maidstone, and sirens are going off in three different directions at once.)

To resume: you know I am not a person to push my books unduly on to an unwilling reader, but I should very much like you to read a book I wrote about Persia, not because it's *my* book but because I should like you to share something of what I feel about that divine country, especially in these days when one can escape from England only in imagination. If you haven't come across it, shall I send it to you? (It is called *Passenger to Teheran*). Tell me when you next write.

Curious how war has drawn the strands of our lives together again. I was so worried about you when France collapsed; I couldn't bear to think of you in danger and distress. One travels far, only to come round to the old starting point. I realised then that we might still be sitting on the leather fire-seat at 30 Portman Square,[1] when I went home to Hill Street saying to myself, like an incantation, "I have a friend. I have a friend."

And thousands of other things as well.

Do you remember spending a night at Plymouth, when we went to the music hall and saw "Lily" who enchanted us? "I'm not like my mother. I'm not like my brother. But they're all like me."

I believe that the enclosed postcard which I received this morning represents that very hotel. It gave me what's called a jump.

Your
Mitya

---

1. The Keppels' London home when Violet and Vita were children. See p. 15.

LETTER No. 55 (*extract*)

Sissinghurst Castle
Friday 1941

Darling,

If you really want to get a house in the Salisbury plain country, why don't you write and ask my cousin Eddy who is now living in Kenneth Clark's house (Upton near Tetbury, Wilts). He knows various people living all round there, e.g., Stephen Tennant, and might easily hear of something you would like. I was only joking about Long Barn — which anyway is filled with 50 children from Hoxton and Shoreditch till the end of the war. I love Wiltshire and the Cotswolds too, and would probably have lived there if I didn't belong to Kent. How I wish you could have the Manor House at Avebury!

Have you, by the way, done what I told you to do and got Dorothy[1] to take you to Brympton d'Evercy? Half of it is too Richard Coeur de Lion for your taste, but you would like the Inigo Jones part. It demands a heavy summer evening — though I daresay that dripping woods might suit its melancholy as well.

Such a battle has been raging round my tower this morning that I quite thought a Spitfire was going to collide with it. I nearly sent you some photographs of Sissinghurst but refrained as I thought of the plight of your own tower. I don't know if you would like it: it is Henry VIII — is that too primitive? It has I think a certain *Belle au bois dormant*[2] quality which I think you would appreciate.

I am appalled to hear of the destruction of Holland House. Is it as bad as they say?

You sound so unhappy, my sweet; I *do* mind. It doesn't surprise me to hear that your life is full of complications. I've never known it to be anything else, but you used to like to choose them for yourself and now they must rather have taken charge. Do make a real effort to find somewhere of your own to live, for if this damned war is going on for another year or longer it is the only thing to do. A poor consolation, I know, but a practical one.

---

1. Dorothy Heneage, Violet's friend and Somerset neighbor (see page 105).
2. *Sleeping Beauty.*

I am trying to write a book (*puisque tu me demandes*[3]) about Arizona which I think the most beautiful country I have ever seen. And the strangest. No, it's *not* a Wild West story — nor are there any cowboys in it. I don't know if you read my books, do you? I should rather like to send you a poem called "Solitude," which you might like. No obligation to say you like it if you don't. Shall I?

Write to me.

Your<br>Mitya

3. At your request.

## LETTER NO. 56

(Undated)

We simply could not have this nice, simple, naif, childish connexion without its turning into a passionate love-affair again.

If you have any honesty in your nature, you will agree with me.

You and I cannot be together. I go down country lanes and meet a notice saying 'Beware. Unexploded bomb'.

So I have to go around another way.

You are the unexploded bomb to me.

I don't want you to explode.

I don't want you to disrupt my life.

My quiet life is dear to me. I hate being dragged away from it. Like Dorothy, I have become *maniaque*.

Just as Dorothy gets the doors left open for fear of germs, so do I stick at home among my cabbages.

This letter will anger you. I do not care if it does, since I know that no anger or irritation will ever destroy the love that exists between us.

And if you really want me, I will come to you, always, anywhere.

You see, you said we might have two sorts of capital to draw on: the great tragedy sort and the childhood-friendship sort. That is true in a way — but not wholly true. You know quite well, if you face it honestly, that although the childhood-friendship link between us is strong and important, the other sort matters equally.

Mitya

LETTER NO. 57 (*extract*)

Sissinghurst Castle
January 27, 1941

Lushka,

I write to you in a bad temper with nearly all my world, always excepting Harold who is a permanent delight — but whom I see only at weekends. He is so refreshing, so unpetty, so amusing, so much the best of the French and English temperaments combined. You would like him now that you have no personal cause to dislike him.

As I said, I write in a bad temper. My world, my life, is getting complicated at this moment and I hate that. I really hate that.

And that is one of the reasons I don't want to get involved with you again: I really dislike the complications and intrigues that your life entails. They bore me.

I love you, and shall always love you, but I would never be bothered with all your maze and labyrinth of life.

I don't want to fall in love with you all over again.

I've said this before: so *"glissons, mortels, n'y attardons nous pas."*[1] (I've quoted incorrectly, I know. You know the quotation I mean. It was a favourite of yours, once.)

1. "Mortal men, let us slip away and not delay ourselves here." The correct quotation is *"Glissez, mortels, n'appuyez pas"* (Pierre-Charles Roy).

LETTER NO. 58

Sissinghurst Castle
February 29, 1941

Darling,

It was nice of you to be concerned instead of being cross. I am touched. As a matter of fact my "complications" were not amorous, — I fear you must be developing a one-track mind! Complications are not necessarily connected with either the heart or the body — and no one wilier than you has again tripped me up, nor shall they.

So your chuckle shall be denied you, but I do thank you for your letter.

I owe you an answer to a letter a fortnight ago, but I can't find it. I live in one room, with my books, my papers and my meals on a tray, so it is not surprising that everything gets lost. Things turn up eventually, but not always at the time one wants them.

I feel sure your manor house is as tidy as its writing papers, West Coker . . . is. I should like to write a poem about it, but it would be a poem intelligible only to you and me. Send me a photograph of it (the house, not the poem) if you have one; then I can visualise you there. Is it true that your Mother and "Papa" are living there with you? Someone told me so. And how about your lost MSS? Are you really struggling with the task of rewriting it?

I myself am trying to finish a novel, a job I loathe, but I committed myself to in a moment of financial crisis.

Have you read Elizabeth Bowen's short stories in a book called "Look at All Those Roses" or something like that? I think you would like them.

I had to make a speech near Lewes, so stayed the night with Virginia[1] and read them there. She has a twist to her mind which I think would please you, — rather like the sudden scratch of a cat's claw. Very un-English.

Virginia and I talked about you. She says she thinks of you as being all chestnut and green in colour. (I fancy she described you something like that in "Orlando"? I must look it up.) She is a person of strange penetration. If you had gone to live at Coke's House, which is not very far from where she lives, I would have arranged to take you over to see her again.

I wish I had had your letter before going there. The idea of Catherine the Great's ring would have been just her cup of tea. I can't remember what I left you in my will. It was made years ago and has been spending the war somewhere in Devonshire. In any case, if I died, I should like you to recover our red lava ring.[2] I shouldn't like it to belong to anybody else. I will give myself the morbid pleasure of leaving instructions to that effect.

1. Virginia Woolf.
2. See pp. 16 and 246.

Goodbye — my darling Lushi — write to me again and this time I won't let your letter get mislaid under piles of agenda.

Yours    M

LETTER NO. 59

Sissinghurst Castle
March 16, 1941

Lushka mine,

You may remember that some months ago I got worried about a letter I had written to you. It got lost — and I didn't know what had happened to it.

Well, I found it under a heap of paper, so here it is — very out-of-date now, but I send it all the same to prove my bona fide. I opened it myself to reread it and although it is scarcely worth sending now, so long after it was written, I send it all the same. I am glad it has turned up.

I got a letter from you today. Yes, of course (idiot that you are) it upsets me to see you or hear your voice. I hate you for having this effect on me. I resent knowing that if I were suddenly to see a photograph of you it would disturb me for at least 24 hours.

Damn you. You have bitten too deeply into my soul. I love you perennially in the odd way we both realise. That doesn't mean that I trust you — or would ever commit myself to you again. I know better than that now. But I do love you.

It was rather startling, your letter saying our story ought to be written. Only half an hour before the postman arrived with your letter, I had been rung up by somebody saying that I simply must write a novel on that subject. I objected the loathesome example of "The Well of Loneliness" — and was told (quite rightly) that I could do it differently. Which is true. I *could* do it differently!

Could we (you and I) collaborate?

No, I don't think we could. It would be one person's book.

I do feel that it is a great and new subject and I would like to do it. The vivid feelings that I have undergone throughout my life would make a worthwhile story of it.

How much I would like to talk to you about this — quite dispassion-
ately and with all the objective intelligence that you and I could bring
to bear on it. I only wish that I could trust myself (and you) to come
and stay with you.

But I don't, so I won't.

Your
Mitya

LETTER NO. 60

Sissinghurst Castle
March 30, 1941

Darling

I loved your letter about your so suddenly Spanish day. Yes, I have
been to Wells. There is a Bishop's Palace hidden behind high walls.
Have you also been to Glastonbury, not far from Wells? It is one of
the most romantic places in England, partly because so little remains of
it and the rest is left to the imagination. Just stumps of columns sticking up out of the turf. And, if I remember rightly, a miraculous rose
tree without thorns.

But I may have invented this.

Have you read "For Whom the Bell Tolls," by Ernest Hemingway?
If not, I recommend it to you. It is just your book, and mine. I wish
I had written it, when I suppose is the greatest compliment one can
pay a book.

Do you know Hemingway? I have a particular reason for asking,
so R.S.V.P. (Refusez si vous pouvez)[1]

Oh no, I won't be tiresomely mysterious, but will tell you the reason:
I would like him to read "Pepita".[2] Only as I am not a person who
goes in for fan mail ("Dear Mr. Hemingway, I admire your work so
much, I want you to read this little book of mine as you are interested
in Spain and Spanish Gypsies,") I would rather get it sent to him by
somebody else, not me. I do think it might amuse him. Because Pepita

1. Refuse if you can.
2. Vita's book about her Spanish grandmother.

is *actualité*[3] like a newsreel. Do you know his book about bullfighting, called "Death in the Afternoon"?

That, also, would be very much your cup of tea.

Have you ever seen a bullfight at Nîmes? I have. It is superb. Spanish bullrings are cheap and ugly, being made of wood painted Pompeian red, not even blood red, but the Provence bullrings are of stone, with the magnificence of Roman architecture added to the dangerous beauty of the fight and *sol y sombra*.[4] I arrived in Nîmes by mistake one day and found a corrida going on . . .

Darling, I've just heard the most terrible news which has put everything else out of my head. Virginia[5] has killed herself. It is not in the papers yet but I heard from Leonard.[6] You know how absolutely devoted I was to her.

Yours
Mitya

3. News.
4. Half sun and half shade. The expression relates to seats in the ring for bullfights.
5. Virginia Woolf.
6. Leonard Woolf, Virginia's husband.

LETTER No. 61 (*extract*)

Sissinghurst
July 5, 1941

Darling

I am thrilled to hear you are writing your memoirs. Oh Duntreath!! . . . how that is mixed up with my own memories. The owls . . . The armoury . . . and our own young innocent loves. I think you ought to dedicate this book to me? . . . yes? no?

I should be flattered and gratified if you did.[1]

Well, I must stop now, but I will send you a more detailed typewritten note on your book[2] when I have got Harold's secretary here to type it. I hope I haven't taken too many liberties with it.

Your
Mitya

1. *Don't Look Round* was dedicated "To the Memory of My Beloved Mother."
2. Vita had been reading *Pirates at Play*.

LETTER NO. 62

Sissinghurst Castle
July 28, 1942

Darling,

There are owls here too. Many years ago — 50, 60 years — a farmer lived here who loved owls, and every man on the place was threatened with instant dismissal if he destroyed an owl. The result is that they hoot and cry all day and all night. There is one pair in particular which I love: the great white barn-owl, which rears a brood every year in the same shed. I have just been watching them on the hunt, and then the soft noiseless return, and then the shrill welcome from the nest, and then the hunt begins again. Two of the babies fell out of the shed once and I caught them: They were very angry and fluffed themselves out and threw themselves backwards whenever I approached, hissing with rage and their talons lifted to strike.

The parents have been a fine sight tonight, flying across an enormous orange moon.

It was a night when I would have liked you to be here. There are practically no flowers now, and the garden is dark green. One gets an impression of long green vistas and statues, all dominated by the pink tower.

Do you ever see "Country Life"? If so, look out for 3 articles on this place which are due to appear in August. As a Somersetshire squire, I feel sure you take in "Country Life"? and if you don't, I expect Dorothy does.

I hear of you from Harold from time to time — brief appearances in London and gone again. What are you *really* doing? Much as I like your *à la recherche du temps perdu*[1] letters, I could wish that they contained some reference to your present.

Are you reconciled to England at all? Are you happier? Are you in love? Are you writing?

To all these inquiries I should like an answer — but a truthful one. So write.

Mitya

1. Reference to Proust's *In Search of Lost Time.*

LETTER No. 63 (*extract*)

April 28, 1947
Sissinghurst Castle/
Kent

I met your friend Mme. Massigli[1] the other day who told me you were still contemplating marriage, not with Marchese Picenardi but the French prince.[2] She seemed amused by this. We met in odd circumstances: on a launch following the Boat Race. It rained as I have seldom seen it rain, and the extremely distinguished company dressed up in travelling rugs thoughtfully provided by the Port of London Authority, and were suddenly transformed from Cabinet Ministers, Ambassadors, and Princes of the Church into a group of apparently Red Indians. I watched the Archbishop of Canterbury being introduced to Mme. Massigli, when the water which had collected in the brim of his shovel hat shot suddenly all over her as he politely bowed. This cut short the delectable indiscretions about you on which she was just about to embark.

1. Madame René Massigli, wife of the French ambassador.
2. Rolphe de Faucigny-Lucinge.

LETTER No. 64

October 13, 1948

My darling dear,

This is the endearment by which Dame Julian of Norwich supposed Our Lord to have addressed her sometime during the Middle Ages — I forget the exact date — but no matter — it will serve me now as a pretty endearment for you, my Lushka.

Oh Lushka, I echo what you said in your letter — though you have probably forgotten it now. I loved Casimir Perier[1] and St. Loup. Above all, I loved St. Loup: Seldom has a place suddenly taken me as St. Loup did. It was a queer feeling — almost as though I belonged there — I can't enlarge on this, even to you — it is too private a feeling. It did, however, make me realise that curious bond between us,

1. Violet had a flat in Paris in the rue Casimir Perier.

— our intense sense of the character of places. We both have it so strongly that it becomes a pain.

I don't even know if you will understand what I mean as I write all this — but I expect you will.

I've just been down to Montacute where I am responsible for the garden. What a lovely house, all grey and golden. If only the interior were equal to the exterior, it would be one of the loveliest houses in England. But there isn't a single room which is well proportioned or sympathetic . . .

Raymond[2] spent the weekend here. He brought with him the prospectus of the crematorium in California which forms the background of "The Loved One." It is, if anything, funnier than the story itself.

Have you read "Christ stopped at Eboli"? (You probably read it in Italian.) What an impression that book made on me! I think it would be your book too.

Bless you, my Lushka.

Your Mitya

2. Raymond Mortimer.

LETTER NO 65 (*extract*)

October 4, 1949

My darling Lushka,

This is a rather difficult letter to write. It is about Saint Loup. You know I loved Saint Loup. I took to it — and I think it took to me.

When I first came there, I had no idea that you had it in your mind to leave it to me — if you died.

When you told me about this idea of yours, my first reaction was that you ought to leave it to Sonia or to one of her children, and I told you so. You then said that neither Sonia nor her children would want it or appreciate it, and that you would rather I had it. So that cleared my conscience so far as Sonia and her children were concerned: you had turned them down, in favour of me who took an instant love to the place and an understanding of it.

Well, that is that — and I have said my bit — in all honesty — and you further eased my conscience when I saw you last Monday by saying that if you didn't have it then, you would leave it to your Bowes-Lyon cousin, and in no case to Sonia or her children. I was worried about them, because after all they are your nearest relations.

You are younger than I am (I know you dismissed the fact when I mentioned it) and a dozen things may arise to make you change your mind which anyhow I know isn't really made up, so nothing may ever come of this. One thing I do know, is that you know me well enough to realise that I am not materialistic or mercenary or worldly — and that my love of Saint Loup is genuinely *for its own sake* — as well as for yours.

Your Mitya

LETTER No. 66

December 19, 1949

Darling my Lushka,

How can I send anything, to you who have so many things? So I send you just a one-and-sixpenny Penguin book — and I send it not so much for the sake of the Sonnets as for the *Lover's Complaint* which is so seldom read and which may or may not be by Shakespeare.

I have marked lines in it which I feel sure *must* be by Shakespeare, and I hope it may interest you, and even if it doesn't, you may turn back to those sonnets which are surely the extreme expression of poetry and love.

Oh my sweet: you'll never tempt me to Paris. Cities terrify me. I get odder and odder, as my life goes on. I shall end up as a complete eccentric hermit, living here and not venturing even as far as Cranbrook, which is my equivalent of your Provins. Cities are not for me. Sissinghurst and St. Loup are my spiritual homes — and of course Knole, which is denied to me forever, through "a technical fault over which we have no control" as they say on the radio. Do you know Queen Elizabeth's magnificent phrase: "Had I been crested and not cloven, my Lords, you had not treated me thus."

This all brings me to your idea of a Spanish excursion next Spring.

Much as I would love to go with you, 'me nerves' wouldn't stand up to your Polish chauffeur. The Continental tempo is too fast for me, who can scarcely bear to go in a London taxi. But you say you will be in London on January 11. So let us meet then.

Your Mitya

LETTER NO. 67

September 3, 1950

My darling,

It was a real event in my life and my heart to be with you the other day. We do matter to each other, don't we? however much our ways may have diverged. I think we have got something indestructible between us, haven't we? Even right back to the library seat in your papa's room at Grosvenor Street — and then at Duntreath — and then to everything that came afterwards. *Glissons, mortels*[1] . . . but what a bond, Lushka darling; a bond of childhood and subsequent passion, such as neither of us will ever share with anyone else.

It has been a very strange relationship, ours; unhappy at times, happy at others; but unique in its way, and infinitely precious to me and (may I say?) to you.

What I like about it is that we always come together again however long the gaps in our meetings may have been. Time seems to make no difference. This is a sort of love letter I suppose. Odd that I should be writing you a love letter after all these years — when we have written so many to each other. *Parceque c'était lui, parceque c'était moi.*[2]

Oh, you sent me a book about Elizabeth Barrett Browning. Thank you, darling generous Lushka and you gave me a coal-black briquet. It lights up into the flame of love which always burns in my heart whenever I think of you. You said it would last for three months, but our love has lasted for forty years and more.

Your
Mitya

1. See p. 226.
2. Because it was him, because it was me.

*APPENDICES*
*INDEX*

# *Violet's Letters from Ceylon: Original Versions*

LETTER NO. 1

A mon incomparable soeur
Aux yeux de velours.
A la peau de nacre,
Aux cheveux d'ébène,
A la lèvre de grenade,
Au souffle de trèfle,
A l'inspiration d'aurore
Salut et Prosperité!

Je t'écris sous un balancement éperdu de bambous gigantesques, tout au fond d'un jardin qui doit faire partie des Mille et Une Nuits, ou, si tu préfères, on se croirait en plein El Dorado. Aimes-tu les orchidées? Moi, je les adore.

Toi, tu ferais de même si tu pouvais les voir telles que moi je les vois en ce moment: c'est à dire, en grappes, empourprées, narcotiques, avec par ci par là, quelques mésalliances rougissantes comme il convient à des orchidées plébéiennes . . .

N'est-ce pas que j'ai la bosse des descriptions, chérie?? Mais je pense que tu ne t'attendras point à mieux quand je te dirai qu'il fait 90 degrés à l'ombre et que mon pauvre corps endolorié est dans un état complet d'anéantissement moral et physique.

— Que ne-suis-je, hélas, la fille d'un "loup de mer" pour aller me balader avec des pantoufles aux pieds, un collier au cou et c'est tout!!!
Je deviens incoherente, je ferai bien de m'arrêter.

Sous un ciel flamboyant de midi tropical la route de Maradane poudroie . . . de chaque côté s'élèvent des arbres imprévus au feuillage tour à tour sombre, chatoyant, où lustré. La chaleur est telle que le moindre geste est une corvée . . . Plus loin dans un tourbillon de poussière, on aperçoit de grands boeufs las, à l'oeil injecté de sang, à l'échine balafrée d'horions. A côté, noirs luisants, fourbus, les bouviers.

Partout du reflet, partout de la lumière — et puis, de temps à autre, une noix de coco qui se détache, lentement, avec un bruit mat, sur la terre brune. Une terre de tout repos, une terre de toute beauté, une terre pleine, une terre inouï, exhalant tous les fruits, toutes les épices — les candeurs d'une terre vermeille éprise de la lumière, ivre de soleil . . .

*Postscript:* Que dis-tu de mon style oriental? Quant à moi, j'en suis abasourdie! I flatter myself I am the possessor of one of the most adaptable natures in existence.

> Dambatenne à 5000, 200 pied de sol.
> 4 décembre 1910.

J'ai le vertige, l'éblouissement des hauteurs.

Je me sens petite, toute petite . . . tu n'as pas idée . . . d'un moment à l'autre il semble que je dois être engoufrée. Toutes les montagnes d'alentour conspirent pour m'écraser de leur poids. D'immensès rochers velus s'entassent pêle-mêle autour de la maison. La vue est superbe. 2000 pieds au dessous de nous de riantes collines dégagent en pentes floues, sylvaines.

Tu le vois. Adam's Peak s'estompent dans la brume du lointain! Plus près, c'est la jungle, plus loin, c'est la mer. De place en place des étangs cernés de bananiers, de cactus, de grenadiers, de camphriers, d'eucalyptus et de muscadiers fument au soleil comme d'immenses cuves.

Inutile de t'affirmer que je suis d'une souveraine paresse et que rien au-dessous d'une mousson ne me ferait abandonner mon divan!! Tout cela est sous-entendu.

Que l'Angleterre est donc loin! Vita mia!

Comment se fait-il que tu ne sois pas ici? ...

Il m'est arrivé parfois durant mon séjour de me demander pourquoi, en effet, tu ne faisait aucun effort pour venir ici, malgré tout, malgré tous???? Je ne voudrais pas être à ta place pour un empire! Voilà qui n'est pas mal, ça me semble pour une personne assez dissimulée?

Now for the little matter-of-fact information you love: nous irons peut-être passer quelques jours à Nuwara-Eliya vers la fin de ce mois mais tu n'as qu'à m'écrire ici on fera suivre.

J'ai eu toutes sortes d'aventures sur le bateau que je voudrais bien pouvoir te raconter de vive-voix. Entre autres une fort divertissante avec une dame Espagnole et une autre avec — ma non importa! It will keep. Suffit de te dire que la femme Violetta s'est follement amusée aux dépens d'autrui. Ce qui n'est peut-être pas tout à fait bien, mais on pardonne tant de choses à la jeunesse, surtout à 16½. Voici sans doute ce que tu appelles des puérilités. Moi, je les appelle tout bonnement, inconséquences ce qui revient à peu près au même . . .

Tâche moyen de ne pas te marier avant que je revienne.

                                          Dambatenne.
                                          12 décembre 1910.

On chercherait vainement quelque suite, quelque brin rapporteur dans le labyrinthe inextricable qu'est ta dernière lettre — labyrinthe hélas! où il manque une Ariane pour me remettre le fil conducteur!

Aussi au bout d'une courte recherche, je donne ma langue au chat! — il fait trop chaud pour s'acharner. A moins que tu ne sois devenue subitement amoureuse de quelque bienheureux mortel, je m'avoue incapable de lire entre les lignes. Au fait, cela se pourrait.

En relisant attentivement, voilà que tout à coup une espèce d'angoisse sourde que je ne qualifierais toutefois pas d'appréhension, vient accélérer la vitesse de mon coeur, vient faire trembler ma main un petit peu en t'écrivant . . .

C'est palpitant et c'est triste!

Pour la première fois tes deux années de plus m'apparaissent bien réelles, arrogantes, sinistres . . .

Mais ne vas pas croire que je n'avais pas prévu ce moment: je m'y suis souvent arrêtée.

Ah, de grâce, dis-moi que je n'ai pas raison, que c'est mon imagination endiablée qui m'entraine! . . .

Après tout, je ne suis qu'une femme. J'aurais dû songer que peut-être à ton age une liaison masculine devait s'imposer. Je ferai bien de m'en tenir là. Je sens que je vais dire des inconvenances. Tu ne riras pas, promets que tu ne riras pas. Il y a longtemps que je ne te demande plus rien, accorde-moi cela. It would hurt so. . . .

Nous allons demain à Nuwara Eliya. Nous comptons passer la plus grande partie de cette semaine dans la jungle où ces messieurs en tireurs émérites vont abattre des alligators.

J'espère ardemment qu'on ne me forcera pas à y participer. Ces enormes bêtes tout en sang — pouah! C'est horripilant. Nous irons ensuite voir les buried cities à commencer par Anuradhapura.

Le jungle me fait frémir. Je fais des voeux pour en revenir intacte.

Violetta

LETTER NO. 2

Dambatenne, Ceylon.
le 2 janvier 1911.

I am in a strange mood today, Vita mia. I cannot make up my mind whether I am a freak in every possible respect, ou tout simplement — une enfant dénaturée. Éclaire-moi de tes lumières et dis-moi mon avenir, ô pythonesse!

I have had every conceivable thing in the way of adventures these last two years. Veux-tu que j'en déniche quelques-unes des plus palpitantes pour ton bénéfice?? Tu ne demandes pas mieux, n'est-ce pas? Et c'est précisément parce que je devine ta curiosité — fort naturelle du reste — que j'ai resolu des les garder pour moi . . .

— J'ai plus de souvenirs que si j'avais mille ans. Un gros meuble à tiroirs encombrés de bilans, de vers, de billet-doux, de procès, de romances, avec de lourd cheveux roulés dans des quittances cache moins de souvenirs que mon triste cerveau. C'est une pyramide, une immense caveau qui contient plus de morts que la fosse commune: Je suis un cimetière abhorré de la lune où, comme des remords, se trainent de long vers qui s'acharnent toujours sur mes morts les plus chers.[1]

— et patata patati, je t'en citerai encore pour une demi-heure, si ça pouvait me guérir de mon spleen.

Ta dernière missive m'en a dit long sur ton état, qui, je l'admets sans ombrages m'avait donné joliment du fil à retordre. C'est qu'elle vous en colle, la mâtine! Excusez mon langage. Je m'en sers dans certaines occasions to bury my feelings which are apt to prove too much for me at times.

Voilà je pense qui te fera rire: imaginez-vous, chère amie, que j'ai rapporté un alligator de mon expédition jungale — mais gros comme on en voit pas de nos jours, gros comme la marche du perron!

Hein, ça vous a coupé le sifflet pour de bon cette fois! ( Je vois ta figure scandalisée d'ici: "quel épanchement voyou!")

I killed it with my little rifle and if you are very good ("qu'elle est donc enfant!"), you shall have a purse made out of it for your birthday present!!

Sais-tu que tu as cessé d'être une réalité pour moi? Tu es si si loin, qu'il me semble que tu n'as jamais existé en dehors de mes rêves. Tu es un mirage qui s'éloigne à mesure que l'on s'en rapproche.

À propos de mirages, j'en ai vu un très beau dans le canal de Suez, à l'embouchure de la Mer Rouge. Je regardais d'un oeil distrait le désert qui s'allongeait à l'infini, le grand soleil implacable qui avait des lueurs de fournaise, un chameau marchant de son grand pas inégal vers le sud — quand soudain, je me rappelle avoir poussé un grand cri: "Vous voyez là-bas, les arbres et l'eau?" On regarda; il semble alors qu'un lac

1. Baudelaire.

ceint de dattiers et d'arbustes touffus invraisemblablement bleu et séduisant était passé inaperçu? Aussitôt on se rua sur les cartes, on s'arracha les lunettes, on se porta en masse chez le capitaine qui, la-haut dans sa cabine s'étendait dans une pose accablée. . . .

"Qu'était-ce donc que ce lac qui brillait au loin, si bleu, si solitaire?"
. . .

Le capitaine descendit en bougonnent, braqua son télescope sur la rive egyptienne, et partit d'un grand éclat de rire: "Ça, mesdames, ça, c'est tout simplement un mirage!", et il remonta chez lui, encore, tout secoué de ce bon rire un peu gras, un peu vague, qu'il se payait à chaque instant.

Moi, je restai longtemps accoudée à la balustrade, l'oeil reveur. Il me semblait voir tant de choses dans cette réalité qui, après tout, n'était qu'un mirage.

# *Letters from Harold Nicolson to Violet*

My dear Violet,

We got back last night in blustering rain and dark. We had an easy journey and Vita was not at all tired. Everybody says that she looks so far better than when she left, and I truly believe that she had gained not only in physical health and intellectual stimulus, but also in confidence in her own vigour and interests. She said that she felt "twenty years younger" and I think that was true. It is very good for turnips to be dug up from time to time and put among the orchids. Above all, bless her she was supremely happy and you can feel that you have given her new zest and enjoyment. It is as if she had undertaken some cure — not in a hydro or clinking glasses of hot water with dotards — but absorbing beauty in the company of people she is fond of and who vitalize her. I have never felt so happy about any holiday that I have ever had and believe me your generosity and thoughtfulness have done us both an immense amount of good. We share so utterly an understanding of Vita and a tender solicitude for her that I know that the knowledge that you have really helped her and encouraged her will give you as much pleasure as it does to me. I think she has been invigorated by her holiday in such a way as will enable her to start

1. After a visit to Violet in Florence.

on her novel with more energy and confidence. She has been terribly unhappy about her inability to write — feeling that the springs have all dried up and the old exultation left her for ever. Now she feels that excitement and refreshment have again been given her and that her batteries, which seemed so weak and empty, have again been replenished. All this we owe to you and this is no ordinary letter of thanks but a deep, believe me, expression of gratitude.

I spent the time in the train writing a Spectator article in which I have dragged in Saint Loup, rather incidentally, rather deliberate, but in a way I hope which will cause you pleasure. Not big pleasure but a small warm pleasure. I really felt that charm of Saint Loup and I hope in your sort of way.

No disasters here on our return. We were met by Ben[1] who in his detached manner was quite interested in our experiences. Anyhow he drank a large portion of our Chianti and listened quite appreciatedly to the stories which we told. He sniffed the tuberoses as if they had been a bottle of Molyneux No. 5.

My dear Violet — I do thank you so much for all you have given to us and send you my fondest gratitude.

Yours ever,
Harold

1. Benedict Nicolson, Vita and Harold's older son.

July I mean August 5 1962
Sissinghurst Castle,
Kent

My dearest Violet,

I think Vita would have liked you to have a book of hers as well as the ring. You were her best and oldest friend and she thought much about you and admired your work. Those long and deep affections are the best thing in the world and I am grateful to you for your long and devoted and amused affection for her. I am glad indeed that she had so happy a life and you were a large part in it.

Things will never be the same to me again. But one cannot expect such happiness to continue for ever and the day will come when I shall be able to look back on the last fifty years with gratitude instead of torturing regret.

Your loving,
Harold

C.1. The Albany,
Piccadilly, W.1
22nd August 1962.

My dearest Violet,

I will send you a copy of Vita's Collected Poems so soon as I am able to collect it. I am going to Bergamo tomorrow and shall not be back in Sissinghurst, but I am asking Vita's Secretary to send it to you.

I think it very enterprising of you to follow in the footsteps of Mme. Tallien, and to go to Chimay must be an experience for any woman, however travel-bitten she may be.[1]

It is very sweet of you to invite me to stay with you in Paris, and if I find the winter hangs too heavy on me I may come across. I am nursing the theory that my three weeks in Bergamo will give me renewed strength, health and vigour, but I fear that it is an illusion. I keep on telling myself that one cannot expect to have 50 years of such companionship and not have to pay for it one day. But I did not foresee that the payment would be so harsh and so prolonged.

Bless you, my dearest Violet, and we must keep corresponding. I saw Frank Gwatkin last night and he told me he was seeing you shortly.

Yours ever, & ever
Harold

1. In August 1962 Violet accompanied by John Phillips visited her old friend, the Princesse Ghislaine de Chimay in Chimay, Belgium. One of the ancestors of the Chimay family was the famous Madame Tallien.

# Index